The Dalkey Archive Bibliography Series

II

GILBERT SORRENTINO

The Dalkey Archive Bibliography Series

1. *Thomas Pynchon: A Bibliography of Primary and Secondary Materials.* Clifford Mead

2. *Gilbert Sorrentino: A Descriptive Bibliography.* William McPheron

Gilbert Sorrentino: A Descriptive Bibliography

William McPheron

Dalkey Archive Press

Library of Congress Cataloging-in-Publication Data
McPheron, William
Gilbert Sorrentino: a descriptive bibliography / by William McPheron
(Dalkey Archive bibliography series; 2)
Includes index.
1. Sorrentino, Gilbert—Bibliography. I. Title. II. Series.
Z8826.94.M37 1991
[PS3569.O7]
016.818'5409—dc20 90-3674
ISBN: 0-916583-67-8

First Edition

Partially funded by grants from The National Endowment for the Arts and The Illinois Arts Council.

Dalkey Archive Press
1817 North 79th Avenue
Elmwood Park, IL 60635 USA

Printed on permanent/durable acid-free paper and bound in the United States of America.

Contents

INTRODUCTION

Gilbert Sorrentino's career as poet, novelist, and critic reflects the fate of classic American modernism in contemporary literary culture. Coming to artistic maturity in the 1950s, Sorrentino was a member of that generation which revolted against the dictates of academic verse and consumer fiction by reviving the modernist aesthetics of William Carlos Williams and Ezra Pound. Art's autonomy was the hallmark of this post-World War II avant-garde, and the writers' rejection of realism in fiction and formalism in poetry set them radically at odds with established publishers. Excluded from the usual channels of cultural communication, they looked, like Pound and Williams before them, to little magazines and small presses to print and discuss their work. Sorrentino was typical of the period when he formed his own magazine, *Neon*, contributed heavily to many other little magazines, and published his first two books through presses operated by friends.

But Sorrentino was also different, for he wanted to make literature a profession, and he deliberately sought entry for himself and his work into the world of commercial publishing. In the 1960s this seemed possible. The industry retained a gentlemanly veneer, still proclaiming to prefer literary quality to profits. In addition, there were a few self-consciously radical houses which were successfully issuing innovative writing, like Grove Press, where Sorrentino worked as editor from 1965 to 1970. In the course of the 1970s, this situation changed as conglomerates acquired independent companies and the high profit margins of best-sellers became the industry's financial norm. Tolerance for difference began to disappear, and mainstream publishers became less willing to risk money on books whose marketability was not self-evident.

Sorrentino's career mirrors this erosion of commitment to serious literature. His early novels, perhaps because they could be misread as realistic fiction, found publishers with little difficulty. But beginning with *Mulligan Stew*, which directly challenges readers' expectations, Sorrentino deviated from standards of commercial acceptability. The novel consequently suffered dozens of rejections by trade houses and was forced to wait four years before finding a publisher. When *Mulligan Stew* finally appeared, its enthusiastic critical reception and strong sales seemed to promise greater openness to Sorrentino's unconventional work. But in fact, his next novel, *Crystal Vision*, met with no less antagonism from commercial editors, and was, indeed, even rejected by Grove Press after the company had profited handsomely from *Mulligan Stew.* In the decade since, Sorrentino has steadfastly refused to compromise his artistic vision, and the distance between his writing and the stylistic norms of commodity fiction has grown progressively greater.

The trajectory of Sorrentino's literary life can be tracked in this bibliography, from his first short story in a 1956 issue of his college literary magazine, through his involvement with the New York publishing scene in the 1960s and 1970s, and finally into the 1980s and early 1990, when his work once again is being printed by small presses. The bibliography treats writings both by and about Sorrentino, uniting in one volume descriptive analysis of primary works with annotated treatment of secondary sources. It thereby serves the needs not only of scholars and collectors interested in the physical production of Sorrentino's books but also of literary critics concerned with matters of reception and interpretation.

Section A records Sorrentino's separate publications in chronological order. First editions as well as significant subsequent issues are fully described, with separate paragraphs for collation, contents, paper, binding, dust jacket, text contents, publication information, and background notes. These formularies follow standard practice and are rooted in Fredson Bowers's *Principles of Bibliographic Description,* with modifications drawn from G. Thomas Tanselle's articles on paper, patterns, and color, gathered in his *Selected Studies in Bibliography,* along with his uncollected article, "Book-Jackets, Blurbs, and Bibliographers," *The Library,* 5th ser., 26 (June 1971): 91-134. The formularies have, however, been adapted to the particular demands of the bibliography of contemporary books, and here two other sources have served as models, Robert J. Bertholf's *Robert Duncan: A Descriptive Bibliography* and Stuart Wright's *Randall Jarrell: A Descriptive Bibliography.*

Some specific aspects of Section A bear remarking. Title page transcriptions differentiate roman, italic, Gothic, and boldface types but do not record differences in point size. Transcriptions of copyright pages are intended to convey essential information and have been abbreviated whenever possible. Color designations follow the ISCC-NBS Centroid Color Charts and numbers in parentheses correspond to that system. The accounts of dust jackets are designed to complement the accompanying photographs and consequently are also abbreviated. Publication information has been supplied by the publishers. Background notes are based on the correspondence files of the Gilbert Sorrentino Papers at the University of Delaware (DeU), the Dalkey Archive Press Papers at the Stanford University Libraries (CSt), and personal interviews and correspondence with Sorrentino.

Finally, with regard to Section A, mention should be made of a German edition of *Steelwork,* whose release late in the fall of 1990 was announced just as this bibliography went to press. Translated by Joachin Kalka, *Steelwork: Ein Brooklyn Roman* is to be published by Maro Verlag in Augsburg.

Section B lists chronologically Sorrentino's contributions to books. First appearances as well as reprinted items are duly noted.

Section C provides chronological coverage of Sorrentino's contributions to periodicals, with notations of the subsequent as well as previous appearances of items. Variants in the poems are fully recorded, with the superscript $^{+}$, following a title abbreviation, indicating that the variant continues in all subsequent printings of the poem. The nature of variants in prose pieces is briefly characterized.

Section D offers separate chronological lists of Sorrentino's book jacket copy and his book blurbs. The former were mostly done for Grove Press during his tenure as editor in 1965-1970; a few were freelance jobs completed shortly after his departure from Grove. All the jacket copy appeared anonymously. Identification relied on Sorrentino's personal review of hundreds of dust jackets, copies of which were supplied from the Grove Press Archive at the Syracuse University Library. Only jacket copy that is wholly from Sorrentino's hand is included. Whenever the exact relation between dust jacket and later paperback wrapper copy could be established, it has been noted. This was, however, not always possible, and it is clear from the documented instances that the wrapper copy was not routinely reprinted from the jackets.

Section E lists chronologically and annotates published interviews with Sorrentino and commercially available taped readings by him. The annotations indicate topics discussed and works read.

Section F records and annotates reviews of Sorrentino's books. Arrangement is chronological, in the order of the books' publication, then alphabetical by reviewers. To provide as complete an account as possible of the reception of Sorrentino's work, even brief notices are included. Much of this material derives from publishers' clipping files, and in some cases it has been impossible to provide full citations. Rather than deleting such items, they have been included with partial references. Annotations typically draw on the language of the review itself and are intended to summarize both the tone and substance of the reviewer's judgment. The approximate number of words in each review is indicated in parentheses at the entry's end.

Section G lists and annotates critical commentary about Sorrentino, including dissertations. Entries are arranged alphabetically, first by critics' names, then by the item's title. The scope is restricted to sustained, substantive discussions of Sorrentino and his work, though sometimes briefer references are entered when these make significant or unusual points. Critical pieces that only mention Sorrentino in passing are excluded.

ACKNOWLEDGMENTS

Of all types of humanistic scholarship, bibliography is, perhaps, the most communal. Its success depends at almost every point on the cooperation and goodwill of others, and this project is no different. Many people generously gave their time and knowledge, and the opportunity to thank them for their support is especially welcome.

Foremost is Gilbert Sorrentino himself, without whose willingness to abide and abet a bibliographer's fanatic attention to detail, this book would have been much the poorer. He submitted to endless questions, made available his own collection of little magazines and books, and directed me to other essential contacts.

Among these, Sorrentino's publishers were consistently kind, not only providing information about the publication of his books but also opening their review files. Particularly helpful were Jill Bialosky of W. W. Norton, Marion Boyars of Marion Boyars Publishers, Elisabeth Dyssegaard of Hill & Wang, Pamela Fishman of Viking Penguin, Dan Johnson of Random House, James Laughlin and Griselda Ohannessian of New Directions, Geoffrey Mulligan of Picador Books, Julie Curtiss Voss and John Martin of Black Sparrow Press, Leslie Miller of the Grenfell Press, Gary Fisketjon, formerly of Random House, now at Alfred A. Knopf, John O'Brien and Steven Moore of the Dalkey Archive Press, Jack Shoemaker of North Point Press, Barbara Spielman of the University of Texas Press, and Theodore Wilentz, publisher of Corinth Books.

Libraries also housed much crucial information that would have remained inaccessible without the assistance of conscientious librarians. Especially important were Robert J. Bertholf, Curator of the Poetry/Rare Books Collection at SUNY-Buffalo, who provided data from the Jargon Society Archive, Maggie Kimball, Manuscripts Librarian at the Stanford University Libraries, who facilitated use of the Dalkey Archive Press Papers, Kathleen Manwaring at the George Arents Research Library, Syracuse University, who supplied records and dust jacket copy from the Grove Press Archive, and Timothy Murray of Special Collections, University of Delaware, who made available the Gilbert Sorrentino Papers.

Others whose contributions were indispensable include Richard Aaron of Am Here Books, Norman Finkelstein of Xavier University, and Tom Goldwasser of Serendipity Books, and Linda Long of Special Collections at Stanford University Libraries. The David C. Weber Librarians Research Fund also offered some much needed support. And finally, a word of special appreciation to Sonia H. Moss of Stanford University Libraries' Interlibrary Loan Department, whose care and persistence made this a better book than it otherwise would have been.

A. BOOKS AND OTHER SEPARATE PUBLICATIONS

GILBERT
SORRENTINO
THE
DARKNESS
Ecclesiastes 2:14
SURROUNDS
US

THE
DARKNESS
SURROUNDS
US
GILBERT
SORRENTINO
JONATHAN WILLIAMS
PUBLISHER
HIGHLANDS
1960

A1 THE DARKNESS SURROUNDS US 1960

First edition

THE | DARKNESS | SURROUNDS | US | GILBERT | SORRENTINO | JONATHAN WILLIAMS | PUBLISHER | HIGHLANDS | 1960

COLLATION: $[1]^{24}$ = 24 leaves; [1-48].

CONTENTS: [1] blank; [2] frontispiece: ink drawing of GS by Fielding Dawson; [3] title page; [4] [nine lines of acknowledgments] | Copyright 1960 by Gilbert Sorrentino | Printed in the United States of America: | Heritage Printers, Inc., Charlotte, North Carolina | Designed by Jonathan Williams | Highlands, North Carolina; [5-6] **THIS BOOK** | [two-page introduction by Joel Oppenheimer]; [7] dedication: **THIS BOOK FOR ELSENE**; [8] blank; [9-47] text; [48] blank.

PAPER: Leaf measures 22.8 x 14.8 cm.; yellowish white (92), wove, unwatermarked.

BINDING: Stapled into stiff black, wove, unwatermarked wrappers. Unstamped. All edges trimmed.

DUST JACKET: Total measurement 22.5 x 50.8 cm.; stiff, yellowish white (92), wove, unwatermarked paper printed in black and grays, reproducing a collage by Fielding Dawson. On the inside front flap is a 12-line autobiographical statement by GS, specifying Ezra Pound, William Carlos Williams, and Robert Creeley as his "great literary markers." The inside back flap lists other Jargon titles.

TEXT CONTENTS: A Fixture—The Fights—The Survivor—An Action—The Crisis —3 Quatrains—Van Wyck Expressway—Memorial Day—A Benediction at Autumn—The Man in the Moon—The Spouse—Man and Wife—Midnight Special—Tilt—"Sunny Down South"—The Zoo—The Vendetta—Mafiosi—The Totem—The Closet—The Photograph: Ca. 1920—El Bronx—A Señorita's Bouquet—Ancient Musick—The Girl—The Whole World Coal—The Rose—The Asphalt Jungle—The 5 Day Week—Nightpiece—A Classic Case—Lullaby of the Leaves—Folk Song—The Tournament—Thus Spake Zarathustra—Calling Dr. Dunninger—Hello Again—The Darkness Surrounds Us—The Outset.

PUBLICATION: Published October 1960 at $1.50. 1000 copies printed by Heritage Printers, Inc., Charlotte, NC.

BACKGROUND NOTES: *DSU* collects and arranges in roughly chronological order of composition the poems that GS wrote from 1957 to early 1960 and wanted to preserve. Because commercial houses at the time were seldom receptive to work by virtually unknown poets, GS did not submit *DSU* to any trade publishers.

Instead, in April 1960, he offered the book to Jonathan Williams, whom he had met in 1957 and whose Jargon Society had already included his work in its *14 Poets, 1 Artist* (B1). Williams immediately agreed to publish *DSU* but only if GS would finance all costs, in return for which GS would receive all the money Williams took in from sales. GS accepted these terms, posting the manuscript to Williams in early May. By month's end, Williams had secured an estimate of $585 for 1000 copies from Heritage Printers in Charlotte, NC. GS's costs included both this printer's charge and a design fee from Williams.

Production proceeded without problems, and advance copies were available in late September. Of the 1000 copies, GS personally took 500, initially giving many away and then later selling large blocks to the Gotham Book Mart in New York and to Sand Dollar in Berkeley. For the 500 copies Williams handled, promotion was negligible, and distribution consisted of placing copies in selected bookstores in New York and in such small press outlets as the Ashphodel Book Shop in Cleveland, City Lights Books in San Francisco, and the Grolier Book Shop in Cambridge. By June 1964, Williams had sold about 200 copies, but no money was ever paid GS.

Fielding Dawson, at that time GS's close friend, did a collage specifically for the cover, which, however, Williams rejected in favor of another that Dawson had earlier constructed for Stuart Perkoff's *The Suicide Room* but that had gone unused. Williams designed the dust jacket's wraparound format and also decided to place on it the Biblical passage Ecclesiastes 2:14, which GS originally intended as the book's epigraph. *DSU*'s title poem derives from Robert Creeley's short lyric "I Know a Man." GS chose it after he had assembled *DSU:* the poem epitomized for him the book's overall darkness as well as its occasional glimmerings of hope.

A2 BLACK AND WHITE 1964

a. First edition, first printing

BLACK AND WHITE | Gilbert Sorrentino | TOTEM PRESS | in association with | CORINTH BOOKS | New York, N.Y.

COLLATION: $[1]^{24}$ = 24 leaves; [1-48].

CONTENTS: [1] title page; [2] [quotation] *Love is no comforter, rather a nail in the* | *skull* | WILLIAM CARLOS WILLIAMS | For Jesse and Delia | [four lines of acknowledgments] | Copyright © 1964 Gilbert Sorrentino | Manufactured in the United States of America | Library of Congress Catalog No.: 64-22684 | Cover by Morton Lucks | TOTEM PRESS | in association with | CORINTH BOOKS INC. | New York 11, New York; [3-47] text; [48] **CORINTH BOOKS** Modern Writers and Poets | [15-line list of titles] | In association with **TOTEM PRESS/LeROI JONES**: | [12-line list of titles] | In association with | **JARGON BOOKS/JONATHAN WILLIAMS**: | [three-line list of titles]

PAPER: Leaf measures 20.2 x 13.5 cm.; yellowish white (92), wove, unwatermarked.

BINDING: Stapled into stiff, white (263) wrappers.

TEXT CONTENTS: The Transcript—The Charm—Ars Longa—The Fiction—Sinking, Swimming—Ave atque vale—In Arizona: December—The Meeting—The Edges—The Memory—Faces of Doom and Sterility—Maytime—Out of Their Butchered Hearts—The Evening News—Bar Games—Paint—Cards—The Checkers Problem—The Mathematics—Open Your Mouth and Say—Fable, with Zodiac—The Abstraction—Dominoes—Two for Franz Kline: 1. The Gunner; 2. The Dark Hallway—Theme and Variations—The Language Barrier—What I Mean Is—As with a Simple Gesture of the Fingers—The Long Goodbye—The Bare Tree—Counterparts—Who Goes There?—Theme for Painters—The Shadow Knows—The Briefing—Shapes of Winter: 1.-6.; 7. (Dirty Glasses)—Silences—Empty Rooms—The Legend—The Dream, Squared—What Shapes Hide—A Detail.

PUBLICATION: Date of publication not available from publisher. 1000 copies at $1.25, printed and bound by Noble Offset Printers, New York.

b. First edition, second printing
Identical to A2a.

PUBLICATION: Date of publication not available from publisher. 1000 copies at $1.25, printed and bound by Noble Offset Printers, New York. Theodore Wilentz, co-publisher of Corinth Books, reports that no effort was made to differentiate the first and second printings.

c. First edition, third printing (1969)
BLACK AND WHITE | **Gilbert Sorrentino** | **TOTEM PRESS** | *in association with* | **CORINTH BOOKS** | *New York, N.Y.*

COLLATION: Identical to A2a.

CONTENTS: Identical to A2a, except: [2] [first 10 lines identical to A2a] | Third Printing 1969 | [five lines identical to A2a] | *29 Perry Street* | *New York, N.Y. 10014* | Distributed by CITADEL PRESS | 222 Park Avenue South | New

York, N.Y. 10003; [48] CORINTH BOOKS/POETRY & CRITICISM | [23 lines listing titles] | *Limited signed editions available at $5.00.

PAPER: Identical to A2a, except white (263).

BINDING: Identical to A2a, except slight changes in the text of the back cover.

PUBLICATION: Date of publication during 1969 not available from publishers. 1000 copies at $1.50, printed and bound by Noble Offset Printers, New York.

BACKGROUND NOTES: *BW* collects the poems that GS wrote in the years 1960-1963 and considered worth preserving. The texts are arranged by tone, a deviation from GS's usual practice of chronological order by date of composition. *BW* was published by Totem/Corinth through the efforts of LeRoi Jones, who had been friends with GS since 1957 and whose Totem Press had earlier printed GS's work in *Jan 1st 1959: Fidel Castro* (B3). Totem was Jones's own press; the Corinth imprint, established by Theodore and Eli Wilentz, owners of the Eighth Street Book Store, had already been publishing avant-garde writers, especially those associated with the Beats and Black Mountain. The Wilentzes funded Totem/Corinth titles, while Jones selected and edited the manuscripts. Another of GS's friends, the painter Morton Lucks, drew the cover specifically for *BW*. According to GS, the drawing represents the poet falling off his stool in a frenzy, which was Lucks's general idea of GS's poems (unpublished interview with William McPheron, 25 October 1989; tape at CSt). The contract with Corinth provided for a $100 advance and a percentage of sales.

A3 THE SKY CHANGES 1966

a. First edition

The Sky Changes | *by Gilbert Sorrentino* | [publisher's device, letter "h" enfolded in letter "w"] HILL AND WANG [diagonal broken line] NEW YORK

COLLATION: $[1\text{-}6]^{16}$ = 96 leaves; [i-ii]; [1-10], 11-181, [182-190].

CONTENTS: [i-ii] blank; [1] half title; [2] The Sky Changes [repeated seven times forming a ladder down from left to right]; [3] title page; [4] © *copyright 1966 by Gilbert Sorrentino* | *All rights reserved* | *Library of Congress catalog card number: 66-15895* | *First edition March 1966* | *Manufactured in the United States of America* | *by American Book-Stratford Press, Inc.;* [5] dedication: *for Victoria—* | *who knows why;* [6] blank; [7] [two quotations] *And so it was I entered the broken world* | *To trace the visionary company of love, its voice* | *An instant in the wind . . .* | HART CRANE | *Divorce is* | *the sign of knowledge in our time,* | *divorce! divorce!* | WILLIAM CARLOS WILLIAMS; [8] blank; [9] half title; [10] blank; 11-181 text; [182-190] blank.

PAPER: Leaf measures 20.2 x 13.5 cm.; yellowish white (92), wove, unwatermarked.

BINDING: Sewn and bound in medium to dark gray (265-266), bead cloth. Front cover: unstamped. Down spine, stamped in gold: The Sky Changes Sorrentino; across spine: [publisher's device, letter "h" enfolded in letter "w"] | HILL | AND | WANG. Back cover: unstamped. All edges trimmed. Yellowish white (92), wove, unwatermarked endpapers.

DUST JACKET: Total measurement 20.8 x 49.6 cm. White (263), wove unwatermarked paper printed in black, grays, strong orange yellow (68), and brilliant yellow (83). Inside flaps include five-paragraph description of *SC* and promotional blurbs by Seymour Krim, Robert Creeley, Donald Phelps, and Robert Gover. Back cover features a photograph of GS by Arthur W. Wang and a five-line biographical statement about GS. Front cover photograph is by Robert Frank.

PUBLICATION: Published 22 March 1966 at $3.95. 3000 copies, printed by American Book-Stratford Press, of which 2,925 were bound. Approximately twenty bound galleys were sent to reviewers prior to publication.

BACKGROUND NOTES: GS wrote the first 40 pages of *SC* in 1961 but then put the manuscript aside until late 1962, when he returned to the novel, radically simplified its conception, and finished the book in 1963. Throughout this period, GS wrote at nights, while during the day he freelanced for publishers—usually as a proofreader—and worked odd jobs at printing companies. When GS completed *SC*, he had no literary agent, but through his friendship with Hubert

Selby, Jr., he knew the journalist Seymour Krim. Krim was fiction editor at *Nugget*, a men's magazine, and was also taking freelance assignments at Grove Press, where by this time GS was working full time as an assistant editor. Krim asked to read *SC* in manuscript and was so impressed that he volunteered to act as GS's agent, commenting at the time: "the writing is so natural and skilled that it can't fail to impress any editor at any bookhouse who cares about the value of language in human intercourse" (letter to GS, 8 October 1964; TLS at DeU).

Three trade houses rejected the novel before Krim placed it with Hill and Wang, where it was accepted without any requests for revisions. There had, however, been conflict about it at the publishing company: though Arthur Wang was thrilled with *SC*, his partner, Lawrence Hill, disliked the novel. Wang's enthusiasm was sufficient to override Hill's objections, and his support extended even further. He personally took GS's photograph for the dust jacket and honored GS's request to feature on the jacket's front cover the Robert Frank photograph. This picture of a lonely New Mexico road GS had admired since its publication in *The Americans* (New York: Grove Press, 1959), and he thought the image particularly appropriate to *SC*. Wang's commitment to *SC* prompted an early promotional campaign for the book, with advertisements in the *New York Times Book Review* and the *New York Review of Books*. His enthusiasm was increased further when *Time* informed him of its intention to run a favorable review, accompanied by a picture of GS to be taken by one of the magazine's own photographers. A very positive review was, in fact, filed with *Time*, and the photographs of GS duly taken, but the coverage was killed. *Time* refused to explain its motives to Wang, after which he lost interest in *SC* and dropped his other promotional plans. Eventual sales were poor.

The publisher later remaindered its stock of the book and in 1972 allowed the title to go out of print. Though GS's new agent, Karen Hitzig, formally requested reversion of the rights on 1 June 1972, Farrar, Straus & Giroux, which now owned Hill and Wang, delayed action for three years before honoring the contract, which had stipulated that the rights to *SC* would revert to GS within six months, if the publisher did not reprint. The contract with Hill and Wang had also provided a $750 advance, which was typical at the time for first novels and ended up being the full extent of GS's financial compensation for the novel.

b. North Point Press edition (1986)
[9.7 cm. rule] | **THE SKY** | **CHANGES** | [9.7 cm. rule] | **Gilbert** | **Sorrentino** | [9.7 cm. rule] | 1986 | north point press | san francisco

COLLATION: [1-5]^{16} = 80 leaves; [i-xiv], [1-3], 4-139, [140-146].

CONTENTS: [i-ii] blank; [iii] [at top right, publisher's device—a sign in calligraphic style of an arrow pointing north]; [iv] blank; [v] [21 lines listing other books by GS]; [vi] blank; [vii] title page; [viii] Copyright © 1966, 1986 by Gilbert Sorrentino | Originally published by Hill & Wang, Inc., New York | Printed in the United States of America | Library of Congress Catalogue Card Number: 85-72984 | ISBN: 0-86547-243-2 | Cover design: David Bullen | North Point Press | 850 Talbot Avenue | Berkeley, California | 94706; [ix] dedication: for Victoria— | who knows why; [x] blank; [xi] AUTHOR'S NOTE | [15 lines discussing the nature of GS's revision of the text] | G.S.; [xii] blank; [xiii] [two quotations] And so it was I entered the broken world | To trace the visionary company of love, its voice | An instant in the wind . . . | *Hart Crane* | Divorce is | the sign of knowledge in our time, | divorce! divorce! | *William Carlos Williams;* [xiv] blank; [1] half title: THE SKY CHANGES; [2] blank; [3]-139 text; [140] blank; [141] Design by David Bullen | Typeset in Mergenthaler Imprint | with Gill Sans display | by Wilsted & Taylor | Printed by Maple-Vail | on acid-free paper; [142-146] blank.

PAPER: Leaf measures 20.9 x 13.8 cm.; yellowish white (92), wove, unwatermarked.

BINDING: Sewn and glued into stiff, white (263) wrapper, printed strong to deep reddish orange (35-36). Back cover includes a three-paragraph description of the novel and blurbs by Robert Creeley and Richard Howard.

TEXT CONTENTS: Identical to A3a except: (1) addition of "Hagerstown, Maryland" and "Wheeling, West Virginia" chapters, pp. 8-10; (2) major revisions, characteristically by deletion and rewriting, to the chapters "Brooklyn, New York," p. 30; "Brooklyn, New York," pp. 74-75; "San Francisco, California," pp. 76-77; and "Santa Fe, New Mexico," pp. 77-82; (3) minor changes in the chapters: "Mississippi," pp. 39-42, notably p. 40; "Brooklyn, New York," pp. 49-50, notably p. 49; "New Orleans, Louisiana," pp. 55-59, notably p. 57; "San Antonio, Texas," pp. 67-69, notably p. 69; "Lawton, Oklahoma," pp. 69-74, notably p. 72; "Taos, New Mexico," pp. 82-85, notably p. 85, "San Francisco, California," pp. 127-34, notably p. 127.

PUBLICATION: Published 10 April 1986 at $12.50. 3928 copies printed and bound by Maple-Vail. No bound galleys were issued, but the publisher reported that a few Xeroxed copies of A3a were made and strip bound for reviewers.

BACKGROUND NOTES: From the time *SC* went out of print in 1972, GS was interested in its reprinting. When the rights reverted to him in 1975, GS took the time to revise the text: "I am remedying all the 'tonal' defects that have always bothered me and the book is tighter and, I think, stronger and better. Not that anyone will reprint it, but it will soothe me to have it the way it should be" (letter to John O'Brien, 18 March 1975; TLS at CSt). Beginning in May 1975, GS's agent, Karen Hitzig, and, later, her successor, Mel Berger, intensively sought a new publisher for *SC*, but after numerous houses rejected it, Berger pulled *SC* from circulation in December 1976. GS himself then offered the book to Marion Boyars, but in February 1977 she, too, declined to reprint it.

In the fall of 1983, just a few months after North Point Press had published *BP*, GS submitted *SC* to Jack Shoemaker, North Point's editor. One phase of the house's publishing program involved reprinting works by its authors which were no longer available, and by year's end a contract had been signed for a new edition of *SC*. In January 1984, GS finished the two new chapters he had long wanted to insert in the novel, explaining that he "had to cast them in the same tone and voice as the rest of the book. I quite literally copied the style of the book in writing these pieces" (letter to O'Brien, 30 January 1984; TLS at CSt). Production on the book began in the summer of 1985, with proofs issued in October 1985. North Point attempted in the fall of 1985 to engage Carcanet as co-publisher with British rights, but the deal never materialized. Shoemaker was also unable to secure the rights to reproduce the Robert Frank photograph used on the cover of the first edition.

A4 THE PERFECT FICTION 1968

a. First edition, clothbound issue

THE | PERFECT FICTION | [three decorative devices forming a triangle] | [2.5 cm. centered rule] | *Gilbert Sorrentino* | [publisher's device, capital letter "N" intersected at top and bottom with capital letters "W" and in the middle by a bird image, the whole enclosed in an oval] | W • W • NORTON & COMPANY, INC. | *New York*.

COLLATION: [1-5]^{8} = 40 leaves; pp. [1-10], 11-73, [74-80].

CONTENTS: [1-2] blank; [3] half title: *The* | PERFECT FICTION; [4] blank; [5] title page; [6] [four lines of acknowledgments] | COPYRIGHT © 1968 BY GILBERT SORRENTINO | FIRST EDITION | Library of Congress Catalog Card No. 68-14767 | All Rights Reserved | Published simultaneously in Canada by | George J. McLeod Limited, Toronto | PRINTED IN THE UNITED STATES OF AMERICA | 1 2 3 4 5 6 7 8 9 0; [7] Dedication: IN MEMORIAM | *Ann Marie Sorrentino* | *1903-1960;* [8] blank; [9] *THE* | PERFECT FICTION; [10] blank; 11-73 text; [74-80] blank.

PAPER: Leaf measures approx. 21.3 x 14.2 cm.; yellowish white (92), laid, chain lines 2.5 cm. apart, watermarked "Warren's Olde Style."

BINDING: Sewn and bound in fine calico strong to deep red (12-13) cloth. Across front cover, blindstamped: Gilbert Sorrentino. Down spine, stamped in gold: Sorrentino THE PERFECT FICTION NORTON. Back cover: unstamped. Top edge trimmed; bottom and fore edges roughly trimmed. Yellowish white (92), wove, unwatermarked endpapers.

DUST JACKET: Total measurement 21.7 x 49.5 cm.; white (263) paper printed in black. Front flap includes a description of *PF* as a 52-poem yearbook, with "one poem for each week"; it also includes a statement formally attributed to GS that explain's *PF*'s three-line stanzaic structure. Back flap features a photograph of GS by Cheri Jenkins and a six-line biographical statement about GS. Jacket design by Angel Arnet.

TEXT CONTENTS: "He walks on the street, in"—"In a fantastic light:"—"Where are the rose-colored cities"—"Now the night is here. Blood"—"A particular density: in the center, rises"—"Nothing grimmer than dawn at noon."—"There is no poetry in me tonight."—"L the simple shape"—"In the blue, singa"—"There is 'a sound of birds' "—Gloss on Catullus 58—"Reality is a glass, a glass."—"Her voice speaks black"—"What did he think Hamlet"—"Something plus something is not one thing."—"Come from the whirling zodiac"—"Come all ye Sons of Art"—"On the margins of various papers"—"What intense colloquy with the self"—"There is no instance that was not love:"—(Sonnet with X's)—"Communications are as love"—"What is past is here, as we"—"Still, it is, as if, one may"—"Some hawk-nosed man"—"It is one man alone, what"—"How I loved that melody"—"The world is still:"—"The woman has gone forth"—"The stupid painter paints. He"—"World is a flame, world"—"What is to be understood:"—"People in Hell are clothed"—"A stinking city full of stinking"—"The weight of the rock"—"The troops that move in the sun"—"Here, in the center, a vacuum:"—"There is a woman in it always"—"Take a card, any card"—For W. C. W.—"Happy"—(pentagram)—"Clairvoyant perception of a distant balloon"—"Vivid is the word: of the imagination."—"My Old Hat. I never had."—"In a dogeared deck of cards"—"Such a long walk to get out"—"A door that opens on"—"A red sun is going down somewhere"—For M. F.—"But the light is imagined"—"Mother, this is a ball of color."

PUBLICATION: Published 28 March 1968 at $4.95. 979 copies, printed and bound by Vail Ballow Press. An unknown number of galley sheets, cut, labeled "uncorrected proofs," and spiral bound in printed, light yellowish green (135), stiff paper wrappers, was distributed to reviewers prior to publication.

NOTE: Though the copyright page states that *PF* was published simultaneously by George J. McCleod Ltd., Toronto, this statement is a copyright formality and no Canadian edition was issued.

b. First edition, paperbound issue
Identical to A4a, except:

COLLATION: Perfect bound.

PAPER: Leaf measures 20.9 x 13.4 cm.; otherwise identical to A4a.

BINDING: Glued into stiff, wove, unwatermarked, yellowish white (92), paper wrapper. Front cover is printed identically to the front of the dust jacket of A4a. Back cover reprints in the text of the inside jacket flaps of A4a as well as the photograph by Cheri Jenkins.

PUBLICATION: Published 28 March 1968 at $1.95. 920 copies, printed and bound by Vail Ballow Press.

BACKGROUND NOTES: *PF* was written during 1965-66, while GS was working full time at Grove Press. Conceived from the very beginning as a 52-poem structure, the book originated in the formal challenge of keeping the three-line stanza interesting over so long a textual stretch. In the process of composition, GS wrote about 80-85 poems, then selected the 52 he thought were best.

PF was published by Norton because of Denise Levertov, whom GS had known since 1956. She wrote GS just as he was finishing the volume, asking if he had a book appropriate for the poetry series she was editing for Norton. Levertov had earlier reviewed *DSU* favorably and also had published several of GS's poems when she was poetry editor at the *Nation.* Norton accepted *PF* with no requests for revision. GS's only involvement in the book's design and production was indirect: the dust jacket's flap copy derives directly from GS's response to a publisher's questionnaire he submitted to Norton.

The contract for *PF* involved a $250 advance, which was the full extent of GS's payments, although Norton regularly sent royalty statements, typically indicating the sale of no more than one or two copies every six months. GS attributed this in part to the publisher's failure to promote any of its poetry books, and he eventually wrote George Brockway, Norton's editor-in-chief at the time, complaining about the situation and suggesting that "more copies could be sold by peddling the books on street corners" (unpublished interview with William McPheron, 25 October 1989; tape at CSt).

A5 STEELWORK 1970

First edition

steelwork | **GILBERT SORRENTINO** | [at right, publisher's device, a classical temple] | [10.5 cm. rule] | PANTHEON BOOKS | *A Division of Random House, New York*

COLLATION: $[1\text{-}6]^{16}$ = 96 leaves; [i-vii], vii-xii; [1-3], 4-177, [178-180].

CONTENTS: [i] half title; [ii] blank; [iii] title page; [iv] Some sections of this book have previously been published in | *Grosseteste Review.* | Copyright © 1969, 1970 by Gilbert Sorrentino | All rights reserved under International and Pan-American Copy- | right Conventions. Published in the United States by Pantheon | Books, a division of Random House, Inc., New York, and simul- | taneously in Canada by Random House of Canada Limited, | Toronto. | Library of Congress Catalog Card Number: 79-119484 | Manufactured in the United States of America by | The Haddon Craftsmen, Inc., Scranton, Pa. | Design by Kenneth Miyamoto | FIRST PRINTING; [v] dedication: *to Donald Walsh;* [vi] blank; [vii-xii] contents; [1] half title; [2] blank; [3]-177 text; [178] blank; [179] [unascribed quotation from Henry Vaughan] "They are all gone into the world of light"; [180] blank.

PAPER: Leaf measures 21.1 x approx. 14.4 cm.; yellowish white (92), wove, unwatermarked.

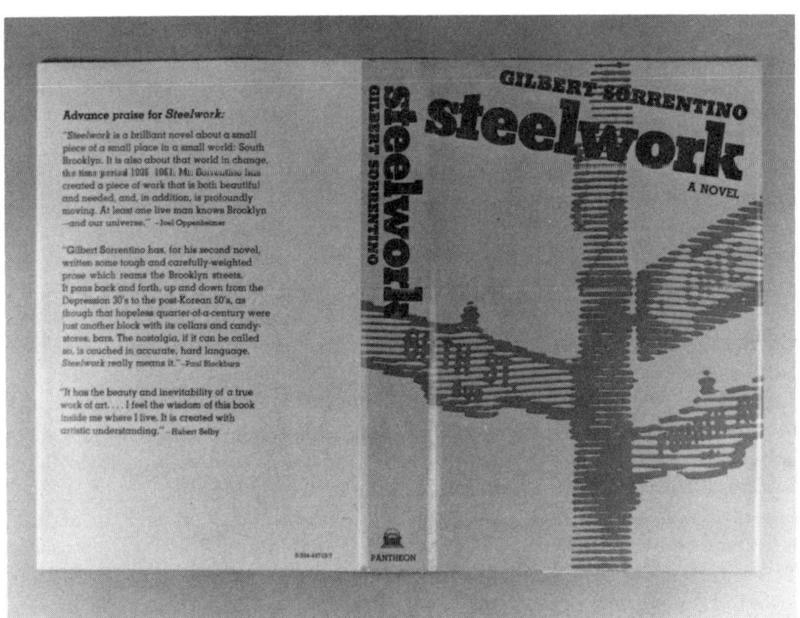

BINDING: Sewn and bound in moderate blue (182), fine calico-texture cloth. Across front cover, stamped at upward angle at top in black: steelwork. Down spine, stamped in gold: steelwork GILBERT SORRENTINO pantheon [final three letters of "pantheon" surmounted by publisher's device, a classical temple]. Back cover: unstamped. Top and bottom edges trimmed; fore-edge roughly trimmed. Yellowish white (92), wove, unwatermarked endpapers.

DUST JACKET: Total measurement 21.6 x 51.8 cm. White (263) paper printed in vivid orange yellow (66), strong blue (178), and cream (no Centroid equivalent). Back cover includes blurbs by Joel Oppenheimer, Paul Blackburn, and Hubert Selby. Front flap has a 24-line description of *SW*. Back flap features a photograph of GS by Cheri Jenkins and a brief biographical statement. Jacket design by Kenneth Miyamoto.

PUBLICATION: Published 16 October 1970 at $5.95. Publisher unable to supply number of copies printed.

NOTE: Though the copyright page states that *SW* was published simultaneously by Random House of Canada, this statement is a copyright formality and no Canadian edition was issued.

BACKGROUND NOTES: *SW* was written at night in 1968-69, while GS was working regular hours at Grove Press. He had previously treated the subject matter of *SW* in a 49-page, unpublished manuscript, "The Light Fantastic," which dates from the mid-1950s and is among GS's papers at DeU. Consisting of a group of "highly subjective impressions" of people GS grew up with in Brooklyn, the piece is marked by a "romanticized style that glamorizes their rather grim lives" (unpublished interview with William McPheron, 25 October 1989; tape at CSt). GS never attempted to publish "The Light Fantastic."

SW proper found its way to Pantheon through a complicated set of events. Sara Blackburn, Paul Blackburn's wife, was then an editor at Pantheon and asked GS if he had a manuscript appropriate to the trade publisher. About the same time, following Hubert Selby's suggestion, GS contacted the literary agency, Sterling Lord, and one of its staff, Karen Schnitzler, later Karen Hitzig, became his agent. At GS's suggestion, she sent *SW* to Pantheon, where André Schiffrin, then the firm's director, accepted it, but only if Pantheon could also publish *IQAT*, which GS had almost completed by this time. GS agreed to these terms, signed the two-book contract, and received a combined $1250 advance for both novels.

Paula McGuire, who served as GS's editor at Pantheon, initially wanted the sections of *SW* arranged chronologically, but when GS refused, she dropped the issue. Otherwise, GS had no involvement in the book's production. Shortly after *SW* was published, John Martin, who had just agreed to print *CS* at his Black Sparrow Press, wrote GS about the novel: "Wonderful book. Everything about it is first rate, down to the way you put the pieces together, dating the sections, etc. You're the first to capture that sensibility of the 40s and 50s—a war-and-profit oriented society with almost nothing to redeem it, no class or flair at all" (letter, 28 December 1970; TLS at DeU).

Although Pantheon promoted *SW* very well, the novel sold relatively poorly.

In early 1973, after Pantheon could not get a remainder price for either *SW* or *IQAT*, the publisher proposed pulping the several thousand copies of each still in their warehouse. But before physically destroying the books, Pantheon offered copies to GS, who in turn arranged for Pantheon to sell them all in April 1973 for $500 to Peter Howard at Serendipity Books in Berkeley, CA. Serendipity, and its subsequent spin-off, Small Press Distribution, distributed *SW* and *IQAT* as their own imprints, selling the volumes through normal trade channels and paying GS a 10% royalty on net sales. Though the rights to both *SW* and *IQAT* should have routinely been reverted to GS, it required frequent requests from GS's agent, Mel Berger, to secure formal reversion, which did not occur until mid-1976. The Donald Walsh to whom GS dedicates *SW* was a boyhood friend.

A6 IMAGINATIVE QUALITIES OF ACTUAL THINGS 1971

First edition

Imaginative | *Qualities* | OF ACTUAL | THINGS | [9.3 cm. rule] | *by Gilbert Sorrentino* | PANTHEON BOOKS | A DIVISION OF RANDOM HOUSE, NEW YORK [publisher's device, a classical temple]

COLLATION: $[1\text{-}8]^{16}$ = 128 leaves; [i-x], [1-3], 4-23, [24-27], 28-54, [55-57], 58-86, [87-89], 90-108, [109-111], 112-151, [152-155], 156-182, [183-185], 186-211, [212-215], 216-243, [244-246].

CONTENTS: [i] half title; [ii] [three lines listing other novels by GS]; [iii] title page; [iv] Copyright © 1971 by Gilbert Sorrentino | All rights reserved under International and Pan-American Copy- | right Conventions. Published in the United States by Pantheon | Books, a division of Random House, Inc., New York, and simul- | taneously in Canada by Random House of Canada Limited, | Toronto. | ISBN: 0-394-47108-3 | Library of Congress Catalog Card Number: 72-155772 | Design by Kenneth Miyamoto | Manufactured in the United States of America | by Haddon Craftsmen, Scranton, Pennsylvania | FIRST EDITION; [v] dedication: *To Morton Lucks and Dan Rice;* [vi] blank; [vii] contents; [viii] blank; [ix] [nine-line quotation from William Carlos Williams]; [x] blank; [1]-243 text; [244] blank; [245] [two-line quotation from Ezra Pound]; [246] blank.

PAPER: Leaf measures 21.1 x approx. 14.1 cm.; yellowish white (92), wove, unwatermarked.

BINDING: Sewn and bound in yellowish white to yellowish gray (92-93), fine calico-texture cloth. Across front cover, stamped in lower right quadrant in very light blue (180): G/S. Down spine, stamped in black: *Imaginative Qualities* of ACTUAL THINGS / *Gilbert Sorrentino;* across spine, in black: [publisher's device, a classical temple] | PANTHEON. Back cover: unstamped. Top and bottom edges trimmed; fore-edges roughly trimmed. Yellowish white (92), wove, unwatermarked endpapers.

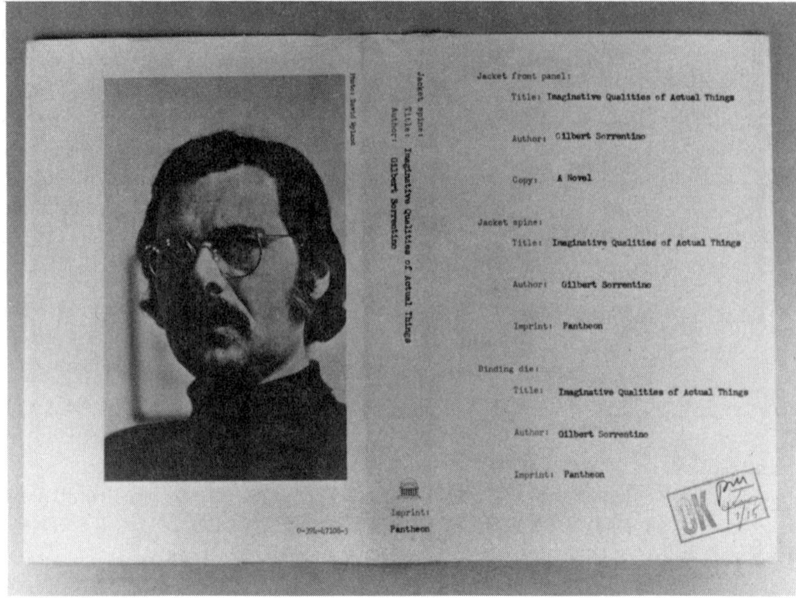

DUST JACKET: Total measurement 21.8 x 52.2 cm. Flaps and outer side are pale yellow (approx. 89), printed in black and brilliant violet (206). Back cover features a photograph of GS by David Wyland. Flaps include a 31-line description of *IQAT* and a four-line biographical statement about GS. Jacket design by Bob Anthony.

PUBLICATION: Publisher announced publication on 21 October 1971 at $6.95; publisher unable to supply number of copies printed. The U.S. Copyright Office's *Register of Copyright Entries* lists 21 September 1971 as the official date of publication.

NOTE: Though the copyright page states that *IQAT* was published simultaneously by Random House of Canada, this statement is a copyright formality and no Canadian edition was issued.

BACKGROUND NOTES: GS began *IQAT* immediately after completing *SW* in 1969 and finished the novel in 1970. Its publication by Pantheon was part of the two-book contract GS had earlier signed for *SW*, and again Paula McGuire acted as his editor, though with *IQAT* there were no suggestions for revisions. Because of the poor sales of *SW*, Pantheon made scant effort to promote and distribute *IQAT*. In fact, on the day of publication, GS was unable even to find copies in New York City bookstores and acquaintances elsewhere in the country also complained of the difficulty of locating copies for sale. GS dedicated *IQAT* to Morton Lucks and Dan Rice because they were two legitimate painters who were outside the "artistic feeding frenzy" that *IQAT* satirizes (unpublished interview with William McPheron, 25 October 1989; tape at CSt). Pantheon remaindered *IQAT* in 1973, along with *SW;* for further information about this arrangement, see the background notes for *SW.*

A7 CORROSIVE SUBLIMATE 1971

a. First edition, clothbound, signed and numbered issue

[in black] **GILBERT SORRENTINO** | [in strong red (12)] CORROSIVE | SUBLIMATE | [in black] **Black Sparrow Press ● Los Angeles ● 1971**

COLLATION: $[1\text{-}4]^8$, $[5]^4$ = 36 leaves; [1-10], 11-67, [68-72].

CONTENTS: [1] blank; [2] [eight lines listing books by GS]; [3] title page; [4] [three-line list of acknowledgments] | Cover illustration by Dan Rice | Copyright © 1971 | by Gilbert Sorrentino | Black Sparrow Press | P.O. Box 25603 | Los Angeles, California | 90025 | SBN 87685-116-1 (paper) | SBN 87685-117-0 (signed cloth); [5] dedication: *This book is for Christopher;* [6] blank; [7-8] contents; [9] half title; [10] blank; 11-67 text; [68] blank; [69] [at left] [publisher's device, pictorial illustration of a black sparrow, followed by GS's signature] | Printed December 1971 in Santa Barbara for | the Black Sparrow Press by Noel Young. Design | by Barbara Martin. This edition is limited to 1000 copies in paper wrappers; 200 hardcover | copies numbered & signed by the poet; & 26 | copies handbound in boards by Earle Gray | lettered & signed by the poet. | [number written in manuscript]; [70] blank; [71] [11.6 x 10.9 cm. black and white photograph of GS by David Wyland] | [10-line biographical statement about GS]; [72] blank.

PAPER: Leaf measures 22.9 x 15.4 cm.; yellowish white (92), wove, unwatermarked.

BINDING: Sewn and quarter bound in deep blue (179), bead cloth and yellowish white (92), shaded toward pale yellow (89) paper covered boards. Front cover printed in black, strong reddish brown (40), and deep blue (179). Down spine, printed on yellowish white (92), shaded toward pale yellow (89) paper label: CORROSIVE SUBLIMATE ● GILBERT SORRENTINO.

Back cover: unprinted. All edges trimmed. Black endpapers.

DUST JACKET: clear acetate.

TEXT CONTENTS: The Morning Roundup—The Poet Tires of Those Who Disparage His City—Land of Cotton—Bluesongo—Rose Room—Long Gone Blues—All the Colors in the World—Some Bright Paintings—Perceive—P.S.—Veterans of Foreign Wars—The Insane Waiters—Blue Turning Grey—Air for Owen and Branca—Poem ("The clear objects")—Apple Scrapple—Toward the End of Winter—1947 Blue Buick Convertible—Marjorie—Pinochle—Country and Western—Now the Leaves—Handbook of Versification—Coast of Texas, 1-16—Old Tale—Another Popular Novel—Research, Again—A Poem for My Wife—They Die Over and Over. In the Movies—*The New York Times:* A Poem for Ross Feld—Another Case o' Wheaties—Figure for Tenor Saxophone—See America First—Give Them Blood—Watteau. The Lady's Slipper—In Preparation for the Cold Season—Yet Another Effort, Frenchmen—Borough of Richmond—A Poem to Read in August—Anatomy—Pail—Rum and Coca-Cola—Prince Rupert's Drop—Address to the National Council on the Arts—Poem ("Living friends live").

PUBLICATION: Published 23 December 1971 at $15.00. 200 copies signed by GS and numbered 1-200, printed and bound by Noel Young, Santa Barbara, CA.

A7b. First edition, clothbound, signed and lettered issue
Identical to A7a, except:

CONTENTS: [69] [manuscript letter, instead of Arabic number].

BINDING: Quarter bound in black bead cloth.

PUBLICATION: Published 23 December 1971 at $20.00. 32 copies, of which 26, signed by GS and lettered A-Z, were for sale, and six, one each marked "Author's Copy," "Artist's Copy," "Publisher's Copy," "Printer's Copy," "Binder's Copy," and "File Copy," were not for sale.

A7c. First edition, paperbound issue
Identical to A7a, except:

COLLATION: perfect bound.

CONTENTS: [69] [no manuscript number or signature by GS].

BINDING: Glued into stiff, yellowish white (92), shaded toward pale yellow (89) paper wrappers. Down spine in black: CORROSIVE SUBLIMATE GILBERT SORRENTINO Black Sparrow Press.

PUBLICATION: Published 23 December 1971 at $4.00. 1000 copies printed and bound by Noel Young, Santa Barbara, CA.

BACKGROUND NOTES: *CS* collects the poems GS wrote after *BW*, arranging them in essentially chronological order of composition. In early fall of 1970, GS offered *CS* to John Martin, publisher of Black Sparrow, who accepted it without any requests for changes. In November, Martin sent the contract, which provided for a $100 advance against 10% royalties on the net price of all copies sold, to GS's literary agent, Karen Hitzig, and it was signed in December. GS arranged for the cover art, which reproduces in its identical size an oil on paper painting Dan Rice did specifically for *CS*. Martin originally planned to issue *CS* in April or May 1971, but production delays postponed page proofs until mid-November and the completed books until 23 December. Initial sales were strong: 300 copies were purchased in the first month after publication, and the royalties statement of July 1972 reported that another 118 had been bought. Subsequently, sales remained steady at about 100-200 copies per year, with the clothbound copies sold out in January 1975 and the paperbound going out of print by September 1978. When Martin decided early in 1979 not to reprint *CS*, the rights reverted to GS.

A8 SPLENDIDE-HÔTEL 1973

a. First edition, signed limited clothbound issue
SPLENDIDE- | HÔTEL | BY | GILBERT | SORRENTINO | [ornament] | A New Directions Book

COLLATION: [1-4]^{8} = 32 leaves; [1-6], 7-61, [62-64].

CONTENTS: [1] half title; [2] [10 lines listing other books by GS]; [3] title page; [4] Copyright © 1973 by Gilbert Sorrentino | Library of Congress Catalog Card Number: 73-78786 | [five-line statement of copyright reservations] | Some of the material in this book was first published in *Grosseteste Review*, to | which grateful acknowledgment is made. | Manufactured in the United States of America | First published clothbound (ISBN: 0-8112-0514-2), in a signed edition limited | to 350 copies, and as New Directions Paperbook 364 (ISBN: 0-8112-0495-2) | in 1973 | Published simultaneously in Canada by McClelland & Stewart, Ltd. | New Directions Books are published for James Laughlin | by New Directions Publishing Corporation | 333 Sixth Avenue, New York 10014; [5] dedication: TO MY OLD FRIEND | HUBERT SELBY; [6] *Et la* [sic] *Splendide-Hôtel* | *fut bâti dans le chaos* | *de glaces et de nuit* | *du pôle* | ARTHUR RIMBAUD; 7-61 text; [62] blank; [63] [compass ornament] | Three hundred and fifty copies | of this edition have been specially | printed and bound at | The Stinehour Press | Lunenburg, Vermont | in September 1973 | and are signed by | the author | [GS's manuscript signature] | This is number | [manuscript number]; [64] blank.

PAPER: Leaf measures 20.5 x 13.6 cm.; yellowish white (92), wove, unwatermarked.

BINDING: Sewn and quarter bound in light to moderate blue (181-182), fine calico cloth and yellowish white (92), wove paper covered boards. Front cover stamped in moderate blue (182) and moderate to dark yellowish green (136-137). Down spine, stamped in gold: GILBERT SORRENTINO SPLENDIDE-HÔTEL NEW DIRECTIONS. Back cover: identical to front cover. All edges trimmed. Pale purplish blue (203) wove, unwatermarked endpapers.

DUST JACKET: Issued in a protective, translucent paper wrapper.

PUBLICATION: Published 24 October 1973 at $25.00. 360 copies, of which 350 were signed and numbered 1-350 and 10 were out-of-series, unnumbered, and unsigned. Printed and bound by the Stinehour Press, Lunenburg, VT.

NOTE: Though the copyright page states that *S-H* was published simultaneously by McClelland & Stewart, Ltd., this statement is a copyright formality and no Canadian edition was issued.

b. First edition, paperbound issue
Identical to A8a, except:

CONTENTS: [63] blank.

PAPER: Leaf measures 20.4 x 13.6 cm.

BINDING: Sewn and glued into stiff, shiny, yellowish white (92) wrapper, printed in light gray (264) and black. Back cover includes three paragraphs that describe *S-H* as an homage to Arthur Rimbaud and William Carlos Williams and provide biographical information about GS. Cover designed by Roderick Stinehour. All edges trimmed.

PUBLICATION: Published at $3.25. 3000 copies printed and bound by the Stinehour Press, Lunenburg, VT.

NOTE: Eight sets of galley proofs were sent out in August to *Kirkus Reviews*, *Library Journal*, John Leonard at the *New York Times*, *Publishers Weekly*, Jerome Klinkowitz at *Fiction International*, Steven Loesk at *Seems*, Ronald Sukenick, and Herman Kogan at the *Chicago Sun-Times*.

BACKGROUND NOTES: Written in late 1970 and early 1971, *S-H* was first named *Hotel Splendide*, and under that title parts of it were published in the *Grosseteste Review*. In early fall of 1972, GS decided to follow Rimbaud's original designation and changed the title to *Splendide-Hôtel*. Under this new designation other parts appeared in *TriQuarterly*.

For book publication, GS initially approached Pantheon, which rejected *S-H* because it was too short. In August 1971, after negative responses from nearly a dozen other trade publishers, GS wrote James Laughlin, owner of New Directions, who agreed to read the manuscript. Laughlin liked *S-H* very much, commenting, "I would be hard put to it to tell what 'Hotel Splendide' is really about, or to write a blurb for it, but I enjoyed it thoroughly, the 'word play' of it, the imagery, the variety, and the sense that here was someone who was really having a good time with the language, and master enough of it to impart the pleasure to a reader, even if a slightly baffled reader" (letter to GS, 24 September 1971; TLS at DeU).

However, Laughlin was also convinced that *S-H* was "quite unmarketable in the commercial sense," and he hesitated to commit New Directions to its publication without finding ways to minimize financial liability. Laughlin first sought a British co-publisher to share production costs, and for the next year New Directions' London agent unsuccessfully circulated the manuscript among English trade houses. In October 1972, doubtful of ever locating a British partner, Laughlin decided to proceed independently with *S-H* but to control costs by reducing the print run and by issuing a signed, limited edition whose higher price could help carry expenses. On this basis the production process began. In November GS submitted his final revisions, in March Laughlin chose Stinehour as the designer and printer, in April GS provided copy for the *S-H* blurb that appeared both in the New Directions catalog and on the paperback issue, and in August the contract was finally worked out and signed. This provided an advance of $500. Copies of both the clothbound and paperbound issues were available by mid-August and distributed to solicit prepublication comments. Some of these, including statements by Luise Varèse and Alice S. Morris, were featured on a mimeographed flier New Directions distributed in October.

c. Dalkey Archive edition, clothbound issue (1984) (photo-offset from A8b) **SPLENDIDE- | HÔTEL | BY | GILBERT SORRENTINO |** [4.7 cm. narrow rule] | AN AFTERWORD | BY | ROBERT CREELEY | [4.7 cm. narrow rule] **THE DALKEY ARCHIVE PRESS**

COLLATION: Identical to A8b, except: [62-64] are numbered, 6^2 [sic]-64.

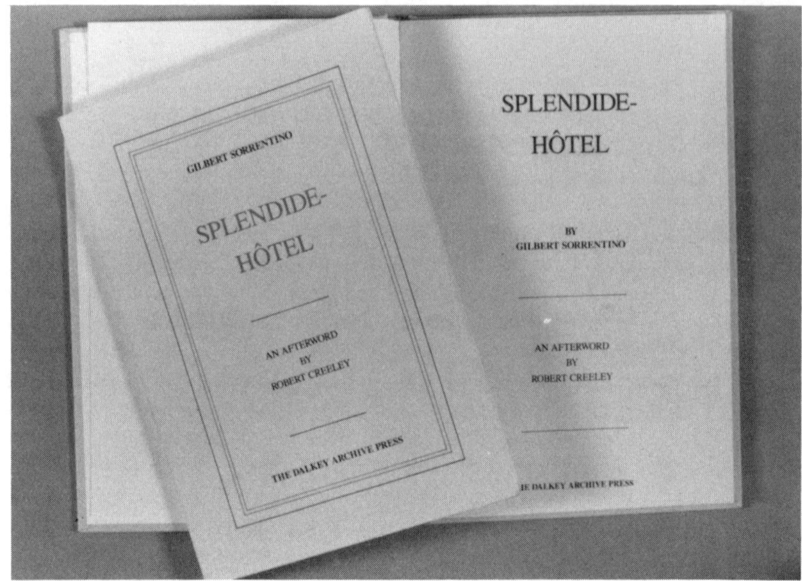

CONTENTS: Identical to A8b, except: [2] [18 lines listing other books by GS]; [3] title page: differences as transcribed; [4] SPLENDIDE-HÔTEL. Copyright © 1973, 1984 by Gilbert Sorrentino | AN AFTERWORD. Copyright © 1984 by Robert Creeley | All rights reserved under International and Pan-American Copyright Conventions. | Printed in the United States by The Dalkey Archive Press for The Review of Contem- | porary Fiction, Inc. Originally published by New Directions. | LIBRARY OF CONGRESS CATALOGING IN PUBLICATION DATA | Sorrentino, Gilbert, 1929- | Splendide-hôtel. | I. Title | PS3569. O7S6 1984 818'.5407 84-3228 | ISBN 0-916583-00-7 | ISBN 0-916583-01-5 | THE DALKEY ARCHIVE PRESS | 1817 N. 79th Avenue | Elmwood Park IL 60635; [6] *Et le Splendide-Hôtel fut bâti dans la chaos* | *de glaces et de nuit du pôle.* | ARTHUR RIMBAUD; 62-64 afterword, by Robert Creeley.

PAPER: Leaf measures 20.4 x 13.9 cm.; yellowish white (92), wove, unwatermarked.

BINDING: Sewn and bound in pale yellow (89), fine calico cloth. Front and back covers: unstamped. Down spine, stamped in black: [single rule] [double rule] GILBERT SORRENTINO SPLENDIDE-HÔTEL THE DALKEY ARCHIVE PRESS [double rule] [single rule]. All edges trimmed. Yellowish white (92), wove, unwatermarked endpapers.

TEXT CONTENTS: Identical to A8b, except for addition of Creeley afterword.

PUBLICATION: Published 26 May 1984 at $12.00. 300 copies printed by McNaughton & Gunn and bound by Heckman Bindery.

d. Dalkey Archive Press edition, paperbound issue (photo-offset from A8b)
Identical to A8c, except:

COLLATION: perfect bound.

BINDING: Glued into stiff, wove, unwatermarked, pale yellow (89) wrapper, printed in vivid to strong red (11-12) and black. All edges trimmed.

PUBLICATION: Published 26 May 1984 at $3.95. 2,026 copies printed by McNaughton & Gunn and bound by Heckman Bindery.

BACKGROUND NOTES: In August 1983 GS proposed to Jack Shoemaker that North Point Press reprint *S-H.* In January 1984 Shoemaker rejected the idea, and John O'Brien, who had just formed Dalkey Archive Press, committed himself to reprinting it. The contract, which provided an advance of $300 to GS, was signed in February, and production started in March, with advanced copies available in early May. "I can't tell you what a wonderful feeling it is to have one of my O.P. books reprinted," GS wrote to O'Brien (letter 20 March 1984; TLS at CSt).

A9 FLAWLESS PLAY RESTORED 1974

a. First edition, clothbound, signed and numbered issue
[within deep greenish yellow (100) 13.4 x 8.9 cm. double rule frame] *Gilbert Sorrentino* | [in vivid to strong red (11-12)] FLAWLESS | PLAY | RESTORED | [deep greenish yellow (100) rampant lion device] | THE MASQUE OF FUNGO | [below double rule frame] BLACK SPARROW PRESS • LOS ANGELES • 1974

COLLATION: $[1]^{18}$, $[2]^{16}$, $[3]^{2}$, $[4]^{8}$ = 44 leaves; [1-8], 9-83, [84-88].

CONTENTS: [1] blank; [2] [11 lines listing other works by GS]; [3] title page; [4] FLAWLESS PLAY RESTORED. Copyright © 1974 by Gilbert | Sorrentino. All rights reserved. Printed in the United States of Am- | erica. [statement of copyright reservations, continuing onto two subsequent lines] | For infor- | mation address Black Sparrow Press, P.O. Box 25603, Los Angeles, | CA, 90025. | LIBRARY OF CONGRESS CATALOGING IN PUBLICATION DATA | Sorrentino, Gilbert. | Flawless play restored: the masque of Fungo. | Part of a novel-in-progress presented in play form, but not intended | for the stage. | I. Title. | PS3569.O7F5 812'.5'4 74-22436 | ISBN 0-87685-198-7 | ISBN 0-87685-197-9 pbk.; [5-6] [alphabetical list of characters]; [7] half title; [8] blank; 9-83 text; [84] blank; [85] [publisher's device, pictorial illustration of a black sparrow, followed by GS's signature] | Printed November 1974 in Santa Barbara & | Ann Arbor for the Black Sparrow Press by | Noel Young & Edwards Brothers Inc. Design | by Barbara Martin. This edition is published | in paper wrappers; there are 200 hardcover | copies numbered & signed by

the poet; | & 26 copies handbound in boards by Earle | Gray lettered & signed by the poet. | [number written in manuscript]; [86] blank; [87] [11 x 10.9 cm. photograph of GS, by David Wyland] | [12-line biographical statement about GS]; [88] blank.

PAPER: Leaf measures 22.5 x 15.3 cm.; yellowish white (92), wove, unwatermarked.

BINDING: Sewn and quarter bound in strong to deep yellow green (117-118) and strong brown (55), coarse linen cloth and yellowish white (92), shaded toward pale yellow (89) paper covered boards. Front cover printed in deep greenish yellow (100) and vivid to strong red (11-12). Down spine, printed on yellowish white (92), shaded toward pale yellow (89) paper label: [in deep greenish yellow (100)] FLAWLESS PLAY RESTORED • Gilbert Sorrentino. Back cover unprinted. All edges trimmed. Dark greenish yellow (103), wove, unwatermarked endpapers.

DUST JACKET: clear acetate.

PUBLICATION: Published 16 December 1974 at $15.00. 201 signed copies, of which 200, numbered 1-200, were for sale, and one copy (marked "File Copy") not for sale; printed and bound by Noel Young, Santa Barbara, CA, and Edwards Brothers, Ann Arbor, MI.

b. First edition, clothbound, signed and lettered issue
Identical to A9a, except:

CONTENTS: Identical except, [85], which has manuscript lettering instead of numbering.

BINDING: Quarter bound in vivid to deep red (11-13), coarse linen cloth.

PUBLICATION: Published 16 December 1974 at $25.00. 31 signed copies, of which 26, lettered A-Z, were for sale, and five, one each marked "Author's Copy," "Publisher's Copy," "Printer's Copy," "Binder's Copy," and "File Copy," were not for sale.

c. First edition, paperbound issue
Identical to A9a, except:

COLLATION: perfect bound.

CONTENTS: Identical except, [85], which lacks GS's signature and the manuscript numbering.

PAPER: Leaf measures 22.8 x 15 cm.

BINDING: Glued into stiff yellowish white (92), shaded toward pale yellow (89) wrapper. Front cover printed overall in pattern identical to cover of A9a. Down spine: FLAWLESS PLAY RESTORED ● Gilbert Sorrentino Black Sparrow Press.

PUBLICATION: Published 16 December 1974 at $3.00. 1536 copies.

BACKGROUND NOTES: On 22 January 1973, John Martin, owner of Black Sparrow Press, wrote GS, referring to the book that would become *MS:* "So you're writing a long novel. Maybe we can publish it in installments!" GS replied at once, asking Martin to consider a section, then titled "Flawless Play Restored to Fungo." Once he read it, Martin was enthusiastic, commenting: "It is an outrageous masterwork, and a 'flawless play' indeed. Of course, I'd love to publish it! It will reduce every author I don't like to whimpering fury. It will enrich and edify all the authors I like. What a lovely sword you wield" (letter to GS, 21 April 1973; TLS at DeU).

Responding to Martin's initial plan to print *FP* immediately, GS suggested in May that his friend Morton Lucks be asked to provide art for the book, and Martin cautiously agreed. But when Martin eventually saw Lucks's drawings, he rejected them, complaining that they looked like "cartoons" and arguing: "I think it would start the book off on the wrong foot to use one of the drawings on the cover. While *Fungo* is very funny, it is NOT slapstick pure and simple, and the drawings suggest this. There's a heroic depth to the text, which must be *preserved* typographically, not detracted from" (letter to GS, 6 June 1973; TSL at DeU).

Paper shortages and related problems postponed production of *FP* until late

July 1974. Black Sparrow's catalog of forthcoming titles for September-December 1974, issued in June, listed *FP* for October, and typesetting was completed in August 1974, with unpaged galleys forwarded to GS in September. But printer's errors further delayed production, and the colophon pages for the signed copies were not ready for GS until 16 December. The contract for *FP* excluded an advance and stipulated royalties of 10% on the sale of all clothbound copies and 5% on the paperbound.

FP was reprinted with minor revisions in *MS*, 178-216.

A10 A DOZEN ORANGES 1976

COLLATION: [1]^{8}; [1-16].

CONTENTS: [1] title page serving as front cover; [2] Copyright © 1976 by Gilbert Sorrentino; [3-14] text; [15] blank; [16] back cover.

PAPER: Leaf measures 23 x 15.2 cm.; yellowish white (92), wove, unwatermarked.

BINDING: Stapled pamphlet in self-wrappers. Front and back covers printed in strong red (12) and black. Back cover lists current Black Sparrow books by authors other than GS.

TEXT CONTENTS: "Remember the story of Columbus and the orange?"—La Vie d'Art—After Montale—King Cole—White Lemons—"O Xmas tree"—Silent Knight—Arthur Rimbaud—Aesthetics—Partial Graph—"Everybody would soon change"—Zukofsky.

NOTE: Text contents reprinted without changes in A13.

PUBLICATION: Published 6 July 1976 at $.75. 1196 copies.

NOTE: Copies of A10 were bound with other first printings of *Sparrow* 37-48 and published by Black Sparrow Press in two issues on 14 October 1976 under the title *Sparrow 37-48*. The book consists of separate issues of *Sparrow* 37-48, trimmed and bound together without a separate title page. The "autographed edition" included copies of the pamphlets signed by their authors and was limited to 60 copies at $40. The trade edition of 146 copies was published at $15.00. Both issues were originally bound in dark grayish reddish brown (47), fine bead cloth with a yellowish white (92) paper label on the front cover, printed in moderate brown (58). The end sheets are brownish cream (no Centroid equivalent), laid, watermarked paper with chain lines 2.5 cm. apart. The dust jacket is clear acetate. Additional copies of the trade edition containing mixed printings were issued in varying bindings as needed.

BACKGROUND NOTES: John Martin, owner of Black Sparrow Press, first invited GS to submit a short manuscript for publication as a *Sparrow* pamphlet in November 1973. GS responded by offering two sections from *MS*, "The Library" and "Perfect Gifts," which Martin declined. In September 1975, a month after accepting *WS*, Martin renewed his invitation, encouraging GS to submit poetry rather than prose. In January GS sent *A Dozen Oranges*, which Martin accepted immediately and scheduled for the July issue of *Sparrow*.

Martin's standard arrangement for issues of *Sparrow* excluded advances and royalties, instead making payment in-kind with 50 copies to the author. These copies were sent to GS on 6 July 1976, along with the unstapled, untrimmed copies that he signed and returned for Martin's subsequent "autograph edition" of *Sparrow 37-48*.

A11 SULPICIÆ ELEGIDIA/ELEGIACS OF SULPICIA 1977

[in light brown (57)] *GILBERT SORRENTINO* | [in dark reddish orange (38)] SVLPICIÆ ELEGIDIA | [in dark gray (266)] ELEGIACS OF SULPICIA | *The Perishable Press Limited • Mt Horeb • Wisconsin Mcmlxxvii*

COLLATION: $[1]^{12}$ = 12 leaves; [1-24].

CONTENTS: [1-2] blank; [3] half title: [in grayish brown (61)] SVLPICIÆ ELEGIDIA; [4] blank; [5] title page, [6] [in dark gray (266)] *copyright 1977 by Gilbert Sorrentino;* [7-19] text; [20] blank; [21] [in grayish brown (61)] work on this small gathering started january thirtieth when | Mary began setting the Saban Antiqua. one hundred thirty | seven copies were printed on our manual Vandercook SP/15 | during the arrival of spring & the simultaneous flowering of | everything. this paper is Perusia sewn into Roma, both made | at the Fabriano mill by hand. this copy is press-numbered [number in strong reddish brown (40)] [period, in grayish brown (61)]; [22-24] blank.

PAPER: Leaf measures approx. 12.2 x 16.5 cm.; cream (no Centroid equivalent), laid, with chain lines approximately 2.7 cm. apart, watermarked with "PERVSIA" below a griffin.

BINDING: Sewn into grayish brown (61) laid wrappers, chain lines varying between 3.7-4.4 cm. apart. Unstamped. Edges deckled.

DUST JACKET: Total measurement 12.3-12.6 x 65.8 cm. Grayish brown (61) laid paper, chain lines varying between 3.7-4.0 cm. apart, watermarked

"ROMA" below a figure of a wolf nursing Romulus and Remus enclosed within an oval. Front cover stamped in strong brown (55) and dark gray (266). Back cover unstamped.

TEXT CONTENTS: I Tandem venit amor, qualem texisse pudori / At last comes love of such a quality that it would shame me—II Invisus natalis adest, qui rure molesto / My hated birthday looms. In the rude and wretched country—III Scis iter ex animo sublatum triste puellae? / Do you know that sad journey is lifted from your darling's heart?—IV Gratum est, securus multum quod iam tibi de me / That you allow yourself this vast neglect of me—V Estne tibi, Cerinthe, tuae pia cura puellae / Cerinthus, don't you have some soft thought for your girl—VI Ne tibi sim, mea lux, aeque iam fervida cura / Light, my light, let me never be again.

NOTE: *SP* 153-55 reprints GS's English versions.

PUBLICATION: Production completed 7 May 1977. 137 numbered copies, printed and bound by Perishable Press, Ltd. Copies 1-20 were GS's, paid as royalty in-kind; remaining copies were for sale at $32.50.

BACKGROUND NOTES: "I am enamored of this woman, Sulpicia, her Latin falls as simply as English, almost," GS wrote John O'Brien (letter, 20 September 1976; TLS at CSt), and continued, "the cadence is utterly sophisticated as the words fall, almost as spoken. I am having a hell of a time with her because of her plainness." Just over a month later, on 28 October 1976, GS wrote Walter Hamady to ask if the Perishable Press would be interested in publishing his translations of Sulpicia. Hamady, who already knew of GS's work through his friendships with

Paul Blackburn and Robert Creeley, received the manuscript from GS in early December and replied almost immediately, praising the translations and agreeing to print them with Latin facing (letter to GS, 11 December 1976; TLS at DeU). Hamady proposed an informal arrangement of payment of royalty in-kind, with GS to receive copies 1-20 of the edition. GS reviewed the first set of proofs in mid-February 1977 and the second set in early April. Hamady sent GS his copies on 8 May 1977.

A12 WHITE SAIL 1977

a. First edition, clothbound, signed and numbered issue

[dark yellow (88), in hollow type] WHITE | SAIL | [light olive gray (112) thick swirling rule] | [dark yellow (88) in hollow type] GILBERT | SORRENTINO | [black] *Santa Barbara* | BLACK SPARROW PRESS | 1977

COLLATION: [1^2 2^{16} 3^2 4^4 5^8] = 32 leaves; [1-8], 9-59, [60-64].

CONTENTS: [1] blank; [2] [11 lines listing other books by GS]; [3] title page; [4] WHITE SAIL. Copyright © 1977 by Gilbert Sorrentino. | [four lines stating copyright reservations] | Black Sparrow Press, P.O. Box 3993, Santa Barbara, CA 93105. | [four lines recording acknowledgments] | LIBRARY OF CONGRESS CATALOGING IN PUBLICATION DATA | Sorrentino, Gilbert. | White sail. | I. Title | PS3569.07W5 811'.5'4 77-7474 | ISBN 0-87685-282-7 (paper edition) | ISBN 0-87685-283-5 (cloth signed edition); [5-6] contents; [7] half title; [8] blank; 9-59 text; [60] blank; [61] [publisher's device,

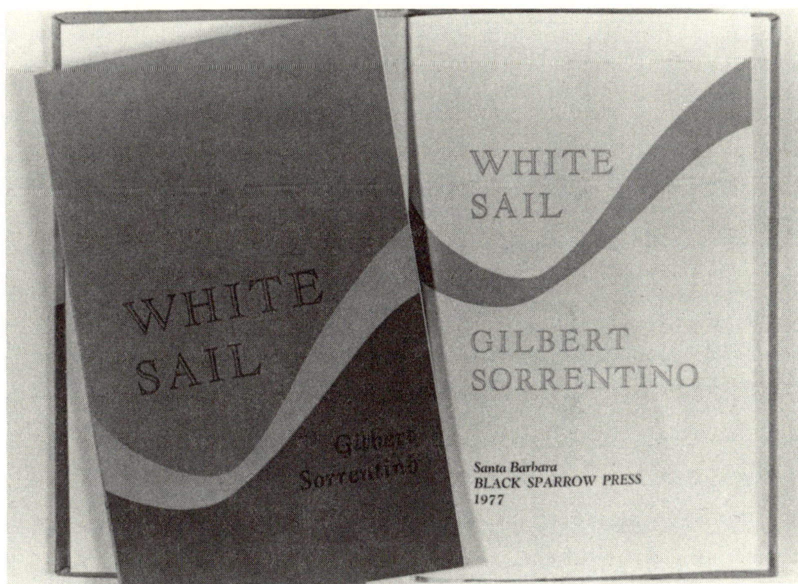

pictorial illustration of a black sparrow, followed by GS's signature] | Printed May 1977 in Santa Barbara & Ann Arbor | for the Black Sparrow Press by Mackintosh and Young | & Edwards Brothers Inc. Design by Barbara Martin. | This edition is published in paper wrappers; there | are 200 hardcover copies numbered & signed by the poet; | & 26 copies handbound in boards by Earle Gray lettered | & signed by the poet. | [number written in manuscript]; [62] blank; [63] 10.7 x 10.5 cm. black and white photograph of GS by Victoria Sorrentino | [seven-line biographical statement about GS]; [64] blank.

PAPER: Leaf measures 22.8 x 15.2 cm.; yellowish white (92), wove, unwatermarked.

BINDING: Sewn and quarter bound in white (263), fine bead cloth along spine and light grayish to grayish olive (109-110), wove paper covered boards. Front cover printed in moderate brown (58), light gray (264), and light to moderate olive (106-107). Down spine on light grayish to grayish olive (109-110), wove paper label, printed in black: WHITE SAIL Gilbert Sorrentino. Back cover: unprinted. All edges trimmed. Dark greenish yellow (103), wove, unwatermarked endpapers.

DUST JACKET: Clear acetate.

TEXT CONTENTS: Beautiful Soup—Paul Blackburn—Orange Sonnet ("She whom no one ever found")—Deluxe Assorted—Boilermakers—Cynical—Charles and Arthur—Oleo Strut—A Hit Album—Feature Story—Four Songs—Orange Sonnet ("She was all in black. A statement")—The Ambassador—New Programs—Fashion—A Silk Ascot for the Terroist—Navy Blue Room—Gimlet—The S.S. Sahara—You Are My Heart's Bouquet—Glass Mind—Let's Call This—Miniature Gifts—Lost in the Stars—Captain Marvell—Orange Sonnet ("*In Memoriam P. B.*")—Drifting Blue Canoe—Mosquitoes in New Jersey—Loony Tune—Clarinet Marmalade—Orange Sonnet: 1939 World's Fair—George C. Tilyou Smiles—They R in Season—The Assumption of Black Sambo—Billy McCoy—Try to Write a Good Poem About Niagara Falls—Blazing Neon Sign—Orange Sonnet: Seminar—Cautious Circumspection Does Not Win the West—Another Meerschaum—Orange Sonnet: Canta Naranja—16 Lines—Hotcha—Orange Sonnet: Chez Macadam—September in Kittery—Orange Sonnet: Broadway! Broadway!—Orange Sonnet ("Now. Tell me how much I am to respect")—Orange Sonnet ("Across this water sits a shore")—Blackburn's Dream.

PUBLICATION: Published 5 July 1977 at $15.00. 201 signed copies, of which 200 copies (numbered 1-200) were for sale and one copy (marked "File Copy") was not for sale; printed and bound by Mackintosh and Young & Edwards Brothers, Inc. in Santa Barbara, CA, and Ann Arbor, MI.

b. First edition, clothbound, signed and lettered issue
Identical to A12a, except:

CONTENTS: Identical except, [61], which has manuscript lettering instead of numbering.

BINDING: Quarter bound in floral patterned cloth, printed in light brown (57), dark grayish reddish brown (47), deep reddish brown (41), black, white, dark yellowish green (137), deep red (13), and strong orange (50).

PUBLICATION: Published at $25.00. 31 signed copies, of which 26 copies were lettered A-Z and were for sale, and five copies, one each marked "Author's Copy," "Publisher's Copy," "Printer's Copy," "Binder's Copy," and "File Copy," which were not for sale.

c. First edition, paperbound issue
Identical to A12a, except:

COLLATION: perfect bound; [1-2], [1-8], 9-59, [60-66].

CONTENTS: [1-2], [65-66] both of these leaves are blank dark greenish yellow (103) paper, identical to endpapers of A12a.

PAPER: Leaf measures 22.7 x 14.5 cm.

BINDING: Glued into stiff, wove, unwatermarked light grayish to grayish olive (109-110) paper wrapper. Front cover: printed identically to A12a. Down spine: [printed in black] WHITE SAIL Gilbert Sorrentino *Black Sparrow Press.* Back cover: unprinted.

PUBLICATION: Published at $3.50. 1586 copies.

BACKGROUND NOTES: "I've collected enough poems (since 1970) to put a new book together, which I will call *White Sail,*" GS wrote John O'Brien (letter, 24 July 1975; TLS at CSt). That summer GS assembled and completed the typescript for *WS,* which arranges in essentially chronological order of composition the poems that he had written since *CS* and wanted to preserve. GS explained his choice of the title: "There are a lot of poems in that book which are about people who are dead, especially Paul Blackburn. I thought of 'white sail' as being sort of a cenotaph" (unpublished interview with William McPheron, 25 October 1989; tape at CSt).

Initially, GS approached New Directions with the volume, but James Laughlin discouraged him, saying, "I'm afraid we are very 'long' on poetry in the schedule of commitments for the next year or so" (letter to GS, 23 July 1975; TLS at DeU). In August GS offered the manuscript to John Martin at Black Sparrow, who accepted it by month's end, originally planning to publish it in the late summer or fall of 1976. Production was, however, delayed for more than a year. In November 1976 Martin asked GS for a brief description of *WS* to be incorporated as the author's statement in the Black Sparrow catalog. The first set of proofs reached GS in late April 1977, and the volume was printed in May, with clothbound copies ready by the end of June.

The book sold moderately well. The first royalty statement, issued by Martin in April 1978, reported 688 paperbound and 113 clothbound copies sold. Six months later, Martin reported another 70 copies sold, but returns in this instance offset royalties. The contract, which was not signed until January 1977, paid no advance and provided for royalties of 10% on clothbound copies and 5% on paperbound.

A13 THE ORANGERY 1978

a. First edition, clothbound issue

The Orangery | Gilbert Sorrentino | [drawing of an orange tree branch, with leaves and fruit] | University of Texas Press | Austin and London

COLLATION: [1-6]^8 = 48 leaves; [i-viii], [1-2], 3-86, [87-88].

CONTENTS: [i] half title: **The Orangery** | [12.3 cm. narrow rule] The University of Texas Press Poetry Series, No. 3 | [12.3 cm. narrow rule]; [ii] blank; [iii] title page; [iv] [12.3 cm. narrow rule] | [in double column] Library of Congress Cataloging | in Publication Data | Sorrentino, Gilbert. | The orangery. | (The University of Texas Press | poetry series; no. 3) | 1. Sonnets, American. I. Title. | PS3569.0707 811'.5'408 77-13099 | ISBN 0-292-76008-6 | ISBN 0-292-76009-4 pbk. | Copyright © 1978 | by the University of Texas Press | All rights reserved | Designed by Rod Parker | Illustration: Bettmann Archive | Printed in the United States of America | [48 lines of acknowledgments] | [12.3 cm. narrow rule]; [v] dedication: [within 12.3 cm. narrow rules] To Vicki and Chris | "the Orange bright"; [vi-viii] contents; [1] half title; [2] blank; 3-86 text; [87-88] blank.

PAPER: Leaf measures 17.8 x 15.1 cm.; yellowish white (92), wove, unwatermarked.

BINDING: Sewn and bound in vivid to brilliant orange (48-49), fine calico-texture cloth. Front and back: unstamped. Down spine, stamped in black: The Orangery Gilbert Sorrentino Texas Press. All edges trimmed.

DUST JACKET: Total measurement 18.7 x 52.1 cm. White (263) paper printed in vivid green (139) and vivid reddish orange (34). Front flap includes one-paragraph description of *O*, promotional blurbs by Carl Rakosi and William Bronk, and a six-line biographical statement about GS. Back cover lists and describes other books published by the University of Texas Press. Jacket printed by University of Texas Printing Division.

TEXT CONTENTS: 1939 World's Fair—"Everybody would soon change"—Saying the Beads—King Cole—Fragments of an Old Song 1—Simplicity—Silent Knight—After Montale—Chez Macadam—Lone Star—Deux morceaux en forme de banane—Drifting South—"Nothing whatever to see"—The Mansion of the Moon—Zukofsky—Imitation of the Greek—"She whom no one ever found"—Cento—Broadway! Broadway!—"Remember the story of Columbus and the orange?"—One Negative Vote—"Across this water sits a shore"—In Memoriam P.B.—Canta Naranja—"Mr. America last seen crossing the road"—Fragments of an Old Song 2—Homage to Arnaut—"White moons are blank. Blank moons"—"She was all in black. A statement"—Variations 1—"On the street that stands"—Nadie come naranjas—Moon Moon—Americana—Trav'lin' Light—"That the mouth speak not daggers"—Variations 2—Marvellous—Variations 3—Canzone—Arthur Rimbaud—Aesthetics—Annie from Miami—Sept morceaux en forme d'orange—Sappho in Paris—"Now. Tell me how much I am to respect"—"The King of the dark tower is a lug."—"Gold and oranges"—Seminar—To David Antin—Big Brown Eyes—Un morceau en forme de lime—The Oranges Returned—Je connais gens de toutes sortes—"The white rockers on the porch" Partial Graph—"Rosy. Azure."—Provence—Footnote—Interlude—Trois morceaux en forme de poire—"O Xmas tree"—To William Bronk—White Lemons—Breakfast—California—Make 'Em Laugh—To Sulpicia—A Word for Paul Goodman—Imitation of the Chinese—A Tour of Duty—Villanette—"At twenty love disintegrates"—Vapid Transit—Vision of the City from a Window—La Vie d'Art—Pastorale—The Crown, 1-7.

PUBLICATION: Published April 1978 at $7.95. 774 copies, printed by Edwards Brothers, Ann Arbor, MI, and bound by Universal Bookbindery, San Antonio, TX.

b. First edition, paperbound issue
Identical to A13a, except:

COLLATION: perfect bound.

PAPER: Leaf measures 17.8 x 14.8 cm.

BINDING: Glued into stiff, wove, unwatermarked, yellowish white (92) paper wrapper, printed identically to the dust jacket of A13a, with the text from the jacket's front and back flaps reproduced on back cover of paperbound wrapper.

PUBLICATION: Published at $3.95. 748 copies, printed and bound by Edwards Brothers, Ann Arbor, MI.

BACKGROUND NOTES: When in the early spring of 1975 GS first began writing sonnets that turned on the word "orange," he had "no sense that I wanted to do a whole book of them." But after a number were in hand, GS realized, "I could do a book with the poems all interdependent, one poem recalling other poems and then wrapping it up by making a crown." Regarding the title, GS explained: "*The Orangery* is lovely because an orangery is a greenhouse where only oranges are grown, and what I wanted as a cover was a photograph of Anthony Caro's sculpture *L'Orangerie*, a great, great sculpture" (unpublished interview with William McPheron, 25 October 1989; tape at CSt). In early February 1977 GS completed the typescript of *O*, remarking to John O'Brien at the time: "It's my best poetry. When I finished the last poem, I felt as if I had been walking for miles in twenty-pound boots, and, as usual, I was exhilarated and depressed in equal measure. Don't let anyone ever tell you that the finished product is what pleases the writer; it is the making of it that is worth everything" (letter, 4 February 1977; TLS at CSt). GS wrote numerous "orange" poems that he chose not to include in the book, the manuscripts for which are among his papers at DeU.

GS's decision to offer *O* first to the University of Texas Press had been made the preceding year in March 1976, when a senior editor, Iris Tillman Hill, had written him to announce the press's formation of a new poetry series and to invite him to submit an unpublished manuscript. In late February 1977 GS sent the final revised typescript to Hill; by mid-April the series' two advisors, the poets Christopher Middleton and David Wevill, had strongly endorsed the book and later that month the Faculty Advisory Committee formally accepted it, enabling the contract to be issued on 28 April 1977 and signed by GS on 2 May.

Production proceeded without problems. The copy-edited manuscript was sent to GS in July and the proofs in late August 1977. Though the designer rejected GS's suggestion of the Caro sculpture for the jacket, he honored GS's request for an orange cloth cover and orange end papers. Texas issued a promotional flier, which included the quotations from William Bronk and Carl Rakosi reprinted on the dust jacket, as well as a longer statement by John Ashbery. GS received advanced copies in early March 1978.

A14 MULLIGAN STEW 1979

a. First edition, clothbound issue

MULLIGAN | STEW | [10 cm. wavy rule] **| A Novel by | GILBERT | SORRENTINO | GROVE PRESS, INC. | New York**

COLLATION: perfect bound, 234 leaves; pp. [i-xviii], 1-445, [446-450].

Mulligan Stew
A Novel by
Gilbert Sorrentino

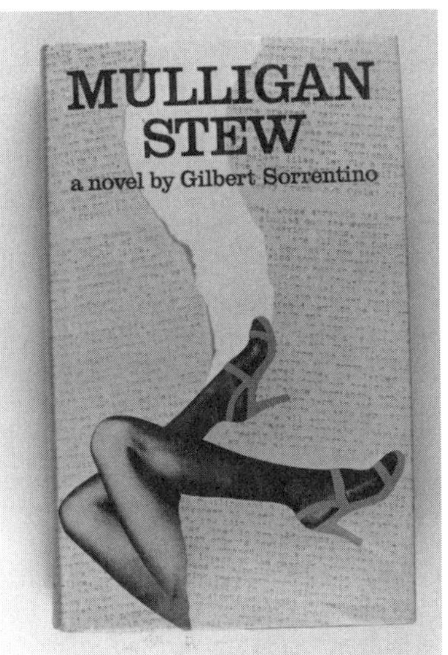
MULLIGAN
STEW
a novel by Gilbert Sorrentino

PICADOR
MULLIGAN STEW
GILBERT SORRENTINO
'An abundant and extravagantly decorated display of the pleasures of the imagination'
MALCOLM BRADBURY, author of THE HISTORY MAN

GILBERT SORRENTINO
Mulligan
Stew
"Utterly dazzling. . . . Sustains a display of linguistic virtuosity that takes your breath away."
—Michael Dirda, Washington Post Book World

CONTENTS: [i-xi] [texts of fabricated letters of rejection and other invented correspondence regarding *MS*]; [xii] blank; [xiii] half title; [xiv] [15-line list of other books by GS]; [xv] title page; [xvi] To the memory of Brian O'Nolan | [1.3 cm. elongated dash] his "virtue *hilaritas*" | [three paragraphs acknowledging previous publication of sections of the novel and foundation support during its composition] | Copyright © 1979 by Gilbert Sorrentino | [four lines stating copyright reservations] | First edition 1979 | First Printing 1979 | ISBN: 0-394-50717-7 | Grove Press ISBN: 0-8021-0173-9 | Library of Congress Catalog Number: 78-67419 | First Evergreen Edition 1979 | First printing 1979 | ISBN: 0-394-17086-5 | Grove Press ISBN: 0-8021-4255-9 | Library of Congress Catalog Card Number: 78-67419 | Library of Congress Cataloging in Publication Data | Sorrentino, Gilbert. | Mulligan stew. | I. Title. | PZ4.S717Mu [PS3569.07] 813'.5'4 78-67419 | ISBN 0-394-50717-7 | ISBN 0-394-17086-5 pbk. | *Manufactured in the United States of America* | GROVE PRESS, INC., 196 West Houston Street, New York, N.Y. 10014; [xvii] epigraphs from Flann O'Brien, Philip Vogel, and James Joyce; [xviii] blank; 1-445 text; [446] quotation from Emile Fion; [447-450] blank.

PAPER: Leaf measures 23.3 x 15.4 cm.; pp. [i-xii] are very pale purplish blue (202), laid, chain lines 23 cm. apart; pp. [xiii-xviii], 1-445, [446-450] are yellowish white (92), wove, unwatermarked.

BINDING: Quarter bound in fine black calico-texture cloth and moderate greenish blue (approx. 173) wove paper covered boards. Front cover: unstamped. Down spine, stamped in silver: [in two lines] MULLIGAN STEW | [4.7 cm. wavy rule] GILBERT SORRENTINO; [in two lines] GROVE PRESS | NEW YORK. All edges trimmed. Medium greenish blue (approx. 173) wove endpapers.

DUST JACKET: Total measurement 24 x 54.2 cm. White (approx. 263), glossy paper, printed silver gray (no Centroid equivalent), black, strong blue (178), and vivid reddish orange (34). Back cover lists other works by GS and reprints blurbs about *SC* from Robert Creeley and the *New Leader*, about *SW* from the *Nation* and *Library Journal*, and about *IQAT* from *Publishers Weekly*. Front inside flap includes two-paragraph description of *MS*. Back inside flap features photograph of GS by Victoria Sorrentino and a 17-line biographical statement about GS. Cover design by Kenneth R. Deardoff.

PUBLICATION: Published 26 May 1979 at $14.95. 2000 copies in first printing. Typesetting was by Com Com of Allentown, PA, and printing and binding were by Haddon Craftsmen of Scranton, PA. Publisher ordered 50 bound galleys from Crane Duplicating in November 1978. Grove Press distributed 14 of these in December 1978 to selected critics and editors, soliciting promotional statements and reviews. GS himself sent the remaining uncorrected galley proofs to prospective reviewers. The proof copies were bound in vivid red (11) paper wrappers, printed with copy from the title page, with the words "Uncorrected Proof" appearing on both the cover and title page.

A second printing was ordered 24 May 1979 for an additional 2000 copies. "Second printing" is designed on the verso of the title page, [xvi]. The paper for preliminary pages [i-xii], in contrast to the first printing, is light yellowish brown (76), wove, unwatermarked.

b. First edition, paperbound issue
Identical to A14a, except:

BINDING: Glued into stiff, wove, white (263), unwatermarked paper wrapper, printed identically to the dust jacket of A14a, except the back cover carries the text of the dust jacket's inside flaps instead of the blurbs about GS's previous novels.

PUBLICATION: Published at $7.95. 8000 copies in first printing. A second printing was ordered 24 May 1979 for an additional 10,000 copies, of which 7000 were bound for Grove and the remaining 3000 reserved for the Quality Paperback Book Club. The paper for preliminary pages [i-xii], in contrast to the first printing, is light yellowish brown (76), wove, unwatermarked.

BACKGROUND NOTES: GS began writing *MS* in November 1971 and by November 1974 was sketching the novel's last sections. He completed the final revisions in February 1975 and late that same month gave the manuscript to his agent, Karen Hitzig. At this point, the novel was called *Synthetic Ink*, and over the next three years it was rejected by nearly thirty trade publishers, including all the major New York houses. The publishers typically praised the novel, often extravagantly, but doubted its commercial viability, fearing that a book so long and so literary would not earn enough profits to justify production costs. James Laughlin, publisher of New Directions, who never himself considered the manuscript but who knew of its length, explained the problem: "The size of your new work worries me for you a bit, I don't know where you are going to find a publisher, composition costs being what they are, who will be willing to finance such a large book. . . . With union rates and all other production costs skyrocketing as they are now, I think that 'serious' literature is going to have to go underground" (letter to GS, 21 May 1974; TLS at DeU).

Early in 1978 the manuscript was submitted to Grove Press, which finally accepted it, with the contract forwarded to GS by his new agent, Mel Berger, on 21 April. Before production began, GS made two important changes, both instigated by Barney Rosset, Grove's owner. First, Rosset wanted GS's text prefaced by a selection of the other publishers' rejection letters. Instead of following Rosset's advice literally, GS wrote the parodies that precede the title page. Second, Rosset disliked the name *Synthetic Ink*, insisting on a less arcane title that would be more attractive to buyers, and in May GS proposed *Mulligan Stew*. While the new title satisfied Rosset's demands, it is, in fact, no less difficult, for it deliberately contains a pun on *Ulysses*'s Buck Mulligan, "Mulligan's Too," thus clandestinely announcing the novel's homage to Joyce. Rosset also asked GS to delete the entire section, "Flawless Play Restored: The Masque of Fungo," pp. 178-216, but GS refused.

Even before *MS* was published, it was well known in literary circles, for since 1973 sections had been appearing in a variety of magazines.

c. Quality Paperback Book Club issue

NOTE: The Quality Paperback Book Club reported that its issue, made from 3000 copies of the second printing of A14b, was identical to A14b, except that the price and ISBN were deleted from the cover. No copy of the issue was located to confirm this information. *MS* was featured in the club's monthly magazine, *QPB Review*, in December 1979.

d. Marion Boyars (First British) edition, clothbound issue (1980) (photo-offset and reduced from A14a)

MULLIGAN | STEW | [9.6 cm. wavy rule] | **A Novel by | GILBERT | SORRENTINO | MARION BOYARS | London . Boston**

COLLATION: perfect bound, 232 leaves; [i-xviii], 1-445, [446].

CONTENTS: Other than lacking one of the blank leaves at the end, identical to A14a, except (a) heading on p. [xiv], which reads **Books By Gilbert Sorrentino | Published in the United States,** instead of **Books By Gilbert Sorrentino;** and (b) the portion of p. [xvi] that follows the three paragraphs of acknowledgments, which reads: First published in Great Britain in 1980 | By Marion Boyars Publishers Ltd. | 18 Brewer Street, London W1R 4AS. | Australian distribution by Thomas C. Lothian | 4-12 Tattersalls Lane, Melbourne, Victoria 3000. | © Gilbert Sorrentino 1979 | British Library Cataloguing in Publication Data | Sorrentino, Gilbert | Mulligan stew. | I. Title | 823'.9'1F PS3569.O7M/ 78-67419 | ISBN 0 7145 2700 9 Hardcover edition | [two paragraphs stating copyright reservations] | Printed and bound in Great Britain by | REDWOOD BURN LIMITED | Trowbridge & Esher.

PAPER: Leaf measures 21.6 x 13.3 cm. Yellowish white (92), wove, unwatermarked paper.

BINDING: Bound in strong to deep red (12-13), fine diaper cloth boards. Front and back: unstamped. Down spine, stamped in gold: [on parallel lines] MULLIGAN STEW | Gilbert Sorrentino; across spine: Marion Boyars. Yellowish white (92), wove, unwatermarked endpapers. All edges trimmed.

DUST JACKET: Total measurement 22.2 x 50 cm. White (263), glossy paper printed in black, grays, and deep pink (3) shading toward vivid red (11). Front inside flap includes 29-line paragraph describing *MS* and excerpts of reviews of *MS* from the *Washington Post*, *New York Times Book Review*, and *New York Times*. Back inside flap features a photograph of GS, a 13-line biographical statement about him, and excerpts of reviews of *MS* from the *Chicago Sun-Times*, *Chronicle of Books & Arts* [i.e., *Chronicle of Higher Education*, "Books and Arts" sect.] and *St. Louis Post-Dispatch*. Jacket design and photography by Michael Werner.

PUBLICATION: Published April 1980 at £7.95. 1500 copies bound and printed by Redwood Burn Ltd., Trowbridge and Esther, Great Britain.

BACKGROUND NOTES: Marion Boyars—without reading the manuscript—had originally rejected *MS* in February 1977 because she could not afford to do so large a book. But in October 1979, after its publication by Grove, she did read the book and formally acquired British rights to the novel, writing GS in November to express her enthusiasm and assure him that *MS* was to be her major novel in 1980 (TLS at DeU). Prior to publication, Boyars expected *MS* to be commercially quite successful, and in November 1979 she concluded an arrangement with Picador, the mass-market paperback house. Initial sales of *MS* in England were, however, poor, with only 395 clothbound copies sold by the end of 1980. Despite the weak market, Boyars decided to issue her own paperbound version. By August 1981 three editions of *MS* were in print in the British Isles, a degree of competition that effectively prevented the profitability of all.

e. Marion Boyars (First British) edition, paperbound issue (1981) (photo-offset from A14a)
Identical to A14d, except:

PAPER: Leaf measures 21.4 x 13.3 cm.

BINDING: Glued into stiff white (263) wrapper. Front cover and spine printed identically to A14d. Rear cover includes a photograph of GS, a one-paragraph description of *MS* extracted from the inside front flap jacket copy of A14d, a one-paragraph biographical statement about GS, and excerpts of reviews of *MS* from the *Scotsman*, *Washington Post*, and *New York Times*. Printed on the wrapper's front and rear insides are 29-line lists, respectively, of other fiction and of criticism published by Marion Boyars. All edges trimmed.

PUBLICATION: Published June 1981 at £4.50. 1500 copies, printed and bound by Redwood Burn Ltd., Trowbridge and Esher, Great Britain.

f. Pan/Picador (Second British) paperback issue (1981) (photo-offset and reduced from A14a)
GILBERT SORRENTINO | **MULLIGAN STEW** | [8.9 cm. wavy rule] | [within 1.9 cm. narrow rules] **PICADOR** | published by Pan Books

COLLATION: perfect bound, 232 leaves; [i-xviii], 1-445, [446].

CONTENTS: Other than lacking the two blank leaves at the end, identical to A14a, except: [xiii] [10-line biographical statement about GS]; [xiv] blank; [xvi] [first four paragraphs identical] | First published in Great Britain 1980 by Marion Boyars Publishers Ltd | This Picador edition published 1981 by Pan Books Ltd | Cavaye Place, London SW10 9PG | © Gilbert Sorrentino 1979 | ISBN 0 330 26444 3 | Printed in Great Britain by | Richard Clay (The Chaucer Press) Ltd, Bungay, Suffolk | [six lines stating copyright reservations].

PAPER: Leaf measures 19.6 x 12.8 cm. Yellowish white (92) wove, unwatermarked.

BINDING: Glued into stiff, white (approx. 263), glossy wrapper, printed brilliant blue (177), vivid red (11), vivid to brilliant yellow green (115-116), light to moderate reddish purple (240-241), and vivid to brilliant yellow (82-83). Back cover includes four-paragraph excerpt from John Leonard's *New York Times* notice of *MS* and a four-line excerpt from Malcolm Bradbury's *New York Times Book Review* review, with the latter's place of publication unacknowledged. Cover illustration by Peter White. All edges trimmed.

PUBLICATION: Published 14 August 1981 at £2.50. 10,000 copies in first and only printing, of which 7,000 copies were priced at £2.50 and 3,000 copies were unpriced. No uncorrected proofs were distributed. The rights of Pan Books to publish *MS* in England reverted to Marion Boyars on 9 November 1985.

g. Second Grove paperback issue (1987) (photo-offset from A14a)
MULLIGAN | STEW | [8.3 cm. irregularly jagged rule] **| A Novel by | GILBERT | SORRENTINO | GROVE PRESS/New York**

COLLATION: perfect bound, 232 leaves; [i-xviii], 1-445, [446].

CONTENTS: [i-xiii] identical to A14a; [xiv] [23 lines listing other books by GS]; [xv] title page; [xvi] identical to A14a except (a) the three paragraphs of acknowledgments are bracketed by 8.6 cm. irregularly jagged rules, and (b) the portion following the acknowledgments reads: Copyright © 1979, 1987 by Gilbert Sorrentino | All rights reserved. | [four lines stating copyright reservations] | Published by Grove Press, Inc. | 920 Broadway | New York, N.Y. 10010 | First Evergreen Edition 1979 | Library of Congress Cataloging-in-Publication Data | Sorrentino, Gilbert. | Mulligan stew. | I. Title. | PZ4.S717Mu [PS3569.O7] 813'.5'4 78-67419 | ISBN 0-394-62361-4 | Manufactured in the United States of America | 10 9 8 7 6 5 4 3 2 1; [xvii-xviii], 1-445, [446] identical to A14a.

PAPER: Leaf measures 20.9 x 13.6 cm.; yellowish white (92), wove, unwatermarked.

BINDING: Glued into stiff, white (approx. 263), glossy wrapper, printed in black, vivid purplish red (254), deep yellow green (approx. 118), strong blue (178), dark reddish orange to strong reddish brown (38-40), strong reddish orange (35). Back cover includes four paragraphs of excerpts of reviews, from Michael Dirda of the *Washington Post Book World*, John Leonard of the *New York Times*, Malcolm Bradbury of the *New York Times Book Review*, and the *Chronicle of Books & Arts* [i.e., *Chronicle of Higher Education*, "Books & Arts" sect.]. Cover design by Cindy LaBreacht. Cover art is Stuart Davis's *Semé*.

PUBLICATION: Printed July 1989. Publisher refuses to disclose information about the precise date of publication and the number of copies in the edition.

BACKGROUND NOTES: In early 1985, the Grove Press edition of *MS* went out of print. When Grove decided not to reissue the novel, the rights reverted to GS, whose agent, Mel Berger, discussed the book with several paperback houses before Fred Jordan, senior editor at Grove, reconsidered. In November 1986 GS signed a contract with Grove, which reacquired rights to *MS* for $500. The figure was below GS's expectations but was accepted because, as he explained, "All I really wanted is to see the old horse back in print" (letter to John O'Brien, 12 November 1986; TLS at CSt). Copies of the new issue reached GS in late July 1987.

A15 ABERRATION OF STARLIGHT 1980

a. First edition

GILBERT | **SORRENTINO** | [6.3 x 3.4 cm. rectangular frame enclosing mirror images of geometrically rendered radiating bursts of light] | **ABERRA-TION** | **OF** | **STARLIGHT**

COLLATION: $[1^{17}\ 2\text{-}6^{16}\ 7^{15}]$ = 112 leaves; [i-x]; [1-3], 4, [5-6], 7-10, [11], 12-17, [18], 19, [20], 21-23, [24], 25-27, [28], 29-35, [36], 37-40, [41], 42-50, [51-53], 54-55, [56], 57, [58], 59-63, [64] 65-69, [70], 71-72, [73], 74-77, [78], 79-82, [83], 84-94, [95], 96-98, [99], 100-106, [107-109], 110, [111], 112, [113], 114-115, [116], 117-119, [120], 121-124, [125], 126-130, [131], 132-135, [136], 137-146, [147], 148-150, [151], 152-157, [158-161], 162-163, [164], 165, [166], 167-169, [170], 171-176, [177], 178-181, [182], 183-185, [186], 187-188, [189], 190-200, [201], 202-203, [204], 205-211, [212-214].

CONTENTS: [i] blank; [ii] [17 lines listing other books by GS; [iii] half title; [iv] [publisher's device, a drawing of a house] | RANDOM HOUSE | NEW YORK; [v] title page; [vi] Copyright © 1980 by Gilbert Sorrentino | All rights reserved under International and Pan American Copyright | Conventions. Published in the United States by Random House, Inc., | New York, and simultaneously in Canada by Random House | of Canada Limited, Toronto. | Library of Congress Cataloging in Publication Data | Sorrentino, Gilbert. | Aberration of starlight. | I. Title | PZ4.S717Ab [PS3569.O7] 813'.54 80-5280 | ISBN 0-394-51189-1 | [20 lines acknowledging previously published materials] | *Manufactured in the United States of America* | 23456789 | FIRST EDITION; [vii] dedication: *To Jack O'Brien;* [viii] [nine-line definition of "aberration of starlight" quoted from *The New Columbia Encyclopedia*]; [ix] epigraphs from César Vallejo, Guillaume Apollinaire, and Erik Satie; [x] blank; [1] half title; [2] blank; [3]-211 text; [212] blank; [213] one-line quotation from Brian O'Nolan; [214] [14-line biographical note about GS].

PAPER: Leaf measures 20.8 x 13.9 cm.; yellowish white (92), wove, unwatermarked.

BINDING: Quarter bound in dark purplish red (259), fine bead cloth and very light to light purple (221-222) paper on boards. Front cover, blind stamped: 6.3 x 3.4

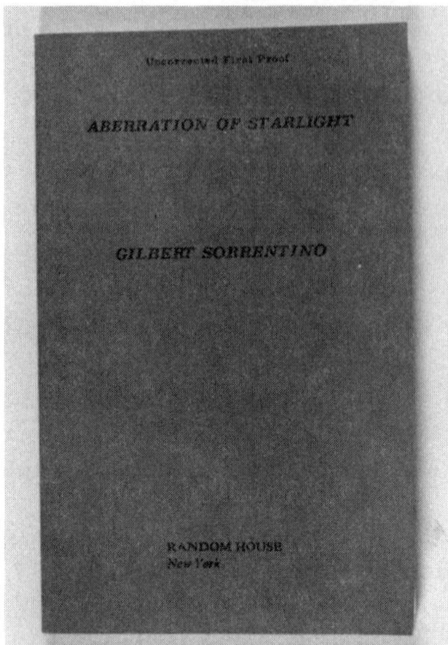
Uncorrected First Proof
ABERRATION OF STARLIGHT
GILBERT SORRENTINO
RANDOM HOUSE
New York

ABERRATION
OF
STARLIGHT
GILBERT
SORRENTINO

ABERRATION OF STARLIGHT
BY GILBERT SORRENTINO
Author of Mulligan Stew
"Lively with narrative ingenuity—yet right to the heart of ordinary life"—Philip Roth
The Penguin Contemporary American Fiction Series

Aberration of Starlight
a novel by Gilbert Sorrentino

cm. rectangular frame enclosing mirror images of geometrically rendered radiating bursts of light. Down spine, stamped in gold: ABERRATION OF STAR-LIGHT | GILBERT SORRENTINO [publisher's device, drawing of house] RANDOM HOUSE. Back cover: unstamped. All edges trimmed. Yellowish white (92), wove, unwatermarked endpapers.

DUST JACKET: Total measurement 21.2 x 53.4 cm. White (263), wove, glossy paper printed in grayish pink to pinkish gray (8-10), light yellowish pink (28), moderate reddish brown (43), brilliant yellow (83), strong blue (178), deep blue (179), very light blue (180), moderate purplish to deep purplish red (258-259), medium gray (265), and black. Back cover lists other books by GS, with excerpts from reviews of *SC* by Richard Howard, of *IQAT* by Paul Theroux, and of *MS* by John Leonard, Hugh Kenner, and Malcolm Bradbury as well as from the *Chronicle of Books & Arts* [i.e., *Chronicle of Higher Education*, 'Books & Arts" sect.], *San Francisco Review of Books*, *Chicago Sun-Times*, and *Washington Post Book World*. Inside front flap has a four-paragraph description of *AS*; inside back flap features a photograph of GS by Thomas Victor and an eight-line biographical statement about GS. Jacket design is by David Tamura.

PUBLICATION: Published 22 August 1980 at $9.95. 7,500 copies. Typeset by Com Com of Allentown, PA; printed and bound by Haddon Craftsmen of Scranton, PA. An undetermined number of proof copies, labeled "Uncorrected First Proof" and bound in vivid red (11) paper wrappers, were distributed prior to publication.

NOTE: Though the copyright page states that *AS* was published simultaneously by Random House of Canada Ltd., Toronto, this statement is a copyright formality and no Canadian edition was issued.

BACKGROUND NOTES: GS began *AS* in June 1977, while *MS* and *CV* were both looking for publishers, and completed the first draft in March 1978. By September 1978, the final, revised typescript was in the hands of GS's literary agent, Mel Berger, who began circulating it among major New York trade houses. During the late summer of 1979, in the months immediately after *MS*'s publication by Grove Press, Random House read and accepted *AS*. In December GS signed the contract, which provided an advance of $7500, royalties of 10% on the first 5000 copies, 12½% on the next 5000, and 15% on all sales above 10,000. The contract also stipulated Random House's option on GS's next novel. The editor at Random House assigned to *AS* was Gary Fisketjon, to whom GS explained at their first meeting that "I do not allow my books to be 'edited' . . ." (letter to John O'Brien, 17 September 1979; TLS at CSt).

The production of *AS* began in February. GS made minor changes on the first set of proofs in April 1980 and read the second set in May, after which he remarked on "how quiet and summery this book is. I like it more than I did when I first completed it. It's like an old photograph album, i.e. what is happening *outside* the edges of the photos? I also like it because it is, though set in summer 1939, devoid of the nostalgic" (letter to O'Brien, 16 May 1980; TLS at CSt). In May GS also reviewed Fisketjon's flap copy. By mid-July advanced copies were available.

To maximize the novel's attention from reviewers, Random House pushed the publication date forward to the end of August, strategically releasing it between the end of summer and the beginning of the fall season rush. Random House also issued a prepublication flier that included promotional statements from Philip Roth, Wallace Markfield, Stanley Elkin, and Don DeLillo. In March 1981, *AS* was nominated for the first annual PEN/Faulkner Award for Fiction, with the citation printed in the 15 March 1981 *New York Times Book Review* and other literary magazines. Though *AS* was reviewed very widely, Random House did not immediately sell out the first printing and in February 1982 sold its remaining copies to Daedalus Books, the mail order discount outlet located outside Washington, D.C.

b. Marion Boyars (First British) edition (1981) (photo-offset from A15a)
Identical to A15a, except:

COLLATION: perfect bound, 114 leaves; [i-xiv]; otherwise identical to A15a.

CONTENTS: [i-v] blank; [vi] By the same author | *Mulligan Stew (a novel);* [vii] half title; [viii] MARION BOYARS | LONDON . BOSTON; [ix] title page; [x] Published in Great Britain in 1981 by | Marion Boyars Publishers Ltd. | 18 Brewer Street, London W1R 4AS | Australian and New Zealand distribution by | Thomas C. Lothian | 4-12 Tattersalls Lane, | Melbourne, Victoria 3000. | [11 lines stating copyright reservations] | British Library Cataloguing in Publication Data | Sorrentino, Gilbert | Aberration of starlight | I. Title | 813'.54[F] PS3569.O7 | ISBN 0-7145-2731-9 | Printed and bound in Great Britain by | Redwood Burn Limited, Trowbridge & Esher; [xi] dedication: *To Jack O'Brien* | [xii] [nine-line definition of "aberration of starlight," quoted from *The New Columbia Encyclopedia*] | [xiii] epigraphs from César Vallejo, Guillaume Apollinaire, and Erik Satie; [xiv] blank. Otherwise identical to A15a.

PAPER: Leaf measures 21.3 x 13.4 cm.; yellowish white (92), wove, unwatermarked.

BINDING: Glued into fine diaper, black cloth over boards. Front cover: unstamped. Stamped down spine in gold: Aberration of Starlight Gilbert Sorrentino [across spine] Marion Boyars. Back cover: unstamped.

DUST JACKET: Total measurement 22.1 x 46.6 cm. White (263), wove, glossy paper printed in black and grays. Back cover includes a two-paragraph description of the novel that also provides basic biographical information about GS, accompanied by brief excerpts of earlier American reviews of *AS* from the *New York Review of Books, New York Times Book Review, Chicago Sun-Times, Los Angeles Times* and *Newsday.* Inside flaps list other works of fiction published by Marion Boyars. Jacket design and photography by Michael Werner.

PUBLICATION: Published July 1981 at £6.95. 1000 copies printed and bound by Redwood Burn Ltd., Trowbridge and Esher, Great Britain.

BACKGROUND NOTES: Marion Boyars first read *AS* in August 1980 and immediately began negotiating for British rights. The contract, dated 21 October 1980, paid an advance of £300 against 10% royalties on the first 3000 copies, 12½% on the next 2000, and 15% on all copies over 5000.

c. Penguin (first American paperbound) edition (1981) (photo offset from A15a)
GILBERT | **SORRENTINO** | [5.2 x 3.8 rectangle enclosing mirror images of geometrically rendered radiating bursts of light] | **ABERRATION** | **OF** | **STARLIGHT** | [publisher's logo, drawing of a penguin enclosed in oval] | PENGUIN BOOKS

Otherwise identical to A15a, except:

COLLATION: perfect bound, 112 leaves; [i-x], [1-2], 3-50, [51-52], 53-106, [107-108], 109-157, [158-160], 161-211, [212-214].

CONTENTS: [i] THE PENGUIN CONTEMPORARY AMERICAN FICTION SERIES | ABERRATION OF STARLIGHT | [eight-line biographical statement about GS]; [ii] [17 lines listing other books by GS]; [iii] title page; [iv] Penguin Books Ltd, Harmondsworth, | Middlesex, England | Penguin Books, 625 Madison Avenue, | New York, New York 10022, U. S. A. | [six lines listing names and addresses of Penguin's Commonwealth subsidiaries, none of which distributed *AS*] | First published in the United States of America by | Random House, Inc., 1980 | Published in Penguin Books 1981 | Copyright © Gilbert Sorrentino, 1980 | First published in Canada by | Random House of Canada Limited 1980 | All rights reserved | LIBRARY OF CONGRESS CATALOGING IN PUBLICATION DATA | Sorrentino, Gilbert. | Aberration of starlight. | I. Title. | [PS3569.O7A73 1981] 813'.54 80-29457 | ISBN 0 14 00.5879 6 | Printed in the United States of America by | Offset Paperback Mfrs., Inc., Dallas, Pennsylvania | Set in Times Roman | [16 lines acknowledging permissions] | [six lines stating copyright reservations]; [v] dedication: *To Jack O'Brien;* [vi] blank; [vii] nine-line definition of "aberration of starlight," quoted from *The New Columbia Encyclopedia;* [viii] blank; [ix] epigraphs from César Vallejo, Guillaume Apollinaire, and Erik Satie; [x] blank; [1] half title; [2] blank; 3-211 text; [212] blank; [213] quotation from Brian O'Nolan; [214] blank.

PAPER: Leaf measures 19.7 x 12.7 cm.; yellowish white (92), wove, unwatermarked paper. All edges trimmed.

BINDING: Glued into stiff, wove, glossy, white (263) paper wrapper, printed in black and light to medium grays (264-265). Back cover includes excerpts of earlier reviews of *AS* that appeared in the *Saturday Review* and the *New York Times Book Review* and a 14-line description of *AS.* Cover design by Neil Stuart.

PUBLICATION: Published 28 May 1981 at $3.95. 7500 copies, printed by Offset Paperback Mfrs., Inc., Dallas, PA. Subsequent to publication, Penguin pasted black labels over the original price statement on the wrapper's back cover, raising the price to $5.95.

BACKGROUND NOTES: Penguin acquired the American paperback rights to *AS* in October 1980 for $4000. The Penguin editor for the book was Daniel Weaver, who told GS that the edition's cover art was taken from an issue of *Liberty Magazine* from the late 1930s. But *Liberty*, as GS observed at the time, "was a Depression hit because it sedulously avoided the fact of the Depression and an illustration like this was intended to take people back to the good old days of high living pre-Crash" (letter to John O'Brien, 12 January 1981; TLS at CSt). Thus Penguin's nostalgic cover conflicts directly with *AS*'s governing tone, of which GS remarked: "What I like most about [*AS*] is the evocation of the past. I don't think there's a false note in it as far as that goes" (letter to O'Brien, 23 April 1980; TLS at CSt). The Penguin edition sold well: in late July 1981, just two months after its release, Penguin informed GS that 6400 of the 7500 copies had sold and that the current rate of sale was 50 copies per week. No second printing, however, was ordered.

d. Marion Boyars (First British) paperbound issue (1982) (photo-offset from A15a).
Identical to A15b, except:

COLLATION AND CONTENTS: Identical, except A15d has only 112 leaves, lacking the two initial blank leaves, [1-4], of A15b.

BINDING: Glued into stiff, glossy, white (263) paper wrapper. Front cover and spine printed identically to the dust jacket of A15b. Back cover slightly revises and reformats text but is otherwise also identical to the dust jacket of A15b.

PUBLICATION: Published May 1982 at £3.95. 1000 copies printed and bound by Redwood Burn Ltd., Trowbridge and Esher, Great Britain.

A16 SELECTED POEMS 1958-1980 1981

a. First edition, clothbound, unsigned trade issue
[within 10.1 x 8.6 cm. brownish orange (54) rectangle] [two .6 cm. square, strong bluish green (160) devices] [in brownish orange (54)] GILBERT | SORRENTINO | [eight .6 cm. square, strong bluish green devices] | [in black] SELECTED | POEMS | 1958-1980 | [at bottom right, two .6 cm. square, strong bluish green (160) devices] [outside square, at bottom] BLACK SPARROW PRESS / SANTA BARBARA / 1981

COLLATION: $[1\text{-}2]^{4}$, $[3\text{-}10]^{16}$ = 136 leaves; [1-12], 13-29, [30-32], 33-71, [72-74], 75-105, [106-108], 109-150, [151-152], 153-155, [156-158], 159-180, [181-182], 183-222, [223-224], 225-266, [269-272].

CONTENTS: [1] [15 lines listing other books by GS]; [2] blank; [3] title page; [4] SELECTED POEMS 1958-1980. Copyright © 1981 by Gilbert Sorrentino. | [five lines stating copyright reservations] | [15 lines acknowledging previous publications and permissions] | LIBRARY OF CONGRESS CATALOGING IN PUBLICATION DATA | Sorrentino, Gilbert. | Selected poems, 1958-1980. | I. Title. | PS3569.O7A17 1981 811'.54 81-1094 | ISBN 0-87685-502-8 AACR2 | ISBN 0-87685-503-6 (signed ed.) | ISBN 0-87685-501-X (pbk.); [5] dedication: *Again, for Victoria;* [6] blank; [7-10] contents; [11]-268 text; [269] [at left, publisher's device, pictorial illustration of a black sparrow] | Printed April 1981 in Santa Barbara & Ann Arbor | for the Black Sparrow Press by Graham Mackintosh & | Edwards Brothers Inc. Design by Barbara Martin. This | edition is published in paper wrappers; there are 500 | cloth trade copies; 200 hardcover copies have been | numbered and signed by the poet; & 26 deluxe copies have | been hand-bound in boards by Earle Gray & are lettered | & signed by the poet.; [270] blank; [271] [11.8 x 10.8 cm. photograph of GS by Victoria Sorrentino] | [seven-line biographical statement about GS]; [272] blank.

PAPER: Leaf measures 23 x 15.3 cm. Yellowish white (92), wove, unwatermarked.

BINDING: Sewn and quarter bound in brilliant bluish green (159), coarse net cloth and cream (no Centroid equivalent) wove paper over boards. Printed in brownish orange (54), strong bluish green (160), and black. Spine carries cream paper label printed in brownish orange (54) and black. Strong to moderate bluish green (160-164), wove, unwatermarked endpapers. All edges trimmed.

DUST JACKET: Clear acetate.

TEXT CONTENTS: *The Darkness Surrounds Us* (1960): A Fixture—Calling Dr. Dunninger—Nightpiece—The Totem—3 Quatrains—The Crisis—The Man in the Moon—The Spouse—Man and Wife—A Señorita's Bouquet—The Closet—Midnight Special—A Classic Case—The Zoo—The Fights—The Whole World Coal—Tilt.

Black and White (1964): Ars Longa—The Transcript—The Fiction—Cards—Dominoes—Sinking, Swimming—Ave atque vale—The Meeting, 1-4—The Evening News—The Charm—Bar Games—As with a Simple Gesture of the Fingers—The Long Goodbye—The Bare Tree—Open Your Mouth and Say—The Memory—The Edges—Out of Their Butchered Hearts—The Mathematics—Maytime—Faces of Doom and Sterility—The Abstraction—The Language Barrier—Who Goes There?—A Detail—Shapes of Winter, 1-7—Silences.

The Perfect Fiction (1968): Something plus something is not one thing—He walks on the street, in—In a fantastic light:—The stupid painter paints. He—What is past is here, as we—Now the night is here. Blood—What intense colloquy with the self—People in Hell are clothed—Nothing grimmer than dawn at noon—A stinking city full of stinking—Where are the rose-colored cities—There is no instance that was not love:—(Sonnet with X's)—A red sun is going down somewhere—A particular density: in the center, rises—A door that opens on—What is to be understood—Come from the whirling zodiac—Come all ye Sons of Art—L the simple shape—In the blue, singa—Some hawk-nosed man—It is one man alone, what—How I loved that melody—But the light is imagined—Mother, this is a ball of color—(pentagram).

Corrosive Sublimate (1971): Handbook of Versification—Address to the National Council on the Arts—The Morning Roundup—Rose Room—The Poet Tires of Those Who Disparage His City—Land of Cotton—Long Gone Blues—Perceive—Poem ("The clear objects")—Toward the End of Winter—Marjorie—Coast of Texas, 1-16—A Poem for My Wife—Old Tale—Research, Again—Pail—Poem ("Living friends live")—A Poem to Read in August—The New York Times: A Poem for Ross Feld—Prince Rupert's Drop—Give Them Blood—They Die Over and Over. In the Movies—Blue Turning Grey—The Insane Waiters—Veterans of Foreign Wars—See America First—Anatomy.

Sulpiciaė Elegidia/Elegiacs of Sulpicia (1977): 1. At last comes love of such a quality that it would shame me—2. My hated birthday looms. In the rude and wretched country—3. Do you know that sad journey is lifted from your darling's heart?—4. That you allow yourself this vast neglect of me—5. Cerinthus, don't you have some soft thought for your girl—6. Light, my light, let me never be again.

White Sail (1977): Boilermakers—Cynical—A Silk Ascot for the Terroist—16 Lines—Captain Marvell—Lost in the Stars—Beautiful Soup—Mosquitoes in New Jersey—George C. Tilyou Smiles—The Ambassador—Oleo Strut—Gimlet—You Are My Heart's Bouquet—Let's Call This—Cautious Circumspection Does Not Win the West—Charles and Arthur—Deluxe Assorted—Blackburn's Dream—Billy McCoy—September in Kittery—A Hit Album.

The Orangery (1978): 1939 World's Fair—Everybody would soon change—She whom no one ever found—Chez Macadam—Mr. America last seen crossing the road—Across this water sits a shore—Canta Naranja—Variations 2—Variations 3—In Memoriam P.B.—Deux Morceaux en Forme de Banane—Drifting South—Big Brown Eyes—Sappho in Paris—Annie from Miami—The King of the dark tower is a lug—Vapid Transit—At twenty love disintegrates—She was all in black. A statement—Simplicity—Canzone—Marvellous—White Lemons—Homage to Arnaut—Zukofsky—Broadway! Broadway!—Remember the story of Columbus and the orange?—The Oranges Returned—Je Connais Gens de Toutes Sortes—Vision of the City from a Window—Fragments of an Old Song 1—Fragments of an Old Song 2—Pastorale—The Crown, 1-7.

New Poems (1978-1980): Twelve Études for Voice and Kazoo: Huge Man in Tight Pants; Some Sap Sings a Poor Pantoum; Waltz of the Empty Roadhouse; Man in Old Blue Suit at the Plaza; 'Ultima Despedida del Príncipe Poniatowski de Su Familia; Impromptu Solo on a Balcony; Jaimie Valeroso y Borracho Consults His Journal; Woman Irritable Because of Her Menses; Girl at Sixteen with Lightning; Le Bateau d'Amour Descried on the Briny; Solitary Man Discovered in a Field of Daisies; In Which There Is Nothing Up the Sleeve—Crool Time—The Iceman, Again—De Pré Est Vénéneux Mais Joli en Automne—Verlaine's Innocents—Diaghilev Did Not Say "Étonnez-moi"—A Celebration of Sorts—The Lemonade Panel—Miss and Hit—"Good Night!"—Où Sont Ils, Où, Vierge Souvrain?—The Lecture on Time and Space—Everything Is a Still-Life—Trouble in Paradise—Mysteries Sacred and Profane—The Disappearance of Oilcloth—From the Journal of Immutable Truths—Cruel Experiments Continue!—Evils of the City—Barely Aware of the Insistent Loud Roars—Strambotto—The Interesting Glass—The Open Boat—Razzmatazz—Brown Nightgown.

PUBLICATION: Published 20 May 1981 at $30.00. 500 copies, printed by Graham Mackintosh and Edwards Brothers Inc. in Santa Barbara, CA, and Ann Arbor, MI. As of 1988, only 300 copies had been bound.

b. First edition, clothbound, signed and numbered issue
Identical to A16a, except:

CONTENTS: Identical, except on [269], where GS's manuscript signature follows the publisher's device and an arabic numeral, handwritten in red follows the printed text.

BINDING: Quarter bound in deep brown (56), fine diaper cloth and wove, cream (no Centroid equivalent) paper over boards.

PUBLICATION: Published at $30.00. 200 copies, of which 30 copies were lost by the binder.

c. First edition, clothbound, signed and lettered issue
Identical to A16a, except:

CONTENTS: Identical, except on [269], where GS's manuscript signature follows the publisher's device and a letter, handwritten in red, follows the printed text.

BINDING: Quarter bound in silk-textured, light grayish reddish brown (45) cloth printed in a pattern of deep red (13), moderate blue (182), and black dots.

PUBLICATION: Published at $40.00. 26 copies signed by GS and lettered A-Z for sale, and five copies, one each marked "Author's Copy," "Publisher's Copy," "Printer's Copy," "Binder's Copy," and "File Copy," which were not for sale.

d. First edition, paperbound issue
Identical to A16a, except:

COLLATION: Perfect bound.

PAPER: Leaf measures 22.8 x 14.8 cm.

BINDING: Glued into stiff, wove, unwatermarked, cream paper wrapper, printed identically to A16a, except spine text is printed directly on the wrapper and adds the publisher's name in brilliant bluish green (159).

PUBLICATION: Published at $7.50. 2509 copies. Price subsequently raised to $8.50.

BACKGROUND NOTES: On 17 April 1980 John Martin wrote GS rejecting *CV*, but in the same letter he also proposed Black Sparrow's publishing a volume of GS's selected poems (TLS at DeU). GS promptly agreed and set about the task almost immediately, commenting at the time: "I hope to do a book of some 250 poems, selected from my previous books, plus a section of maybe 30-35 new poems, work since *The Orangery*" (letter to John O'Brien, 23 April 1980; TLS at CSt). Initially Martin wanted *WS* excluded, since the book was still in print, but he later agreed to a selection from it, explaining "I just didn't want to completely supersede [*WS*]" and then urging GS, "Let this be a 'big' book—don't pare it down to nothing!" (letter to GS, 2 May 1980; TLS at DeU). In July, the manuscript arrived at Black Sparrow, and Martin pushed his desire for a distinctive title: "I still believe we would be INFINITELY better off if you would title the book and use "Selected Poems 1958-1980" as the subtitle. Titles have always been a strong point with you, and surely you could find one that would heighten the occasion. . ." (letter, 24 July 1980; TLS at DeU). GS refused Martin's request and continued to insist on his part that he "wanted a plain, clean, chaste type of cover on a neutral background" (letter to O'Brien, 29 July 1980; TLS at CSt). The contract for *SP* was finalized in October and production proceeded without incident over the next year. In early May 1981 GS signed the colophon pages; a month later he received an advanced copy of the book, remarking "the cover is absolutely elegant—plain and clean and strong" (letter to O'Brien, 1 June 1981; TLS at CSt).

A17 CRYSTAL VISION 1981

a. First edition
Gilbert Sorrentino | **CRYSTAL** | **VISION** [**C** and **V** enlarged and interconnected] | A Novel | North Point Press • San Francisco • 1981

COLLATION: $[1\text{-}8]^{16}$, $[9]^{8}$, $[10]^{16}]$ = 152 leaves; [i-xii], [1-2], 3-289, [290-292].

CONTENTS: [i-ii] blank; [iii] publisher's device in upper right corner; [iv] blank; [v] title page; [vi] Copyright © 1981 by Gilbert Sorrentino | Printed in the United States of America | Library of Congress Catalogue Number: 81-2628 | ISBN: 0-86547-041-3; [vii] [epigraph from Canto IV of Dante's *Inferno*]; [viii] blank; [ix-xi] contents; [xii] blank; [1] half title; [2] blank; 3-289 text; [290] blank; [291] Design by David Bullen | Typeset in Mergenthaler Trump Mediaeval | by Robert Sibley | Printed by Maple-Vail Press | on acid-free paper; [292] blank.

PAPER: Leaf measures 22.7 x 15.4 cm.; yellowish white (92), wove, unwatermarked.

BINDING: Quarter bound in black, fine diaper cloth and light bluish gray (190), fine bead-cloth over boards. Front and back covers unstamped. Down spine, stamped in silver: Crystal Vision   Gilbert Sorrentino; across spine: [publisher's device]. All edges trimmed. Very pale to pale purplish blue (202-203), laid endpapers, with vertical chain lines approx. 5 cm. apart. All edges trimmed.

DUST JACKET: Total measurement 23.3 x 51.8 cm. White (263), wove, unwatermarked paper coated glossy, printed in black, silver, and reproducing a color photograph. Back cover features a black and white photograph of GS by Thomas Victor and a seven-line biographical statement about GS. Front inside flap includes a three-paragraph description of *CV.* Back inside flap lists books published by North Point Press. Jacket design by David Bullen. Jacket photograph by Tracey Pettis and Robert Reiter.

PUBLICATION: Published 30 November 1981 at $14.50. 5090 copies printed by Maple-Vail Press. A sticker was subsequently placed over the original price on the inside front flap of the dust jacket to raise the price to $17.50. A small number (10-20) of uncorrected page proofs were photocopied and strip bound in cream wrappers by North Point Press and distributed to major review and trade outlets. Both the cover and title page of the bound proofs are printed with the phrase, "ADVANCE UNCORRECTED GALLEY COPY."

BACKGROUND NOTES: GS began *CV* in the late spring of 1975, just a few months after finishing *MS,* and completed his first draft in July 1976, commenting to John O'Brien, "I think it is a beauty. I love it" (31 July 1976; TLS at CSt). GS submitted the final, revised manuscript to his agent, Mel Berger, in September. Initially the novel was called *Ghost Talk,* and for the next four years it circulated unsuccessfully among more than twenty major trade publishers, sometimes in tandem with the manuscript of *MS.* The reasons typically given for rejection were the book's lack of a narrative line and its exclusive reliance on dialogue. Characteristic was Gary Fisketjon, who rejected the novel at Random House and who less than two years later acted as GS's editor for *AS:* "*Ghost Talk* dispenses with plot, character development, narrative description–in short, much of the traditional novel's foundation. We are therefore left in an exclusively verbal

Crystal Vision
Gilbert Sorrentino
NORTH POINT PRESS
ADVANCE UNCORRECTED GALLEY COPY
NOVEMBER 30, 1981

Crystal Vision
Gilbert Sorrentino

GILBERT SORRENTINO
AUTHOR OF
MULLIGAN
STEW
"A COMIC ROMP...
A REMARKABLE
ACHIEVEMENT"
–SATURDAY REVIEW
Crystal Vision
The Penguin Contemporary American Fiction Series

CRYSTAL VISION
a novel by Gilbert Sorrentino

world where characters define themselves through their words, words transform events into stories, and stories are essentially a matter of sensibility and style. As an aesthetic investigation of the creation of phrase and story, *Ghost Talk* is intriguing; as a verbal slice of life, it is resourceful and interesting. But I have trouble with it as a novel. Given little beyond dialogue, I cannot *see* these characters, soda fountains, and street corners at all clearly, though I would surely like to" (letter to Mel Berger, 6 February 1979; TLS at DeU). About the rejections, GS remarked: "I am simply nonplussed by the tenor of the rejections. The problem is that nobody ever wrote a book like *CV* before. . ." (letter to O'Brien, 1 July 1980; TLS at CSt).

In September 1978, while *MS* was in production, Grove Press rejected *CV*. A year later, after the commercial success of *MS*, Grove Press reconsidered the book, now carrying the name *In Limbo*, but in October once more turned it down. GS remained dissatisfied with the title. Before trying *In Limbo*, he had briefly considered *Shadowland* and then *Fata Morgana*. In Early 1980 GS again changed titles, this time to *Crystal Vision*. In May 1980, after John Martin had decided in April against publishing it at Black Sparrow, GS sent *CV* to Jack Shoemaker, the editor of the recently established North Point Press. North Point accepted it in late July 1980, offering GS an advance of $5000.

Production began in the fall and proceeded without problems, with GS reviewing the copy-edited manuscript in January 1981, the proofs in July, and bound galleys in September. The dust jacket copy, though written by North Point staff, drew much of its content from a letter GS wrote Shoemaker describing *CV*'s five major divisions. The jacket illustration, however, was conceived independently of GS, who had himself suggested using the Tarot deck, the sequence of whose 78 cards structures *CV*'s 78 chapters. After receiving an advanced copy from North Point in October 1981, GS wrote O'Brien that "it is an absolutely beautiful book, from the jacket to the binding to the typeface and size. . . . I think that it may be the best-looking book that I've ever published" (20 October 1981; TLS at CSt). Though early sales of *CV* were strong, they soon tapered off, and in February 1985 North Point sold its excess stock of the novel to Daedalus Books.

b. Marion Boyars (First British) Edition, clothbound issue (1982) (photo-offset reduction from A17a)

Gilbert Sorrentino | [centered] **Crystal | Vision** [**C** and **V** enlarged and interconnected] | A Novel | [at bottom, left] Marion Boyars ● London ● Boston

COLLATION: $[1\text{-}8]^{16}$, $[9]^{8}$, $[10]^{16}$ = 152 leaves; [i-x], [1-2], 3-289, [290-294].

CONTENTS: [i] [top right] North Point's publisher's device; [ii] blank; [iii] title page; [iv] Published in Great Britain in 1982 by | MARION BOYARS PUBLISHERS LTD. | 18 Brewer Street, London W1R4AS | Australian and New Zealand distribution by | Thomas C. Lothian Pty. | 4-12 Tattersalls Lane, Melbourne, Victoria 3000 | © Gilbert Sorrentino 1981, 1982 | Design by David Bullen | [10 lines stating copyright reservations] | **British Library Cataloguing in Publication Data** | Sorrentino, Gilbert | Crystal vision. | I. Title | 813'.54

PS3569.O7 | ISBN 0-7145-2759-9 cased | Printed and bound in Great Britain at | The Camelot Press Ltd, Southampton; [v] epigraph from Canto IV of Dante's *Inferno;* [vi] blank; [vii-ix] contents; [x] blank; [1] half title; [2] blank; 3-289 text; [290-294] blank.

PAPER: Leaf measures 21.5 x 13.8 cm.; yellowish white (92), wove, unwatermarked.

BINDING: Sewn and bound in black, fine linen cloth. Front and back covers: unstamped. Down spine, stamped in silver: [on two parallel lines] CRYSTAL VISION | Gilbert Sorrentino; across spine: Marion | Boyars. White (263), wove, unwatermarked endpapers. All edges trimmed.

DUST JACKET: Total measurement 22 x 48.5 cm. White (263), wove, paper coated glossy, printed in black, grays, and strong greenish blue (169). Back cover lists other fiction published by Marion Boyars. Inside front flap features a photograph of GS and a 27-line description of *CV* that continues onto the inside back flap. The inside back flap also includes a five-line biographical statement about GS as well as excerpts of reviews of *CV* from *Kirkus,* of *MS* from the London *Times, Literary Review, Washington Post,* and *New York Times,* and of *AS* from the *Chicago Sun-Times, New York Review of Books,* and *Newsday.* Jacket design and photography by Michael Werner.

PUBLICATION: Published June 1982 at £7.95; 1000 copies printed and bound at Camelot Press Ltd., Southampton, Great Britain. Publisher reports issuing no bound galleys prior to publication.

BACKGROUND NOTES: Marion Boyars acquired the British rights to *CV* in November 1981. The contract paid GS a £300 advance and stipulated a 10% royalty on the first 3000 copies sold, 12½% on the next 2000, and 15% on copies over 5000. *TLS* reviewed the American edition of *CV* January 1982, almost six months before the British edition reached the bookstores, a problem in timing that may have hurt sales.

c. Penguin (First American Paperbound) Edition (1982) (photo-offset reduction from A17a)

Gilbert Sorrentino | **Crystal** | **Vision** [**C** and **V** enlarged and interconnected] | [at left] [publisher's device, drawing of penguin within oval] | Penguin Books

COLLATION: perfect bound, 152 leaves; [i-xii], [1-3], 4-5, [6-7], 8-11, [12], 13-15, [16], 17-18, [19], 20-22, [23], 24-26, [27], 28-29, [30], 31-34, [35], 36-38, [39], 40-42, [43], 44-46, [47], 48-49, [50], 51-53, [54], 55-56, [57], 58-61, [62], 63-65, [66], 67-69, [70], 71-72, [73], 74-76, [77], 78-79, [80], 81-83, [84], 85-87, [88], 89-90, [91], 92-94, [95-96], 97-98, [99], 100-101, [102], 103, [104], 105-106, [107], 108-109, [110], 111-113, [114], 115-117, [118], 119-122, [123],

124-126, [127], 128-129, [130], 131-132, [133], 134, [135], 136-138, [139], 140-142, [143], 144-146, [147], 148-149, [150], 151-153, [154], 155-159, [160], 161-163, [164], 165-166, [167], 168-170, [171], 172-173, [174], 175-178, [179], 180-182, [183], 184-186, [187], 188-189, [190], 191-194, [195], 196, [197], 198-200, [201], 202-203, [204], 205-206, [207], 208-210, [211], 212, [213-214], 215-216, [217-218], 219-221, [222], 223, [224], 225-227, [228], 229-234, [235], 236-237, [238], 239-244, [245], 246-249, [250], 251-253, [254], 255-257, [258], 259-260, [261], 262-266, [267], 268-270, [271], 272-275, [276], 277-281, [282], 283-285, [286], 287-289, [290-292].

CONTENTS: [i] THE PENGUIN | CONTEMPORARY AMERICAN | FICTION SERIES | CRYSTAL VISION | [12-line biographical statement]; [ii] blank; [iii] [19 lines listing other books by GS]; [iv] blank; [v] title page; [vi] Penguin Books Ltd, Harmondsworth, | Middlesex, England | Penguin Books, 625 Madison Avenue, | New York, New York 10022, U.S.A. | [six lines listing names and addresses of Penguin's Commonwealth subsidiaries, none of which distributed *CV*] | First published in the United States of America by | North Point Press 1981 | Published in Penguin Books 1982 | Copyright © Gilbert Sorrentino, 1981 | All rights reserved | LIBRARY OF CONGRESS CATALOGING IN PUBLICATION DATA | Sorrentino, Gilbert. | Crystal vision. | I. Title. | PS3569.07C7 1982 813'.54 82-12280 | ISBN 0 14 00.6320X | Printed in the United States of America by | R.R. Donnelley & Sons Company, Harrisonburg, Virginia | Set in Mergenthaler Trump Mediaeval | [nine-line statement of copyright reservations]. Otherwise identical to A17a.

PAPER: Leaf measures 19.7 x 12.7 cm.; yellowish white (92), wove, unwatermarked paper.

BINDING: Glued into thick, wove, unwatermarked, glossy, white (263) paper wrapper, printed in shades from pinkish gray (10) to dark reddish gray (23), dark purplish gray (234), strong red (12), vivid orange (48), and black. Back cover includes a 19-line description of *CV* and an eight-line excerpt of a review of the novel from the *San Francisco Chronicle*.

PUBLICATION: Published 16 December 1982 at $6.95. 10,000 copies printed by R.R. Donnelley & Sons Company, Harrisonburg, VA.

BACKGROUND NOTES: Penguin acquired the paperback rights to *CV* in November 1981 for $4000. The contract stipulated a 12-month delay in publication and limited Penguin's rights to the book to seven years, after which they were to revert to North Point. As with the Penguin edition of *AS*, Daniel Weaver was the editor, and shortly after *CV*'s publication he left Penguin, which effectively ended GS's relation with the house. GS was not involved at all in the production of *CV*. "The cover is OK," he commented, "a little busy maybe, but you can sure *see* the son of a bitch" (letter to John O'Brien, 18 November 1982; TLS at CSt).

d. Marion Boyars (First British) paperbound issue (photo-offset from A17a)
Identical to A17b, except:

COLLATION: Perfect bound.

PAPER: Leaf measures 21.5 x 13.4 cm.

BINDING: Glued into stiff, white (263), glossy, wove paper wrapper. Front and spine printed identically to the dust jacket of A17b; the back cover reformats and slightly revises the material on the front and back inside flaps of the dust jacket of A17b and includes the same photograph and biographical statement about GS, a virtually identical description of *CV*, and excerpts of reviews of *CV* from ***Kirkus Reviews*** and the London *Times*.

PUBLICATION: Published January 1984 at £3.95. 1000 copies printed by Camelot Press Ltd., Southampton, Great Britain.

A18 — BLUE WRITES A MYSTERIOUS AND HAUNTING SONG — 1983

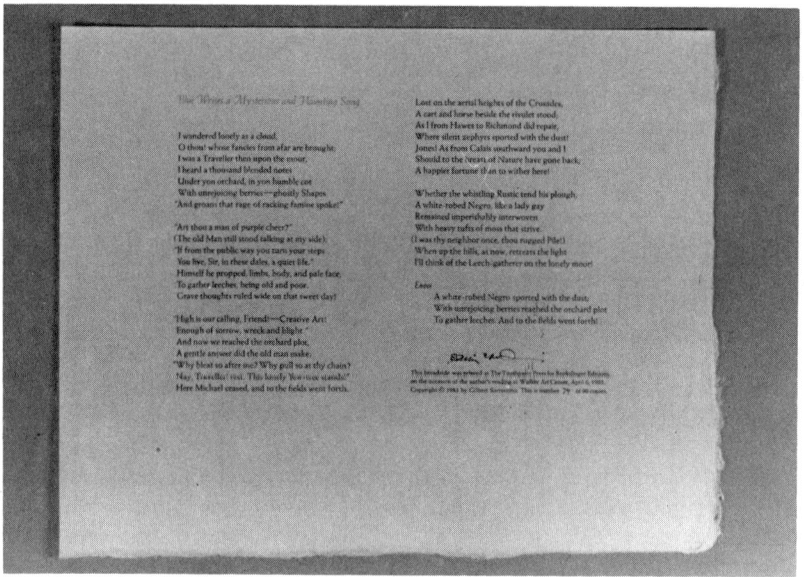

Blue Writes a Mysterious and Haunting Song

I wandered lonely as a cloud,
O thou! whose fancies from afar are brought;
I was a Traveller then upon the moor,
I heard a thousand blended notes
Under yon orchard, in yon humble cot
With unrejoicing berries—ghostly Shapes
"And groans that rage of racking famine spoke!"

"Art thou a man of purple cheer?"
(The old Man still stood talking at my side);
"If from the public way you turn your steps
You live, Sir, in these dales, a quiet life."
Himself he propped, limbs, body, and pale face,
To gather leeches, being old and poor.
Grave thoughts ruled wide on that sweet day!

"High is our calling, Friend!—Creative Art!
Enough of sorrow, wreck and blight."
And now we reached the orchard plot,
A gentle answer did the old man make,
"Why bleat so after me? Why pull so at thy chain?
Nay, Traveller! rest. This lonely Yew-tree stands!"
Here Michael ceased, and to the fields went forth.

Lost on the aerial heights of the Crusades,
A cart and horse beside the rivulet stood;
As I from Hawes to Richmond did repair,
Where silent zephyrs sported with the dust!
Jones! As from Calais southward you and I
Should to the breast of Nature have gone back,
A happier fortune than to wither here!

Whether the whistling Rustic tend his plough,
A white-robed Negro, like a lady gay
Remained imperishably interwoven
With heavy tufts of moss that strive.
(I was thy neighbor once, thou rugged Pile!)
When up the hills, as now, retreats the light
I'll think of the Leech-gatherer on the lonely moor!

Envoi

A white-robed Negro sported with the dust;
With unrejoicing berries reached the orchard plot
To gather leeches. And to the fields went forth!

[In two columns] [at top of left-hand column, in light blue (181)] Blue Writes a Mysterious and Haunting Song | [in black, text in two columns] | [at bottom of right-hand column, GS's manuscript signature] | This broadside was printed at the Toothpaste Press for Bookslinger Editions, | on the occasion of the author's reading at Walker Art Center, April 6, 1983. | Copyright © 1983 by Gilbert Sorrentino. This is number [arabic number in manuscript] of 90 copies.

COLLATION: broadside.

PAPER: Leaf measures approx. 26.2 x 33.5. White (263), Hosho paper, with deckled edges.

TEXT CONTENTS: "Blue Writes a Mysterious and Haunting Song" [poem]. Reprinted in *BP*, 231-232.

PUBLICATION: 6 April 1983 at $15.00. 90 copies, numbered and signed by GS; printed by the Toothpaste Press.

A19 BLUE PASTORAL 1983

a. First edition

Blue Pastoral | GILBERT SORRENTINO | [ornament] | NORTH POINT PRESS | *San Francisco* | *1983*

COLLATION: $[1\text{-}9]^{16}$, $[10]^{8}$, $[11]^{16}$ = 168 leaves; [i-xvi]; 1-315, [316-320].

CONTENTS: [i-ii] blank; [iii] publisher's device in upper right corner; [iv] blank; [v] [18 lines listing other books by GS]; [vi] blank; [vii] title page; [viii] Copyright © 1983 by Gilbert Sorrentino | Printed in the United States of America | Library of Congress Catalogue Card Number: 82-073720 | ISBN: 0-86547-095-2; [ix-xi] contents; [xii] blank; [xiii] [10-line quotation from Drayton's preface to his *Pastorals*] | *Michael Drayton, 1619;* [xiv] blank; [xv] half title; [xvi] blank; 1-315 text; [316] blank; [317] Design by David Bullen | Typeset in Mergenthaler Granjon | by Wilset & Taylor | Printed by Maple-Vail | on acid-free paper; [318-320] blank.

PAPER: Leaf measures 22.7 x 15.2 cm.; yellowish white (92), wove, unwatermarked.

BINDING: Strong to deep reddish purple (237-238), fine bead cloth. Front cover: unstamped. Down spine, stamped in gold: Blue Pastoral GILBERT SORRENTINO [publisher's device]. All edges trimmed. Grayish to dark grayish green (150-151) wove, unwatermarked endpapers.

DUST JACKET: Total measurement 23.2 x 50.9 cm. White (263), wove, unwatermarked paper, coated glossy and printed in dark blue (183), gold, light reddish

DUST JACKET: Total measurement 23.2 x 50.9 cm. White (263), wove, unwatermarked paper, coated glossy and printed in dark blue (183), gold, light reddish purple (240), and black. Back cover includes excerpts of reviews that focus on GS's fiction generally, from the *New York Times Book Review*, *Cincinnati Enquirer*, Robert Creeley, *Review of Contemporary Fiction*, and *Times Literary Supplement*. Inside front flap prints a four-paragraph description of *BP*; inside back flap includes an eight-line biographical statement about GS. Jacket design and illustration by Victoria Hoke.

PUBLICATION: Published 30 May 1983 at $18.00. 5088 copies. Typeset by Wilset & Taylor and printed by Maple-Vail. 60 copies of bound, uncorrected galleys distributed 5 November 1982.

BACKGROUND NOTES: As early as January 1979, GS considered basing a new book on the model of the pastoral. By the summer of 1979, he had settled on the title, *Blue Pastoral*, and was at work on the novel, saying at the time: "I am inventing a syntax so that not even the language has reference to 'reality' " (letter to John O'Brien, 14 August 1979; TLS at CSt). Composition followed *BP*'s geographical structure, with GS writing the chapters in their order along the book's transcontinental route. Originally he planned "a final, 'post-text' *Notes* section . . . commenting on much of the material and the writer, his sources, etc.," (letter to O'Brien, 4 September 1981; TLS at CSt), but by the time GS completed the first draft in November 1981, this chapter had been eliminated.

In January 1982, GS submitted the final revised typescript to his agent, Mel Berger, who forwarded it to Random House in compliance with its option on GS's next novel. Berger asked for a $10,000 advance, and when Random House refused, offering instead $8000, GS decided to pursue other options. He explained: "In light of the fact that *Aberration of Starlight* had done quite well for Random, and that they'd sold rights to Penguin, I thought that my $10,000 advance request was justified. When they turned me down, I thought it time to leave, especially since they'd also earlier rejected *Crystal Vision*. It seemed that they were not really interested" [letter to William McPheron, 21 December 1989; TLS at CSt]. In contrast, North Point, which had published *CV* only a few months before, was very interested in *BP*, and they promptly accepted the novel. The contract, dated 13 April 1982, provided a $5000 advance against 10% royalties on the first 5000 copies sold, 12½% on the next 5000, and 15% on copies over 10,000.

Production proceeded smoothly. The uncorrected galleys, issued in early

November, were first distributed to prospective paperbound publishers of the novel, and by late November Penguin as well as other major paperback houses had expressed interest in the rights. As was typical with North Point, the publisher's staff handled design, jacket copy, and advertising copy. When North Point's Spring 1983 catalog appeared, GS observed that the blurb for *BP* "has about as much to do with the book I wrote as 'a colorful jaunt around quaint Dublin' has to do with *Ulysses*" (letter to O'Brien, 13 January 1983; TLS at CSt). From the beginning, *BP* sold poorly, and by August, just two months after its publication, the earlier interest in paperback rights had evaporated. Penguin did offer $4000 for the rights, but contingent upon cross accounting it with *CV*, "a shabby, sleazy, altogether bush proposal," GS commented at the time the offer was rejected (letter to O'Brien, 1 September 1983; TLS at CSt).

b. Marion Boyars (First British) issue (1984)
Identical to A19a, except:

DUST JACKET: White (263) adhesive label affixed at the bottom of the inside front flap, which reads: *Published in Great Britain and the Commonwealth* | *in 1984 by* | MARION BOYARS PUBLISHERS LTD | LONDON & NEW YORK | ISBN 0-7145-2817-X £9.95.

PUBLICATION: Published May 1984 at £9.95. 500 copies, imported from North Point Press with Marion Boyars labels attached.

BACKGROUND NOTES: In summer 1982 North Point Press proposed that Marion Boyars Publishers share the production costs of *BP* and issue the British edition from sheets printed in the United States. Because *CV* had not been selling well in Britain, Boyars declined. In June 1983 she offered £300 for British rights, with the expectations of purchasing the North Point plates to produce the book in England. This arrangement was rejected and eventually all plans to manufacture a British issue were dropped.

A20 SOMETHING SAID 1984

First edition
Something | [within 2.3 x 7.2 cm. doubled-framed rectangle, two successive lines] ESSAYS BY | *GILBERT SORRENTINO* | **Said** | NORTH POINT PRESS | *San Francisco 1984*

COLLATION: $[1\text{-}9]^{16}$ = 144 leaves; [i-ii], [i-vi], vii-viii, [ix-x], [1-2], 3-266, [267-276]

CONTENTS: [i-ii] blank; [i] [top right corner, publisher's device]; [ii] blank; [iii] title page; [iv] Copyright © 1984 by Gilbert Sorrentino | Printed in the United States of America | Library of Congress Catalogue Card Number: 84-060690 | ISBN: 0-86547-177-0; [v-vi] contents; vii-viii Preface; [ix] epigraph from

Maurice Blanchot; [x] blank; [1] half title; [2] blank; 3-266 text; [267-268] blank; [269] Design by David Bullen | Typeset in Mergenthaler Kennerly | and Goudy Olde Style | by Wilsted & Taylor | Printed by Maple-Vail | on acid-free paper; [270-276] blank.

PAPER: Leaf measures 22.8 x 15.1 cm.; yellowish white (92), wove, unwatermarked. No endpapers. All edges trimmed.

BINDING: Sewn and glued into stiff, white (263), wove, unwatermarked paper wrapper, printed yellowish white (92) and coated glossy. Printed across front cover: [at upward angle, in light gray (264)] Something | [within 2.3 x 7.2 cm. double-framed rectangle, two successive lines] ESSAYS BY | *Gilbert Sorrentino* | Said. Printed down spine, in light gray (264): Something Said *Gilbert Sorrentino;* across spine: [publisher's device]. Back cover: unprinted.

DUST JACKET: Total measurement 22.8 x 50.5 cm. White (263), wove, unwatermarked paper, coated glossy and printed in black, grays, light green (144), and pale green (149). In an undetermined number of jackets, medium gray (265) replaces the light green and pale green. Back cover features a photograph of GS by Thomas Victor and a seven-line biographical statement about GS. Inside front flap includes a 26-line description of *SS;* inside back flap lists other works of criticism and biography from North Point Press. Jacket design by David Bullen.

TEXT CONTENTS: Preface—The Act of Creation and Its Artifact—William Carlos Williams—Jack Spicer—Louis Zukofsky—William Bronk—Kenneth Rexroth—Lorine Niedecker—Jonathan Williams—Edward Dahlberg—Paul Blackburn—Hubert Selby—Coleman Dowell—Michael McClure: Artaud—Max Finstein—Ron Loewinsohn's *Watermelons*—Measure of Maturity—Charles Olson: *The Distances*—Andrew Hoyem: *The Wake*—Neruda: *Residence on Earth*—AN OCTOPUS/of ice—Ross Feld's Plums—Emerald on the Beach—George Oppen: Smallness of Cause—A Glance at West's West—John Hawkes' Oranges—Lost Lives—Larry Woiwode: *Beyond the Bedroom Wall*—Never on Sunday—Blue Gass—García Márquez's Monster—David Antin Talking—Le Style de Queneau—Travels with Calvino—Paul Bowles: The Clash of Cultures—La Guaracha—The Ending Is Wanting—John Gardner: Rhinestone in the Rough—"For my day had passed."—Ross Macdonald: Some Remarks on the Limitations of Form—Moderns—Ten Pamphlets—Black Mountaineering—Empty, Empty Promises, Promises—Dan Rice—Mort Lucks—A Note on William Anthony—Genetic Coding.

PUBLICATION: Published 20 January 1985 at $15.50. 3928 copies. Typeset by Wilsted & Taylor; printed and bound by Maple-Vail. North Point reports a very small number (10-20 total) of strip bound Xeroxes were issued for prepublication review purposes.

BACKGROUND NOTES: Jack Shoemaker proposed as early as 1980 that North Point Press publish a collection of GS's critical articles. In late summer 1981, as North Point was finishing production of *CV*, Shoemaker renewed the idea. GS was reluctant, commenting at the time: "I dread this, reading through mounds of stuff from 1960 on, picking, typing, xeroxing, etc. . . . What a bore to read all that crap" (letter to John O'Brien, 4 September 1981; TLS at CSt). Although at this time GS carefully reviewed the project and decided against revising any material, it was nearly two years later, in September 1983, before he began seriously to work on the volume. By March 1984 GS had scissored and pasted the text, revised North Point's copy-edited version, and settled on the title *Something Said.*

A21 ODD NUMBER 1985

First edition

GILBERT SORRENTINO | [two parallel lines .8 cm. apart, extending 11 cm. from bottom of first line to top of third line, broken by text of second line] **Odd Number** | NORTH POINT PRESS SAN FRANCISCO | 1985

COLLATION: $[1\text{-}4]^{16}$, $[5]^{8}$, $[6]^{16}$ = 88 leaves; [i-viii], [1-3], 4-159, [160-168].

CONTENTS: [i-ii] blank; [iii] [upper right corner, publisher's device]; [iv] blank; [v] title page; [vi] Copyright © 1985 by Gilbert Sorrentino | Printed in the United States of America | Library of Congress Catalogue Card Number: 85-60853 | ISBN: 0-86547-212-2; [vii] [epigraph from Sigmund Freud's *The*

"Uncanny"; [viii] blank; [1] half title; [2] blank; [3]-159 text; [160] blank; [161] Design by David Bullen | Typeset in Mergenthaler Walbaum | by Wilsted & Taylor | Printed by Maple-Vail | on acid-free paper; [162-168] blank.

PAPER: Leaf measures 22.7 x 15 cm.; yellowish white (92), wove, unwatermarked.

BINDING: Bound in dark gray (266), fine bead cloth. Front and back covers: unstamped. Down spine, stamped in silver: Odd Number [on two parallel lines] GILBERT | SORRENTINO; across spine, at bottom: [publisher's device].

DUST JACKET: Total measurement 23.2 x 52.4 cm. White (263), wove, unwatermarked paper, coated glossy and printed in vivid to strong red (11-12), light to medium gray (264-265), medium gray (265), dark gray (266), and black. Back cover features a photograph of GS by Thomas Victor and a five-line biographical statement about GS, as well as three promotional statements—a blurb by Robert Creeley and two excerpts of reviews from the *Cincinnati Enquirer* and the *Review of Contemporary Fiction.* Inside front flap includes a four-paragraph description of *ON;* inside back flap lists other GS titles published by North Point Press, with excerpts of reviews of *BP* from *Magill's Literary Annual* (1984) and the *New York Times Book Review,* of *CV* from the *San Francisco Chronicle* and *Kirkus Reviews,* and of *SS* from the *New York Times Book Review* and the *Los Angeles Times Book Review.* Jacket design and illustration by David Bullen.

PUBLICATION: Published 30 September 1985 at $16.50. 4014 copies. Typeset by Wilsted & Taylor; printed and bound by Maple-Vail. 45 copies of uncorrected proofs prepared by Crane Duplicating were released 16 May 1985.

BACKGROUND NOTES: GS began *ON* in December 1981, early the next month remarking that it was "the most complicated piece of fiction ever devised by mankind" (letter to John O'Brien, 8 January 1982; TLS at CSt). The novel's original working title was *Triad*, a name GS retained throughout the book's composition. The first draft was completed in late July 1983, at which point GS also realized that the book was only the first volume of what was "definitely a trilogy," adding, "tentative titles of the next two woiks [sic]: *Rose Theatre* and *Construction in Metal*" (letter to O'Brien, 29 July 1983; TLS at CSt). In September 1983 GS made what he thought at the time were the final revisions to the manuscript: "I've made a lot of changes, nothing substantive re/structure, character, events, but it is more clearly defined now" (letter to O'Brien, 1 September 1983). But not until the following August did GS actually complete his revisions, at which time he also renamed the novel *Odd Number*, taking his title from a line from Flann O'Brien's *At Swim-Two-Birds:* "Evil is even, truth is an odd number and death is a full stop."

By early 1985 the manuscript was with Jack Shoemaker at North Point Press, where it was accepted in February. The contract, dated 11 March 1985, provided a $3000 advance against 10% royalties on the first 10,000 copies sold and 12½% on subsequent sales. Production began in March, proceeding quickly through the summer. By early September advanced copies were sent to GS, who remarked that "the book looks very good, a rather strange and arty jacket" (letter to O'Brien, 10 September 1985; TLS at CSt). The early reviews were harshly negative, prompting GS to observe "*Odd Number* has apparently approached the condition of poetry" (letter to O'Brien, 24 September 1985; TLS at CSt). The book did not sell well; through April 1987, nearly a year and a half after release, only 1207 copies had been purchased.

A22 A BEEHIVE ARRANGED ON HUMANE PRINCIPLES 1986

a. First edition, arabic numbered issue

Gilbert Sorrentino | [in strong reddish brown (40)] A | Beehive | Arranged | on Humane | Principles | *Linocuts by David Storey*

COLLATION: $[1\text{-}10]^2$ = 20 leaves; [1-40]. The signatures, $[1\text{-}2]^2$ and $[9\text{-}10]^2$, consist of single sheets of trimmed paper folded once, in folio format; the interior signatures, $[3\text{-}8]^2$, consist of sheets with deckled edges in French-folded quarto format, with the top edge uncut, so that each of the interior 16 bibliographic leaves is actually two physical leaves, with the insides blank.

CONTENTS: [1-7] blank; [8] linocut; [9] title page; [10] *All rights to text and artwork reserved by Gilbert Sorrentino and David Storey;* [11] half title; [12] linocut; [13-17] text; [18] linocut; [19-23] text; [24] linocut; [25-30] text; [31-32] blank; [33] 85 copies printed on Whatman paper and published | by The Grenfell Press, New York, January 1986. | Typography by Michael Bixler; binding by | Claudia Cohen. | Copies 1-70 bound in | full paper; copies I-XV bound in | full morocco. All copies signed | by the author and the artist. | This is number [number

in manuscript] | [GS's signature] | [David Storey's signature]; [34-40] blank.

NOTE: On an unattached paper slip: "Erratum: Copies 1-70 are bound in quarter morocco."

PAPER: Leaf measures approx. 27 x 22 cm. [1-4], [37-40] trimmed, bluish white (189), laid paper, chain lines approx. 4 cm. apart; [5-36] bluish white (189) paper with deckled edges, watermarked "J Whatman 1954 Mould Made England."

BINDING: Sewn and quarter bound in black morocco and handmade, black Japanese paper over boards, printed with a linocut in deep reddish orange (36), light gray (264), and grayish purplish blue (204).

DUST JACKET: Clear acetate.

PUBLICATION: Published 1 March 1986 at $165.00. 73 copies, of which 70 were for sale, numbered 1-70, and signed by GS and David Storey. The other three were reserved for the author, the artist, and the publisher and were unnumbered and not for sale.

b. First edition, roman numbered issue
Identical to A22a, except:

BINDING: Sewn and bound in strong orange (50) morocco, with one vivid red (11) and two black morocco onlays, gold and blind stamping, and laid into a full, dark gray (266) cloth tray case.

PUBLICATION: Published at $585.00. 18 copied, of which 15 were for sale, numbered I-XV, and signed by GS and David Storey. The other three copies were reserved for the author, the artist, and the publisher and were unnumbered and not for sale.

NOTE: Prior to publication, Grenfell Press issued a promotional brochure, consisting of a single, French-folded leaf on laid paper with chain lines 2.5 cm. apart, watermarked "Crest" accompanied by a crest emblem. The text, on pp. [2-3], explains the genesis of *Beehive* in a list of 100 nouns drawn from Wallace Stevens and characterizes the work as "a wonderful word game to be unraveled by the reader." This description of *Beehive* was based on GS's own account of his method.

BACKGROUND NOTES: GS explained the publishing circumstances of *Beehive:* "Leslie Miller asked me if I had any work for the Grenfell Press. I'd just finished 'Beehive' and sent it to her; Brad Morrow read it and asked if he could run it in *Conjunctions.* I had no working relationship with David Storey" (letter to William McPheron, 21 December 1989; TLS at CSt). Storey was chosen by Miller and his drawings were conceived with GS's text in hand.

A23 ROSE THEATRE 1987

First edition
[in gothic] **Rose Theatre** | [in Roman] **Gilbert Sorrentino** | The Dalkey Archive Press

COLLATION: $[1\text{-}3]^{16}$, $[4]^{8}$, $[5]^{16}$ = 72 leaves; [i-ii], [1-6], 7-139, [140-142].

CONTENTS: [i] blank; [ii] 25 lines listing other books by GS]; [1] half title; [2] blank; [3] title page; [4] Portions of this work have appeared in *Conjunctions, PsychCritique*, and *The | Review of Contemporary Fiction*, to whose editors the author gives grateful | acknowledgment. | Copyright © 1987 by Gilbert Sorrentino | ISBN: 0-916583-23-6 | Library of Congress Catalog Card Number: 87-071643 | Partially funded by grants from The National Endowment for the Arts and The Illinois | Arts Council | The Dalkey Archive Press | 1817 79th Avenue | Elmwood Park, IL 60635 USA; [5] epigraph from John Ashbery; [6] blank; 7-139 text; [140-142] blank.

PAPER: Leaf measures 22.8 x 15.1 cm.; yellowish white (92), wove, unwatermarked.

BINDING: Sewn and glued into black, fine calico-texture cloth. Front and back covers: unstamped. Down spine, stamped in gold: [in gothic] Rose Theatre | [in Roman] GILBERT SORRENTINO; across spine: The | Dalkey | Archive | Press. All edges trimmed. Thick, yellowish white (92), wove, unwatermarked endpapers.

DUST JACKET: Total measurement 23.6 x 51.4 cm. White (263), wove, unwatermarked paper, coated glossy and printed in black, medium to dark gray (265-266), and vivid red (11). Back cover reprints excerpts of reviews of *ON* from the *Los Angeles Times Book Review*, *Washington Post Book World*, *Review of Contemporary Fiction*, and *Hudson Review*. Inside flaps include a three-paragraph description of *RT* and a 10-line biographical statement about GS. Cover design by Patricia Shields.

PUBLICATION: Published 10 November 1987 at $20.00. 1111 copies, printed by McNaughton & Gunn and bound by John H. Dekker & Sons. 55 sets of uncorrected proofs, in very light greenish blue (171) wrappers, issued approximately 15 July, of which 51 copies were distributed to reviewers.

BACKGROUND NOTES: Early in 1983, while no further than halfway through the first draft of *ON*, GS was already thinking about the book that eventually became *RT*: "I have a feeling that a novel might be made of names only. I know one can be made of lists, and some day I'll write one. Maybe the next one, already in my head, based on an inventory made by Philip Henslowe of the Rose Theatre's props in 1598 in London, when he moved the company to a new location" (letter to John O'Brien, 15 January 1983; TLS at CSt). Six months later, still over a year away from completing *ON*, GS had decided that *RT* was to be the second volume of the trilogy begun with *ON* and had also outlined the book's structure: *RT* "will have 15 chapters titled after Henslowe's inventory.... A remarkable list that begs to be investigated" (letter to O'Brien, 29 July 1983; TLS at CSt).

Though GS continued to sketch the structure of *RT* in the months that followed, it was not until October 1984 that he began seriously writing the book. On 11 April 1985, he commented that *RT* was coming slowly and explained that "it has to be an extension of *Odd Number* but also a mine of new information, or 'information' " (letter to O'Brien; TLS at CSt). Seven months later, GS reported that he was "still working fitfully on *Rose Theatre* and have now got done in various stages of completion, seven of the fifteen chapters," adding: "It looks good, but I'm having trouble with it because I am really trying to work a new language in this book, a kind of demotic, scattered, haphazard, 'style-less' language that falls into and out of cliché, a kind of useless language" (letter to O'Brien, 12 November 1985; TLS at CSt). A year later, with the manuscript now complete, final revisions made, and the finished typescript almost ready, GS remarked: "I don't know if it is good or bad, but I do know that the very act of writing has become a kind of endless questioning of endless choices, none of which ever seem 'right' " (letter to O'Brien, 12 November 1986; TLS at CSt).

In early January 1987, GS submitted the manuscript to Jack Shoemaker at North Point Press. North Point and then Grove Press rejected the book, before John O'Brien proposed in April that his Dalkey Archive Press publish it. The contract was dated 10 May 1987 and provided for a $3000 advance against 10% royalties on all copies sold. GS wrote the first two paragraphs of the jacket copy (O'Brien wrote the third) and suggested the line drawing of a single rose for the jacket art.

A24 MISTERIOSO 1989

First edition

[in gothic] **Misterioso** | [in Roman] **Gilbert Sorrentino** | Dalkey Archive Press

COLLATION: $[1\text{-}9]^{16}$ = 144 leaves; [1-6], 7-282, [283-288].

CONTENTS: [1] half title; [2] [26 lines listing other books by GS]; [3] title; [4] [four lines acknowledging previous publication of portions of *M* and foundation support during its writing] | Copyright © 1989 by Gilbert Sorrentino | All rights reserved | First edition | Library of Congress Cataloging in Publication Data | Sorrentino, Gilbert. | *Misterioso* | by Gilbert Sorrentino. | I. Title. | PS3569.O7M57 1989 813'.54—dc19 89-7707 | ISBN 0-916583-43-0 | Partially funded by grants from The National Endowment for the Arts and The Illinois | Arts Council. | Dalkey Archive Press | 1817 North 79th Avenue | Elmwood Park, IL 60635 USA | *Printed on permanent/durable acid-free paper and bound in the United States of America.* [5] four-line epigraph from Samuel Beckett]; [6] blank; 7-282 text; [283-288] blank.

PAPER: Leaf measures 22.9 x 15.2 cm.; yellowish white (92), wove, unwatermarked.

BINDING: Sewn and glued into black, fine calico-texture cloth. Front and back covers: unstamped. Down spine, stamped in gold: [on parallel lines] GILBERT SORRENTINO | [in gothic] Misterioso | [on parallel lines] DALKEY ARCHIVE. All edges trimmed. Thick, yellowish white (92) wove, unwatermarked endpapers.

DUST JACKET: Total measurement 23.6 x 53.3 cm. White (263) wove, unwatermarked paper, coated glossy and printed in black and strong red (12). Back cover reprints excerpts of reviews of *ON* and *RT* from the *Los Angeles Times Book Review, Hudson Review, New York Times Book Review, Washington Post Book World,* and *American Book Review.* Inside flaps feature a two-paragraph description of *M,* a photograph of GS by Thomas Victor, and a 10-line biographical statement about GS.

PUBLICATION: Published 10 November 1989 at $19.95. 1000 copies, printed and bound by Thomson-Shore. Approximately 50 sets of uncorrected proofs, in brilliant yellow (83) wrappers, were distributed to reviewers.

BACKGROUND NOTES: As early as the summer of 1983, GS began planning *M* as the final book of the trilogy that opens with *ON.* At the time his working title for this concluding volume was *Construction in Steel,* and GS speculated about its nature: "the 3rd, maybe, maybe at long last, a book that is a series of lists and catalogues—no narrative, no characters, no author, and no place or time or action, no nothing but those words that 'tend toward maximum entropy" (letter to John O'Brien, 29 July 1983; TLS at CSt). Three years later, as he was making the final revisions on the manuscript of *RT,* GS wrote O'Brien about the book that would eventually become *M:* "I have worked out a structure for the third book, and my working title is to be *White Shifts*" (letter, 18 September 1986; TLS at CSt). GS started writing *M* in the summer of 1987 and proceeded steadily, completing the first draft of the manuscript in the summer of 1988 and the final revised text in the fall. Regarding the title, GS explained: "I changed the title from *White Shifts* because it seemed not to fit the book at all. I liked *Misterioso* because of itself, and because I wanted to pay subtle homage to Thelonious Monk, one of the great artists of our time, by naming my work after one of his compositions" (letter to William McPheron, 21 December 1989; TLS at CSt).

The contract for *M* was dated 24 December 1988 and provided a $3000 advance against 10% royalties on the sale of all copies. Jacket copy was based on GS's description of *M* but was written by Steven Moore. GS had a hand in the jacket art: "I suggested the jacket illustration of the Double Seal of Solomon. It is a great magical figure, its elements are apparent yet opaque, and it clearly adumbrates the system of the alphabet" (letter to McPheron, 21 December 1989; TLS at CSt).

B. CONTRIBUTIONS TO BOOKS

B1 14 POETS, 1 ARTIST 1958

JARGON 31: 14 POETS, 1 ARTIST | DECEMBER 12-14, 1958, NEW YORK

PUBLICATION: Loose-leaf folio of 14 leaves published in an edition of 1000 copies by the Jargon Society, Christmas, 1958.

CONTRIBUTION: "Ancient Musick" [poem]. First appearance. Separate leaf reproduces GS's manuscript transcription of the poem, accompanied by Fielding Dawson's drawing. Collected in *DSU*, [32].

B2 PATERSON (BOOK FIVE) 1958

PATERSON | (BOOK FIVE) | [within five-rectangle box] A NEW | DIREC- | TIONS | BOOK | WILLIAM CARLOS WILLIAMS

PUBLICATION: New Directions Book published in New York by James Laughlin. Copyright 1958.

CONTRIBUTION: Excerpt from "Bordertown," an otherwise unpublished sketch, [18-19]; signed G.S.

NOTE: In later printings of the collected *Paterson*, GS's text was revised to reflect his original text. James Laughlin's letter of 5 May 1972 to GS explained the circumstances: "I'm pleased indeed that you will be sending us in due course some corrections for that letter [sic] of yours about the Mexican town which Bill used in 'Paterson V'. . . . There were, as I recall, a number of errors in Bill's re-typings of some of the other letters that are included in the poem, and I think we fixed them as we learned of them."

B3 JAN 1ST 1959: FIDEL CASTRO 1959

JAN 1ST | 1959: | FIDEL | CASTRO

PUBLICATION: Issued by Totem Press, New York, as Blue Plate 1. Copyright 1959, by LeRoi Jones.

CONTRIBUTION: "A Classic Case" [poem], [4]. First appearance. Reprinted in B5. Collected in *DSU*, 38; *SP*, 25.

13 his gut.] his gut, *DSU*+

B4 SAVONAROLA'S TUNE 1959

[printed vertically down a tipped-in half page] savonarola's tune by max finstein | [printed vertically up the right-hand margin of the underlying page] SAVONAROLA'S TUNE BY MAX FINSTEIN PUBLISHED BY LAURENCE HELLENBERG 1959

PUBLICATION: Printed by Orion Press and Publishing Company; distributed by Totem Press, New York.

CONTRIBUTION: "A Foreword" [prose], [3]. Collected in *SS*, 138.

B5 THE NEW AMERICAN POETRY 1960

[repeated fleuron forming a rectangular pattern 10.9 x 8.4 cm.] | THE NEW AMERICAN | POETRY: 1945-1960 | EDITED BY DONALD M. ALLEN | [8 cm. rule] | GROVE PRESS, INC. • NEW YORK | EVERGREEN BOOKS LTD. • LONDON

CONTRIBUTIONS: "A Classic Case" [poem], 296. Reprinted from B3.
"The Zoo" [poem], 297. First appearance. Collected in *DSU*, 24; *SP*, 26.
[95w untitled autobiographical statement], 444. First appearance. Uncollected.

B6 POESIA AMERICANA DEL '900 1963

Poesia | *americana* | *del '900* | *con testo a fronte* | *introduzioni* | *e note bibliografiche* | *a cura di Carlo Izzo* | GUANDA

PUBLICATION: Copyright by Ugo Guanda Editore, Parma, 1963. Published as vol. 4 of the series, *Collana fenice.*

CONTRIBUTIONS: "The Memory" [poem, with accompanying Italian translation as "Il Ricordo"], [830-31]. Reprinted from C62. Collected *BW*, [11], *SP*, 52.
"Dominoes" [poem, with accompanying Italian translation as "Domino"], 832-33. First appearance. Collected *BW*, 22, *SP*, 38.
11] painting] paintings *BW*+
"Fable, with Zodiac" [poem, with accompanying Italian translation as "Favola con Zodiaco"], 834-35. First appearance. Collected *BW*, 20.
18] glinting,] glinting.

NOTE: "Gilbert Sorrentino," a two-paragraph biographical statement appears on p. 968 and includes an Italian translation of part of GS's autobiographical statement in B5.

B7 POEMS NOW 1966

POEMS NOW | edited by | HETTIE JONES | Kulchur Press

PUBLICATION: Copyright 1966, Kulcher Press, New York.

CONTRIBUTIONS: "Just Me an' My Guitar" [poem], 51-52. First appearance. Uncollected.
"Down on the Bingo Farm" [poem], 53-54. First appearance. Uncollected.
"from *The Perfect Fiction*" ["Take a card, any card"] [poem], 55. First appearance. Collected in *PF*, 57-58.

B8 ARTISTS AND WRITERS PROTEST AGAINST THE WAR [1967]

ARTISTS AND WRITERS PROTEST | AGAINST THE WAR IN VIET NAM | [19 cm. deep red orange (36) rule] | POEMS | [19 cm. deep red orange (36) rule].

PUBLICATION: 500 copies printed at Profile Press in New York.

CONTRIBUTION: "A Look Askance" [poem], [25]. First appearance. Uncollected.

B9 NEW WRITING IN THE U.S.A. 1967

THE | NEW WRITING | IN | THE USA | EDITED BY DONALD ALLEN AND | ROBERT CREELEY | PENGUIN BOOKS

PUBLICATION: Copyright 1967. Published by Penguin Books Ltd, Harmondsworth, Middlesex, England.

CONTRIBUTIONS: "The Mathematics" [poem], 264. Reprinted from *BW*, [18-19].
"Ars Longa" [poem], 265-66. Reprinted from *BW*, [4].
"Gilbert Sorrentino" [35w autobiographical note], 329. First appearance. Uncollected.

B10 OUT OF THE WAR SHADOW [1967]

1968 PEACE CALENDAR | & | APPOINTMENT BOOK | OUT OF THE WAR SHADOW | *An Anthology of Current Poetry* | *Compiled & Edited by* Denise Levertov | WAR RESISTERS LEAGUE NEW YORK.

PUBLICATION: 64 unnumbered leaves spiral bound. Copyright 1967 by Denise

Levertov Goodman and distributed by Grossman Publishers, New York.

CONTRIBUTION: "Retreat" [poem], [30]. First appearance. Uncollected.

B11 A TRIBUTE TO JIM LOWELL 1967

[at upward angle, silk-screened in vivid purplish blue (194)] a tribute to | JIM [hand-drawn flower design] | LOWELL | [two hand-drawn flower designs] | [in double line red rectangular adhesive label affixed to lower right-hand corner] GHOST PRESS CLEVELAND | TWO DOLLARS.

PUBLICATION: 500 copies, published June 1967, sold and distributed by Asphodel Bookshop in Cleveland. Unpaged leaves, printed on recto only.

CONTRIBUTION: [300w untitled prose statement criticizing the Cleveland police's arrest of Jim Lowell for selling obscene literature at his Asphodel Bookshop], leaves [37]-[38]. First appearance. Uncollected.

B12 EDWARD DAHLBERG: A TRIBUTE 1970

Edward Dahlberg: | A Tribute | Essays | Reminiscences | Correspondence | Tributes | Edited by | Jonathan Williams | A TriQuarterly Book | David Lewis, Inc./New York

PUBLICATION: Copyright 1970. This book reprints in its entirely *TriQuarterly* 19 (Fall 1970). Verso incorrectly identifies the issue reprinted as *TriQuarterly* 20.

CONTRIBUTION: [untitled memoir of Edward Dahlberg], 90-91. Reprints C155.

B13 BALLAD 1 1971

[Within 7.1 x 20.7 cm. rectangle] bernard rands | ballad 1 | score | universal edition

PUBLICATION: Copyright 1971 by Universal Edition (London) Ltd. This is a score for mezzo-soprano, flutes, trombone, double bass, piano, and percussion, set to the words of GS's poem "(pentagram)."

CONTRIBUTION: "(pentagram)" [poem], [6]. Reprinted from *PF*, 61. Text integrated into score, [7]-18.

B14 A CATERPILLAR ANTHOLOGY 1971

[Double spread title page] A CATERPILLAR ANTHOLOGY | A Selection of Poetry and Prose from CATERPILLAR Magazine | Edited by CLAYTON ESHLEMAN | Anchor Books | Doubleday & Company, Inc. | Garden City, New York | 1971

CONTRIBUTIONS: "Coast of Texas" [suite of sixteen poems], 106-15. Reprinted from C126.

[untitled, 100w autobiographical statement], 502. First appearance. Uncollected.

B15 EQUAL TIME 1972

EQUAL TIME | Editors | Hugh Seidman | Frances Whyatt | EQUAL TIME PRESS | 1972

PUBLICATION: Copyright 1972 by Equal Time Press, New York. Printed by Villiers Publications Ltd, London.

CONTRIBUTIONS: "Charles and Arthur" [poem], 84. First appearance. Collected in *WS*, 16; *SP*, 175.

"September in Kittery" [poem], 84-85. First appearance. Collected in *WS*, 55; *SP*, 179.

"Oleo Strut" [poem], 85. First appearance. Collected in *WS*, 17; *SP*, 169.

14] apart] apart. *WS*+

B16 EPITAPHS FOR LORINE 1973

EPITAPHS FOR LORINE | EDITED AND INTRODUCED | BY JONATHAN WILLIAMS | THE JARGON SOCIETY | PENLAND NORTH CAROLINA | 1973

PUBLICATION: Issued as Jargon 74 under the title *Thirty-Two Poets Celebrate Lorine Niedecker (1903-1970)*. 1000 copies, privately distributed.

CONTRIBUTION: "In Memoriam: Lorine Niedecker" [poem], [39]. First appearance. Uncollected.

B17 POEMS ONE LINE & LONGER 1973

Poems | One Line | & Longer | [8.5 cm. rule] | William Cole | [8.5 cm.

rule] | Grossman Publishers | New York 1973

CONTRIBUTION: "Anatomy" [poem], 148. Reprinted from *CS*, 61.

B18 BALLAD 2 1974

[within 7.1 x 20.5 cm. rectangle] bernard rands | ballad 2 | universal editions

PUBLICATION: Copyright 1974 by Universal Edition (London) Ltd. This is a score for voice and piano, set to the words of GS's poem, "L the simple shape."

CONTRIBUTION: "L the simple shape" [poem], ii. Reprinted from *PF*, 20. Text integrated into score, 2-8.

B19 CAPITALISM: THE MOVING TARGET 1974

LEONARD SILK | Capitalism: | the moving target | With contributions by Kenneth J. Arrow | Thomas Carvel | John Kenneth Galbraith | Andrew Glyn | Gabriel Kolko | Edwin Kuh | Wassily Leontief | David Rockefeller | Paul A. Samuelson | Gilbert Sorrentino | Paul M. Sweezy | & Studs Terkel | Illustrations by Jean-Claude Suarès | [publisher's device, featuring the letters "NYT"] QUADRANGLE | The New York Times Book Co.

PUBLICATION: Copyright 1974.

CONTRIBUTION: "Empty, Empty Promises, Promises" [essay], 73-77. Reprints C180.

B20 SUPERFICTION 1975

SUPERFICTION, | or | THE AMERICAN | STORY | TRANSFORMED | [4.5 cm. decorative rule] | AN ANTHOLOGY | Edited by | JOE DAVID BELLAMY | [publisher's device, anthropomorphic sunburst] | VINTAGE BOOKS | A Division of Random House, New York

PUBLICATION: Copyright 1975.

CONTRIBUTION: "The Moon in Its Flight" [short story], 221-33. Reprints C172.

B21 DAN RICE 1976

DAN RICE | FEBRUARY 17-MARCH 7, 1979 | OWENS ART GALLERY | MOUNT ALLISON UNIVERSITY | SACKVILLE, NEW BRUNSWICK

CONTRIBUTION: "Dan Rice" [prose essay, introducing the exhibit catalog], [2]. First appearance. Collected *SS*, 256-57.

B22 SELF-PORTRAIT BOOK PEOPLE PICTURE THEMSELVES 1976

[20.4 cm. rule] | **SELF-PORTRAIT** | [20.4 cm. rule] | Book People Picture Themselves | *From the collection of* | **BURT BRITTON** | *Random House* [publisher's device, drawing of a house with clouds and sun] *New York* | [20.4 cm. rule]

PUBLICATION: Issued November 1976.

CONTRIBUTION: Signed line-drawn self-portrait, with caption, "Sorrentino registering at the Splendide," 152. First appearance. Uncollected.

B23 BASEBALL I GAVE YOU ALL THE BEST YEARS OF MY LIFE 1977

BASEBALL I GAVE YOU | ALL THE BEST | YEARS OF MY LIFE | Editors: Kevin Kerrane | Richard Grossinger | NORTH ATLANTIC BOOKS

PUBLICATION: Issued as *IO* 24. In 1978 North Atlantic published an enlarged second edition with a different cover and 16 additional pages. In 1980 Doubleday/Anchor reprinted the book.

CONTRIBUTION: "Baseball" [500w prose essay on baseball], 71. Reprinted in *New York Times*, 9 April 1978, sec. 5: 3, under the title "Baseball's Beauty," and in B46. Uncollected.

B24 BALLAD 3 1978

[within 6.9 x 18.5 cm. rectangle] bernard rands | ballad 3 | for soprano and tape | UE15586 | universal edition

PUBLICATION: Copyright 1978 by Universal Edition (London) Ltd. This is a score for soprano and electronic music on tape, set to the words of GS's poem "Come all ye Sons of Art."

CONTRIBUTION: "Come all ye Sons of Art" [poem], [7]. Reprinted from *PF*, 31, with accompanying partial translation into Italian. Text and translated portions integrated into score, [1]-5.

B25 BEST AMERICAN SHORT STORIES 1978

The Best | AMERICAN | SHORT | STORIES | 1978 | [8.5 cm. rule] | Selected from | U.S. and Canadian Magazines | by Ted Solotaroff | with Shannon Ravenel | *With an Introduction by Ted Solotaroff* | *Including the Yearbook of the* | *American Short Story* | [publisher's device, boy on a dolphin] 1978 | Houghton Mifflin Company Boston

CONTRIBUTION: "Decades" [short story], [316]-328. Reprints C232. Uncollected.

B26 BIBLE STORIES 1978

BIBLE STORIES | WILLIAM ANTHONY | Texts & Drawings by William Anthony | Introduction by Gilbert Sorrentino | THE JARGON SOCIETY, HIGHLANDS, NORTH CAROLINA, 1978.

PUBLICATION: Issued as Jargon 85.

CONTRIBUTION: "A Note on William Anthony" [prose], 7-9. First appearance. Collected in *SS*, 260-62.

B27 IN THE WAKE OF THE WAKE 1978

In the Wake | of the **Wake** | Edited by | David Hayman and Elliott Anderson | *The University of Wisconsin Press*

PUBLICATION: Copyright 1977; published 1978. The contents of this book are identical to *TriQuarterly* 38 (Winter 1977).

CONTRIBUTION: "O'Mara of no fixed abode" [fiction], 179-190. Previously appeared as C236 and was later reprinted under the heading "O'Mara" in *MS*, 66-75.

B28 THE LITTLE MAGAZINE IN AMERICA 1978

[10.9 cm. rule] | THE LITTLE MAGAZINE | IN AMERICA: | A MODERN

| DOCUMENTARY HISTORY | [10.9 cm. rule] | edited by Elliott Anderson and Mary Kinzie | [publisher's device, rounded rectangle enclosing the figure of a man pushing a hand cart] | PUSHCART

PUBLICATION: Copyright 1978. The contents of this book are identical to *Tri-Quarterly* 43 (Fall 1978); the book and the journal issues were published simultaneously.

CONTRIBUTION: "*Neon, Kulchur,* Etc." [critical article], 298-316. Simultaneously appeared as C241. Uncollected.

B29 THE POETRY ANTHOLOGY 1978

THE | *POETRY* | ANTHOLOGY | 1912-1977 | [6.4 cm. rule] | Sixty-five years of America's Most | Distinguished Verse Magazine | [magazine's logo, a drawing of Pegasus] | EDITED BY | Daryl Hine & Joseph Parisi | HOUGHTON MIFFLIN COMPANY | BOSTON 1978

CONTRIBUTION: "Handbook of Versification" [poem], 425. Reprints C147.

B30 YARDBIRD LIVES! 1978

Yardbird | Lives! | EDITED BY | ISHMAEL REED and AL YOUNG | GROVE PRESS, INC./NEW YORK

PUBLICATION: Copyright 1978.

CONTRIBUTION: [Excerpt from *SW,* describing Charles Parker's music], [7]. Reprints parts of the chapter "1945: Koko" from *SW,* [3].

B31 POEMS FROM A FORGOTTEN BOOK 1979

POEMS FROM | A FORGOTTEN | BOOK | Edited by | [6.5 cm. rule] | Charles Shahoud Hanna | [Arabic inscription] | DAMASCUS ROAD PRESS | Wesconville, Pennsylvania

PUBLICATION: Issued as the eighth volume of the Damascus Road series of books of modern writing. Copyright 1979. Second printing 1981.

CONTRIBUTION: "The Memory" [poem], 44. Reprinted from *BW,* [11].

B32 MANY WINDOWS 1982

Many | Windows | [9.2 cm. rule] | 22 Stories from *American Review* | [9.2 cm. rule] | *Edited by Ted Solotaroff* | [publisher's device, a torch flame] | HARPER COLOPHON BOOKS Harper & Row, Publishers | New York, Cambridge, Philadelphia, San Francisco | London, Mexico City, Saõ [sic] Paulo, Sidney [sic]

PUBLICATION: Copyright 1982.

CONTRIBUTION: "The Moon in Its Flight" [short story], 34-43. Reprints C172. Uncollected.

B33 CONTEMPORARY AMERICAN FICTION 1983

Contemporary | American | Fiction | Edited and introduced | by Douglas Messerli | Sun & Moon Press | Washington, D.C. | 1983

CONTRIBUTION: "The Gala Cocktail Party" [fiction], 162-68. Reprinted in B40 and *BP*, 113-17.

B34 IN PRAISE OF WHAT PERSISTS 1983

In Praise of | What Persists | [11.5 cm. double rule] | Stephen Berg, Editor | [publisher's device, torch emblem enclosed in rectangle, above the date, 1817] | HARPER & ROW, PUBLISHERS, New York | Cambridge, Philadelphia, San Francisco, | London, Mexico City, São Paulo, Sydney

PUBLICATION: Copyright 1983.

CONTRIBUTION: "Genetic Coding" [prose essay], 252-55. Essay is prefaced by brief, untitled autobiographical statement. Collected in *SS*, 263-66.

B35 WILLIAM CARLOS WILLIAMS: MAN AND POET 1983

[Double spread title page] WILLIAM CARLOS WILLIAMS Man and Poet | Edited | with an introduction by | Carroll F. Terrell | [in left bottom corner] [publisher's device, rectangular logo with lyre] NATIONAL | POETRY | FOUNDATION | UNIVERSITY OF MAINE AT ORONO

PUBLICATION: Copyright 1983.

CONTRIBUTION: "Polish Mothers and 'The Knife of the Times' " [critical essay], [391]-395. Collected in *SS*, 44-48.

B36 WRITER'S CHOICE 1983

[within rounded rectangular border] WRITER'S CHOICE A LIBRARY | OF REDISCOVERIES | with an Introduction by Doris Grumbach | *Linda Sternberg Katz* | *Bill Katz* | [publisher's device: capital letter, "R," on open book] | Reston Publishing Company, Inc. | *A Prentice-Hall Company* | Reston, Virginia

PUBLICATION: Copyright 1983 by Reston Publishing Company.

CONTRIBUTIONS: Brief critical comments interpolated in entries describing *Cadenza*, by Ralph Cusack [40w], *Teitlebaum's Window*, by Wallace Markfield [60w], *The Flanders Road*, by Claude Simon [30w], *The March of Literature*, by Ford Maddox Ford [35w], and *The Maximus Poems*, by Charles Olson [25w], 29, 77, 111, 154, 165. First appearances. All uncollected.

B37 BLAST 3 1984

[within 26 x 19 cm. brilliant yellow (83) rectangle] [in approx. strong red (12)] BLAST 3 | [7.5 cm. thick, brilliant yellow (83) rule] | EDITED BY SEAMUS COONEY | [7.5 cm. thick, brilliant yellow (83) rule] | CO-EDITED BY | BRADFORD MORROW, BERNARD LAFOURCADE | AND HUGH KENNER | BLACK SPARROW PRESS • 1984

CONTRIBUTION: "John Gardner: Rhinestone in the Rough" [critical article], 340-[344]. Collected, with minor revisions and without the concluding footnote in *SS*, 213-18.

B38 CADENZA 1984

CADENZA | BY | RALPH CUSACK | [3.5 cm. rule] | AN AFTERWORD | BY | GILBERT SORRENTINO | [3.5 cm. rule] | THE DALKEY ARCHIVE PRESS

PUBLICATION: Issued in November 1984.

CONTRIBUTION: "An Afterword," 225-27. First appearance. Uncollected.

B39 INWARD JOURNEY: ROSS MACDONALD 1984

INWARD JOURNEY | Ross Macdonald | EDITED BY | Ralph B. Sipper | 1984 | Cordelia Editions : Santa Barbara

PUBLICATION: *Inward Journey* was reprinted, with the identical pagination. New York: Mysterious Press, 1987.

CONTRIBUTION: "Ross Macdonald: Some Remarks on the Limitation of Form" [critical essay], 148-53. First appearance; collected in *SS*, 221-26.

B40 THE PUSHCART PRIZE, IX 1984

[Double spread title page] [three decorative devices] THE PUSHCART PRIZE, IX: BEST OF THE SMALL PRESSES | . . . WITH AN INDEX TO THE FIRST NINE VOLUMES | *An annual small press reader* | EDITED BY BILL HENDERSON | with The Pushcart Prize editors | [on left, publisher's device, a man with a pushcart] Introduction by Jayne Anne Phillips | published by THE PUSHCART PRESS | 1984-85 Edition | BEST OF THE SMALL PRESSES THE PUSHCART PRIZE, IX: [three decorative devices]

PUBLICATION: Copyright 1984.

CONTRIBUTION: "The Gala Cocktail Party" [fiction], [246]-251. Reprints B33.

B41 POETI ITALO-AMERICANI 1985

FERDINANDO ALFONSI | della Fordham University di New York | POETI ITALO-AMERICANI | ITALO-AMERICAN POETS | Antologia bilingue - A Bilingual Anthology | ANTONIO CARELLO EDITORE | CATANZARO (ITALIA)

PUBLICATION: Copyright 1985.

CONTRIBUTION: "Pinochle" [poem], 376, accompanied by a translation into Italian under the title "Pinnacolo," 377. Reprinted from *CS*, 31.

B42 EPIPHANIES 1987

EPIPHANIES | THE Prose Poem Now | [10.2 cm. rule] | George Myers Jr., editor | [5.3 cm. rule] | [21-line quotation] | —Ralph Waldo Emerson, | Journals & Miscellaneous | Notebooks, 1836-1842 | [5.3 cm. rule]

PUBLICATION: Copyright 1987; published by Cumberland, Westerville, OH.

CONTRIBUTION: "Selection from *Splendide-Hôtel* ["J" section], 64-65. Reprinted from *S-H*, 27-28.

B43 ROBERT CREELEY'S LIFE AND WORK 1987

Robert Creeley's Life and Work: *A Sense of Increment* | Edited by John Wilson | *Ann Arbor* | THE UNIVERSITY OF MICHIGAN PRESS

PUBLICATION: Copyright 1987.

CONTRIBUTION: "From 'Black Mountaineering' " [critical review], 67-69. Reprints Creeley sections from C153.

B44 THE MEANING OF LIFE 1988

The Meaning of | **Life** | Collected by Hugh S. Moorhead | Chicago Review Press

PUBLICATION: Copyright 1988.

CONTRIBUTION: [one-line, "La vida es sueño," untitled statement in answer to the question, "What is the meaning or purpose of life?"], 182-83. Page 183 reproduces GS's manuscript response, inscribed in the editor's copy of *AS*. First appearance. Uncollected.

B45 COLLECTED FICTION 1990

Louis Zukofsky | *Collected Fiction* | with a Foreword by Gilbert Sorrentino | and an Afterword by Paul Zukofsky | Dalkey Archive Press

PUBLICATION: Issued in May 1990.

CONTRIBUTION: "Foreword," vii-ix. First appearance. Uncollected.

B46 INTO THE TEMPLE OF BASEBALL 1990

[figure of a baseball player] | [within a rectangle] **INTO** | the | [at an upward angle] **TEMPLE** | *of* | BASEBALL | [within 12.8 cm. rules] EDITED by RICHARD

GROSSINGER & KEVIN KERRANE | **CELESTIALARTS** [sic] | Berkeley, California

PUBLICATION: Copyright 1990; published by Celestial Arts.

CONTRIBUTION: "Baseball" [500w prose essay on baseball], 132-33. Reprinted from B23.

C. CONTRIBUTIONS TO PERIODICALS

1956

C1 "Last Rites." [short story] *Landscapes* 2.1 (Spring 1956): 6-8. Uncollected. NOTE: GS's first publication provoked considerable controversy on the Brooklyn College campus. A review in the 11 May 1956 number of the student newspaper, the *Kingsman*, described it as "a smooth, rather perceptive story . . . ruined by its painfully self-conscious modernity, its straining to be right in fashion with the stream of consciousness technique." Under the title "Collegians Insult Religion," the lead editorial of the 23 June 1956 *Tablet*, a local Catholic newspaper, attacked it as "a travesty on the Catholic priesthood, shockingly insulting to all Catholics." This was followed by a letter from a Reverend Healy, printed in the 30 June 1956 *Tablet*, charging that the publication of GS's story was "indefensible." These objections were answered by the magazine's editors and staff in a 10-leaf mimeographed pamphlet, *The Position of Landscapes on the Present Controversy and a Statement of Policy in Matters Editorial.*

C2 "A Note on Neon." [prose] *Neon* 1 ([1956]): [1]. Uncollected.

C3 "A Pastoral/ Part of a Novel in Progress." [fiction] *Neon* 1 ([1956]): 6-13. Uncollected.

C4 "An Editorial." [prose] *Neon* 2 (1956): [1]. Uncollected.

C5 "Two Vignettes: Holidays." [fiction] *Neon* 2 (1956): 11-13. Uncollected.
CONTENTS: "Noel Noel Noel."
"Should Auld Acquaintance Be Forgot—?"

C6 "Nor Heed My Craft or Art." [poem] *Neon* 2 (1956): 14. Uncollected.

1957

C7 "An American Comedy." [short story] *Emergent* 1.2 (Spring 1957): 5-7. Uncollected.

C8 "A Translation from the Old Spanish Romances." [poems] *Shenandoah* 8.2 (Spring 1957): [39]; and 8.3 (Summer 1957): [61]. Uncollected. NOTE: GS's translations into English of "Romance del Prisionero" and "Romance de Julianesa" precede the texts in Spanish.

C9 "Lyric | From the Spanish of Gil Vicente." [poem] *Spectrum* 1.2 (Spring-Summer 1957): 43. Uncollected.

C10 "Roundsong | From the Spanish of Diego Hurtado y Mendoza." [poem]

Spectrum 1.2 (Spring-Summer 1957): [42]. Uncollected.

C11 "And I Also Think I Shall Never See." [poem] *Existaria* 6 (July-August 1957): 14. Uncollected.

1958

C12 "Hymn among Ruins." [poem, translated from the Spanish of Octavio Paz, "Donde espumoso el mar siciliano . . . Góngora"] *Colorado Review* 2 (Spring 1958): 17-18. Uncollected.

C13 "The Rose." [poem] *Supplement to Now* (August 1958): [8]. Collected: *DSU,* [35].
11 Pile] Pile,

C14 "10 P.M." [poem] *Supplement to Now* (August 1958): [6]. Uncollected.

C15 Untitled editorial statement. *Supplement to Now* (August 1958): [1]. Uncollected.

C16 "Little Oranges." [poem, translated from the Spanish of Lope de Vega] *Nation* 187 (6 December 1958): 435. Uncollected.

C17 "The Darkness Surrounds Us." [poem] *Yugen* 3 (1958): 13-14. Collected: *DSU,* [45-46].

1959

C18 "Brown Mountain." [poem, translated from the Spanish of Rafael Alberti] *Nation* 188.21 (23 May 1959): 482. Uncollected.

C19 "The Lover." [poem] *Neon* 4 (1959): [25]. Uncollected.

C20 "A Fixture." [poem] *Yugen* 4 (1959): 27. Collected: *DSU,* [9]; *SP,* 13.

C21 "A Note on Gregory Corso's *To Black Mountain*" [letter to the editor] *Yugen* 5 (1959): 38. Uncollected.
NOTE: Responds to Gregory Corso's poetic advertisement, "For Black Mountain." *Yugen* 4 (1959): 28.

C22 " 'Sunny Down South.' " [poem] *Neon* 4 (1959): [26]. Collected: *DSU,* [23].

1960

C23 "Memorial Day (For Elsene)." [poem] *White Dove Review* 2.4 (1960): [4]. Collected: *DSU,* [16].
Memorial Day (For Elsene)] Memorial Day | for Elsene *DSU*

C24 "Hello Again." [poem] *White Dove Review* 2.5 (Summer 1960): [16]. Collected: *DSU,* [44].

C25 "And Younger Blood." [poem] *Nomad* 8 (Autumn 1960): 20. Uncollected.

C26 "The Cabinet of Dr. Caligari." [poem] *Nomad* 8 (Autumn 1960): 21. Uncollected.

C27 "Defense of Rhyme." [poem] *Hearse* 8 [1960]: 7. Uncollected.

C28 Review of *Watermelons,* by Ron Loewinsohn. *Kulchur* 2 (1960): 91-92. Collected: *SS,* 139-40.

C29 "The Totem." [poem] *Neon Obit* (1960): [8]. Collected: *DSU,* [27]; *SP,* 16.
For the American troops killed in Korea] *omitted SP*

1961

C30 Letter dated 5 April 1961 to "Roi" [i.e., LeRoi Jones] regarding William Burroughs's novel *Naked Lunch. Floating Bear* 11 ([July] 1961): [2-4]. Signed: Gil. Uncollected.

C31 "In the Grave." [poem] *Nation* 193 (30 September 1961): 214. Uncollected.

C32 "ave atque vale." [poem] *Outsider* 1 (Fall 1961): 35. Collected: *BW,* [6]; *SP,* 40.
15 now slowly] now, slowly *BW*+

C33 "Rollins' Return." *Floating Bear* 16 ([December] 1961): [12]. Review of Sonny Rollins in performance, 14 November 1961. Signed: G. Sorrentino. Uncollected.

C34 Review of *Kaddish and Other Poems, 1958-1960,* by Allen Ginsberg. *Kulchur* 3 (1961): 85-87. Signed: G.S. Uncollected.

C35 Review of *Like I Say* and *Memoirs of an Interglacial Age,* by Philip Whalen. *Kulchur* 3 (1961): 79-81. Signed: G.S. Uncollected.

C36 Review of *The Misfits* [film], screenplay by Arthur Miller, directed by John Huston. *Kulchur* 3 (1961): 89-90. Signed: G.S. Uncollected.

C37 "A Note." [preface as guest editor to the issue] *Kulchur* 4 (1961): [2]. Signed: G.S. Uncollected.

C38 Reviews of *L'Avventura* [film], directed by Michelangelo Antonioni, and *Rocco and His Brothers* [film], directed by Luchino Visconti. *Kulchur* 4 (1961): 90-93. Signed: G.S. Uncollected.

C39 Review of *The End of It,* by Mitchell Goodman. *Kulchur* 4 (1961): 96-97. Signed: G.S. Uncollected.

C40 Review of *Life Studies,* by Robert Lowell, and *Heart's Needle,* by W. D. Snodgrass. *Yugen* 7 (1961): 5-7. Uncollected.

C41 "Some Notes Toward a Paper on Prosody." [critical article] *Yugen* 7 (1961): 34-37. Uncollected.

1962

C42 "Measure of Maturity." *Nation* 194.10 (10 March 1962): 220-21. Review of *The Jacob's Ladder,* by Denise Levertov. Collected: *SS,* 141-43.

C43 "The Shadow Knows." [poem] *Nation* 194.12 (24 March 1962): 271. Collected: *BW,* [34].

C44 "Who Goes There?" [poem] *Nation* 194.17 (28 April 1962): 388. Collected: *BW,* [32]; *SP,* 62-63.

C45 "The Jester." *Nation* 194.22 (2 June 1962): 500-501. Review of *Amen Huzza Selah,* by Jonathan Williams. Collected: *SS,* 91-93.

C46 "From 'Shapes of Winter.'" [poem] *Poetry* 100.3 (June 1962): 162-63. Collected: *BW,* [36], [39]; *SP,* 65, 68-69—as sections 1 and 4 of the suite "Shapes of Winter."

C47 "In Quest of Ugendun." [prose poem] *Floating Bear* 22 ([August] 1962): [11]. Signed: Abe Harvard. Uncollected.

C48 "Cards." [poem] *Nomad/New York* 10-11 (Autumn 1962): 16. Collected: *BW,* [17]; *SP,* 37.

C49 "The Checkers Problem." [poem] *Nomad/New York* 10-11 (Autumn 1962): 15. Collected: *BW,* [17-18].

C50 "Paint." [poem] *Nomad/New York* 10-11 (Autumn 1962): 17. Collected:

BW, [16].

C51 "Reflections on *Spring and All.*" [critical article] *Kulchur* 5 (1962): 40-46. Collected: *SS*, 13-19.

C52 "The Savage Eye (or, Fun with Your Camera)." *Kulchur* 5 (1962): 87-88. Review of the film *The Savage Eye*, screenplay by Ben Maddow; directed by Maddow, Sidney Meyers, and Joseph Strick. Uncollected.

C53 Review of *My Friend Tree: Poems*, by Lorine Niedecker. *Kulchur* 7 (Autumn 1962): 86-87. Signed: G.S. Collected: *SS*, 87-88.

C54 Review of *The Shell Game*, [poems] by Joe Early and [collages] by Fielding Dawson. *Kulchur* 7 (Autumn 1962): 85-86. Signed: G.S. Uncollected.

C55 "Statement." [prose] *Nomad/New York* 10-11 (Autumn 1962): 14. Uncollected.
NOTE: Describes GS's principles of poetic composition.

C56 Contribution to "Little Magazines: A Symposium." [prose] *Mainstream* 15.12 (December 1962): 37-52, esp. 42-43. Uncollected.

C57 "Kitsch into 'Art': The New Realism." [critical article] *Kulchur* 8 (Winter 1962): 10-23. Uncollected.

C58 Review of *Burning Conscience: The Case of the Hiroshima Pilot*, by Claude Eatherly and Gunther Anders. *Kulchur* 8 (Winter 1962): 86-87. Signed: G.S. Uncollected.

C59 Review of *The Distances*, by Charles Olson. *Kulchur* 8 (Winter 1962): 91-95. Signed G.S. Collected: *SS*, 144-49.

C60 "Out of Their Butchered Hearts." [poem] *Massachusetts Review* 3.2 (Winter 1962): 347. Collected: *BW*, [14]; *SP*, 54.
9-10 And one can quietly be seated / speak of it in a civilized] And one can quietly be seated, speak / of it in a civilized *BW*$^{+}$

C61 "The Meeting." [poem] *Yugen* 8 (1962): 35-36. Collected: *BW*, [8-10]; *SP*, 41-44.
18 of part III deep",] deep," *BW*$^{+}$
3-7 of part IV were water, there was a smell of water | on them | [stanza break] in your hair, your hands | were quick and nervous | fragile to hold and there was water] were water, there was a smell of water | in your hair, your hands | were quick and nervous | [stanza break] fragile to hold and there was water | on them *BW*$^{+}$

C62 "The Memory." [poem] *Yugen* 8 (1962): 37. Collected: *BW*, [11]; *SP*, 52.

C63 Review of *The Opening of the Field*, by Robert Duncan, and *Billy the Kid*, by Jack Spicer. *Yugen* 8 (1962): 11-15. Partially collected: *SS*, 49-50 [Spicer section only].

1963

C64 "Poetry Chronicle." *Kulchur* 9 (Spring 1963): 69-82. Review of *The Love Bit*, by Joel Oppenheimer, *Four Young Lady Poets* [Carol Bergé, Barbara Moraff, Rochelle Owens, and Diane Wakoski], *Red Cats*, by Anselm Hollo, *The Materials*, by George Oppen, *By the Waters of Manhattan*, by Charles Reznikoff, *Pictures from Brueghel*, by William Carlos Williams, *Mexico & North*, by Clayton Eshleman, *We All Have Something to Say to Each Other*, by David Meltzer, *The Seven Hells of the Jigoku Zoshi*, by Jerome Rothenberg, and *The Heads of the Town up to the Aether*, by Jack Spicer. Partially collected, with minor revisions: *SS*, 50-52 [Spicer section only].
NOTE: Anselm Hollo's "Letter to the Editors and Readers of *Kulchur*," *Kulchur* 10 (Summer 1963): 101-2, and Jerome Rothenberg's "A Letter to the Editors of *Kulchur*," *Kulchur* 11 (Autumn 1963): 103-5, took vigorous exception to this review.

C65 "Silences." [poem] *Poetry* 102.5 (August 1963): 299. Collected: *BW*, [42]; *SP*, 71.

C66 "Two for Franz Kline I: The Gunner II: The Dark Hallway." [poems] *Poetry* 102.5 (August 1963): 300-301. Collected: *BW*, [23-24].

C67 "Remembrances of Bop in New York, 1945-1950." [critical article] *Kulchur* 10 (Summer 1963): 70-82. Uncollected.

C68 Review of *The Lion's Tail and Eyes: Poems Written out of Laziness and Silence*, by James Wright, William Duffy, and Robert Bly. *Kulchur* 10 (Summer 1963): 84-86. Signed: G.S. Uncollected.

C69 "Voices from the Art World (or, Bright Sayings)." [prose] *Floating Bear* 26 ([October] 1963): [8-9]. Signed: Duke Mantee. Uncollected.

C70 Review of *The Collected Later Poems* (Revised Edition), by William Carlos Williams. *Kulchur* 11 (Autumn 1963): 82-83. Signed: G.S. Collected, with minor revisions: *SS*, 19-20.

C71 Review of *In England's Green &*, by Jonathan Williams. *Kulchur* 11 (Autumn 1963): 87-88. Signed: G. S. Collected: *SS*, 93-94.

C72 Review of *To Mix with Time*, by May Swenson. *Kulchur* 11 (Autumn 1963): 86-87. Signed: G. S. Uncollected.

C73 "A Note on the Muslims." [critical article] *Kulchur* 12 (Winter 1963): 19-21. Uncollected.
NOTE: GS's contribution to a forum entitled "Rights: Some Personal Reflections."

C74 Review of *Residence on Earth*, by Pablo Neruda, translated by Clayton Eshleman. *Kulchur* 12 (Winter 1963): 90-92. Signed: G.S. Collected, with minor revisions: *SS*, 154-56.

C75 Review of *The Wake*, by Andrew Hoyem. *Kulchur* 12 (Winter 1963): 88-90. Signed: G.S. Collected: *SS*, 150-53.

C76 "Open Your Mouth and Say." [poem] *Wild Dog* 4 (1963): 21. Collected: *BW*, [19]; *SP*, 51.

1964

C77 "Yorick's Song for the New Year." [poem] *Nation* 198.1 (4 January 1964): 18. Uncollected.

C78 "Some from the Forge, Some Slightly Forced." *Book Week*, 1 March 1964: 6, 19. Review of *Poems 2*, by Alan Dugan, *Collected Poems*, by Elder Olson, *Selected Poems*, by Octavio Paz, translated by Muriel Rukeyser, and *Natural Numbers: New and Selected Poems*, by Kenneth Rexroth. Partially collected: *SS*, 83-84 [Rexroth section only].

C79 "The Rugged Individualist." [poem] *Nation* 198.16 (13 April 1964): 382. Uncollected.

C80 "Thoreau Runs Out of Sterno." [poem] *Nation* 198.6 (13 April 1964): 382.

C81 "The Art of Hubert Selby." [critical article] *Kulchur* 13 (Spring 1964): 27-43. Collected: *SS*, 114-128. Reprinted: *Review of Contemporary Fiction* 1.2 (Summer 1981): 335-46.
NOTE: Parts of this essay were reprinted as a flier distributed to reviewers by the publisher of Selby's *Last Exit to Brooklyn;* the dust jacket blurb for the first edition of *Last Exit to Brooklyn* also derived from GS's essay.

C82 "A Good House." *Poetry* 104.3 (June 1964): 179-81. Review of *The Homestead Called Damascus* and *Natural Numbers: New and Selected Poems*, by Kenneth Rexroth. Collected: *SS*, 81-83. Excerpted: *Contemporary Literary Criticism* 49 (1988): 274.

C83 "The Bullpen Is Up and Throwing." [poem] *Wild Dog* 9 (July 1964): 33-36. Uncollected.

C84 "The Shells Aren't Edible, Anyhow." *Book Week*, 16 August 1964: 5. Review of *Powdered Eggs*, by Charles Simmons. Uncollected.

C85 Review of *The Moderns: An Anthology of New Writing in America,* edited by LeRoi Jones. *Kulchur* 14 (Summer 1964): 81-86. Signed: G.S. Collected, with minor revisions: *SS,* 227-34.

C86 "It's Only a Paper Moon." [poem] *Island* 1 (17 September 1964): 8. Uncollected.

C87 "The Stellar Attraction." [poem] *Island* 1 (17 September 1964): 9. Uncollected.

C88 "Tonight: Free Lecture." [poem] *Island* 1 (17 September 1964): 10. Uncollected.

C89 "Old Soldiers Never Die." [poem] *Poetry* 104.6 (September 1964): 360. Uncollected.

C90 Review of *Because I Was Flesh,* by Edward Dahlberg. *Kulchur* 15 (Autumn 1964): 88-89. Signed: G.S. Collected: *SS,* 96-98.

C91 "No More Coffee, No More Pies." [poem] *Peace News* no. 1487 (25 December 1964): 8. Uncollected.

C92 "*Signal:* A New Magazine." [review] *Floating Bear* 29 (1964): [15-16]. Signed: Sorrentino. Uncollected.

C93 "For the *Floating Bear:* Prose of Our Time." [critical article] *Floating Bear* 30 (1964): [11-13]. Uncollected.

1965

C94 "Firing a Flare for the Avant-Garde." *Book Week,* 3 January 1965: 10. Review of *The Yage Letters,* by William Burroughs and Allen Ginsberg, *The Holy Grail,* by Jack Spicer, *Ace of Pentacles,* by John Wieners, and *After I's,* by Louis Zukofsky. Uncollected.

C95 "A Señorita's Bouquet." [poem] *Cenobio: Revista Bimestrale di Cultura* 14.3 (May-June 1965): 171. Reprinted from *DSU,* with an Italian translation by D. M. Pettinella, also on 171. Signed: G. Sorrentino.
1 her] *omitted*

C96 "The Totem." [poem] *Cenobio: Revista Bimestrale di Cultura* 14.3 (May-June 1965): 171. Reprinted from *DSU,* with an Italian translation by D. M. Pettinella, also on 171. Signed: G. Sorrentino.

C97 "From *The Perfect Fiction.*" *Fuck You/A Magazine of the Arts* no. 5, vol. 9 [sic] (June 1965): 12-14.
CONTENTS:

"People in Hell are clothed." Collected: *PF*, 51; *SP*, 85.
6 In that] In the *PF*+
"A stinking city full of stinking." Collected: *PF*, 52; *SP*, 87.
"The stupid painter paints." Collected: *PF*, 47-48; *SP*, 78-79.

C98 "Two Poems from *The Perfect Fiction*." *Wild Dog*, 17 July 1965: 14-15.
CONTENTS:
"Nothing grimmer than dawn at noon." Collected: *PF*, 18; *SP*, 86.
"(Sonnet with X's)." Collected: *PF*, 37; *SP*, 91.
14, an X,], an X: *PF*+

C99 "World and Self: Instances." *Poetry* 106.4 (July 1965): 306-9. Review of *The World, the Worldless*, by William Bronk, *Some Deaths*, by Walter Lowenfels, and *Centering*, by M. C. Richards. Partially collected: *SS*, 77-78 [Bronk section only].

C100 "Pariahs on Parnassus." *Book Week*, 8 August 1965: 15. Review of *The Moth Poem*, by Robin Blaser, *Hands Up*, by Edward Dorn, *Routines*, by Lawrence Ferlinghetti, and *The Love Poems of Kenneth Patchen*, by Kenneth Patchen. Uncollected.

C101 "He walks on the street, in." [poem] *Magazine* 1 (c. September 1965): [13]. Collected: *PF*, 11; *SP*, 76.

C102 "Where are the rose-colored cities." [poem] *Magazine* 1 (c. September 1965): [12]. Collected: *PF*, 13-14; *SP*, 88-89.

C103 "Sons of King Kong (or, The Apes of God Return)." [critical article] *For Now* 4 (c. 1965): 21-27. Uncollected.
NOTE: Essay discusses camp in music and art.

1966

C104 "First Novelists—Spring 1966." [prose] *Library Journal* 91.3 (1 February 1966): 722-37, esp. 734-35. Uncollected.
NOTE: In this 350w untitled statement GS describes *SC*.

C105 "From *The Perfect Fiction*." [poems] *Poetry* 107.6 (March 1966): 369-72.
CONTENTS:
"What intense colloquy with the self." Collected: *PF*, 34-35; *SP*, 83-84.
"On the margins of various papers." Collected: *PF*, 32-33.
"The weight of the rock." Collected: *PF*, 53.

C106 "The New Note." *Book Week*, 1 May 1966: 19. Review of *Lunch Poems*, by Frank O'Hara, *The Beautiful Days*, by A.B. Spellman, and *Language*, by Jack Spicer. Partially collected: *SS*, 52-53 [Spicer section only].

C107 "The Language Barrier." [poem] *Poetry Pilot,* May 1966: 9. Reprinted from *BW,* [26]; here the poem forms the sixth unit (after poems by Paul Blackburn, Cid Corman, Robert Creeley, Robert Duncan, and Denise Levertov) in "A May Suite of an Older Sympathy," selected by Louis Zukofsky.

C108 " 'Words Are . . . Not Mocked.' " *Poetry* 108.2 (May 1966): 134-35. Review of *Language,* by Jack Spicer. Collected: *SS,* 53-54.

C109 "Jack Spicer: Language as Image." [critical article] *For Now* 5 (c. 1966): 28-36. Collected: *SS,* 55-62. Reprinted, as "Gilbert Sorrentino on Jack Spicer": *Invisible City* 23-25 (March 1979): [9-10].
NOTE: Michael Davidson, in his "Incarnations of Jack Spicer: *Heads of the Town up in the Aether,*" *Boundary 2* 6.1 (Fall 1977): 103-34, deems this is "the best single essay on Spicer's work."

C110 "two poems from *The Perfect Fiction.*" *Promethean* 14.2 (1966-1967): 1-2.
CONTENTS:
"Mother, this is a ball of color." Collected: *PF,* 73; *SP,* 104.
3 "life?"] "life"? *PF*+
4 Reach for it] Reach for it. *PF*+
6-7 *separated by asterisks*] *separated by rule PF*+
"Come from the whirling zodiac." Collected: *PF,* 30; *SP,* 96.

1967

C111 "A Glance at West's West." [critical article] *Guerrilla* 1.2 (June 1967): 9. Collected, with major revisions: *SS,* 175-77.
NOTE: Discusses Nathanael West and Ronald Reagan.

C112 "Football Poem I." *Poetry* 110.3 (June 1967): 174. Uncollected.

C113 "Land of Cotton." [poem] *Poetry* 110.3 (June 1967): 175. Collected: *CS,* 13; *SP,* 115.

C114 "Long Gone Blues." [poem] *Poetry* 110.3 (June 1967): 176. Collected: *CS,* 16; *SP,* 116.

C115 "Some Bright Paintings." [poem] *Poetry* 110.3 (June 1967): 177. Uncollected.

C116 "All the Colors in the World." [poem] *Caterpillar* 1 (October 1967): 35. Collected: *CS,* 17.
10 neck is stiff and hurts me.] neck is stiff and hurts me. Send check to E.
13 raining,] raining.

C117 "The clear objects." [poem] *Caterpillar* 1 (October 1967): 38. Collected: *CS*, 25; *SP*, 118.
untitled] Poem *CS*+

C118 "In the paper moon." [poem] *Caterpillar* 1 (October 1967): 37. Collected, under the title "P.S.": *CS*, 20.

C119 "The Insane Waiters." [poem] *Caterpillar* 1 (October 1967): 39. Collected: *CS*, 22; *SP*, 147.
for Mort] *omitted SP*
7 ranging] raging *CS*+
11-12] *stanza break omitted SP*

C120 "Perceive." [poem] *Caterpillar* 1 (October 1967): 36. Collected: *CS*, 19; *SP*, 117.

C121 "The Morning Roundup." [poem] *Ant's Forefoot* 1 (Fall 1967): [26]. Collected: *CS*, 11; *SP*, 112.

C122 "Toward the End of Winter." [poem] *Ant's Forefoot* 1 (Fall 1967): [26]. Collected: *CS*, 27-28; *SP*, 119-20.

C123 "Veterans of Foreign Wars." [poem] *Ant's Forefoot* 1 (Fall 1967): [26]. Collected: *CS*, 21; *SP*, 148.

1968

C124 "Brooklyn-Newark Blue Poem." *Poetry* 111.6 (March 1968): 367-73. Uncollected.

C125 "Ten Pamphlets." *Poetry* 112.1 (April 1968): 56-61. Review of *State of the Union*, by Aimé Césaire, *Lachrymae Mateo*, by Clayton Eshleman, *Sing-Song*, by Paul Blackburn, *Crystals*, by Frank Samperi, *Definitions*, by David Antin, *The Galilee Hitch-Hiker*, by Richard Brautigan, *Voyages*, by Robin Magowan, *Living with Chris*, by Ted Berrigan, *Identikit*, by Jim Brodey, and *Aloud*, by Bill Dodd. Collected: *SS*, 235-41. Excerpted [Brautigan section only]: *Contemporary Literary Criticism* 12 (1980): 57.

C126 "Coast of Texas." [suite of sixteen poems] *Caterpillar* 3-4 (April-July 1968): 102-17. Reprinted: B14. Collected: *CS*, 36-45; *SP*, 122-35.

C127 "Old Tale." [poem] *Noose* 4 (4 May 1968): [3]. Collected: *CS*, 46; *SP*, 136.
8-9 We speak here of a wry, a fragmentary / syllogism] *omitted CS*+

C128 "See America First." [poem] *Noose* 4 (4 May 1968): [3]. Collected: *CS*, 54; *SP*, 149.

C129 "Marianne Moore: AN OCTOPUS/ of ice." *Park* 1 [also cited as *Wivenhoe Park Review* 3] (August 1968): 67-78. Review of *The Complete Poems of Marianne Moore.* Collected: *SS,* 157-66.

C130 "Air for Owen & Branca." [poem] *Haravec: A Bilingual Magazine from Peru* 5 (September 1968): 11-12. Uncollected.

C131 "Now the Leaves." [poem] *Haravec: A Bilingual Magazine from Peru* 5 (September 1968): 11. Uncollected.

C132 "Country and Western." [poem] *Chelsea* 24-25 (October 1968): 135-36. Collected: *CS,* 32-33.
29 success,] success.
30 that] That
31 escarole,] escarole.
32 her] Her

C133 Review of *Aram Saroyan,* by Aram Saroyan. *Grosseteste Review* 1.2 (Autumn 1968): 46-50. Reprinted, under the title, " 'History Is Bunk' ": *Promethean* 16.2 (1968-1969): 45-50. Uncollected.

C134 "The Poet Tires of Those Who Disparage His City." [poem] *Promethean* 15.1 (1967-1968): 1. Collected: *CS,* 12; *SP,* 114.

C135 "Rose Room." [poem] *Promethean* 15.1 (1967-1968): 2-3. Collected: *CS,* 15; *SP,* 113.

C136 "From *The Perfect Fiction.*" [poem] *Intransit: The Andy Warhol-Gerard Malanga Monster Issue* (1968): 213.
CONTENTS:
"A particular density: in the center, rises." Collected: *PF,* 17; *SP,* 93.
"Clairvoyant perception of a distant balloon." Collected: *PF,* 62.
"But the light is imagined." Collected: *PF,* 72.

1969

C137 "Poem" ["Living friends live"]. *Poetry* 113.6 (March 1969): 409. Collected: *CS,* 67; *SP,* 140.

C138 "Another Case o' Wheaties." [poem] *Park* 4-5 (Summer 1969): 70. Collected: *CS,* 52.

C139 "Borough of Richmond." [poem] *Park* 4-5 (Summer 1969): 69. Collected: *CS,* 59.
2 window,] window.

C140 "A Poem to Read in August." [poem] *Park* 4-5 (Summer 1969): 69.

Collected: *CS*, 60; *SP*, 141.
11-13 willows gladioli narcissi | hoenysuckle forsythia crocus | peach plum and cherry] willows, gladioli, narcissi, | honeysuckle, forsythia, crocus, | peach, plum, and cherry *CS*+

C141 "Prince Rupert's Drop." [poem] *Park* 4-5 (Summer 1969): 70. Collected: *CS*, 64; *SP*, 143.

C142 "Research, Again." [poem] *Park* 4-5 (Summer 1969): 67. Collected: *CS*, 48; *SP*, 138.
3 A poetic] (A poetic *CS*+

C143 "Thirty-five / is gone." [poem] *Adventures in Poetry* 4 (Summer 1969): [3]. Uncollected.

C144 "Watteau. The Lady's Slipper." [poem] *Park* 4-5 (Summer 1969): 68. Collected: *CS*, 56.

C145 "Yet Another Effort, Frenchmen." [poem] *Park* 4-5 (Summer 1969): 71. Collected: *CS*, 58.
17 Faces] faces

C146 "Seven Sections from 'Steelwork.'" [fiction] *Grosseteste Review* 2.2 (Autumn 1969): 10-17.
CONTENTS:
"1936 | Big Kid," 10-11. Collected: *SW*, 35-37.
"1937 | Beer," 11. Collected: *SW*, 55-56.
"1938 | Little Mickey," 12. Collected: *SW*, 37-38.
"1938 | The Magnificent Music Machine," 13. Collected: *SW*, 56-57.
"1939 | The Movies," 13-15. Collected: *SW*, 17-19.
"1941 | Ghost Ships," 15. Collected: *SW*, 85-86.
"1943 | Dancing in the Dark," 16-17. Collected: *SW*, 86-88.

C147 "Handbook of Versification." [poem] *Poetry* 115.3 (December 1969): 161. Collected: *CS*, 35; *SP*, 109. Reprinted: B29.

C148 "Address to the National Council on the Arts." [poem] *Promethean* 16.1 (1968-1969): 16-17. Collected: *CS*, 65-66; *SP*, 110-11.
30-31 *no stanza break*] *stanza break CS*+

C149 "Give Them Blood." [poem] *Promethean* 16.1 (1968-1969): 19. Collected: *CS*, 55; *SP*, 144.
2 drink] drunk *CS*+

C150 "The New York Times." [poem] *Promethean* 16.1 (1968-1969): 21. Collected: *CS*, 51; *SP*, 142.
The New York Times] The New York Times: A Poem for Ross Feld *CS*+

C151 "Pail." [poem] *Promethean* 16.1 (1968-1969): 20. Collected: *CS*, 62; *SP*, 139.

C152 "They Die Over and Over. In the Movies." [poem] *Promethean* 16.1 (1968-1969): 18. Collected: *CS*, 50; *SP*, 145.

1970

C153 "Black Mountaineering." *Poetry* 116.2 (May 1970): 110-20. Review of *The Black Mountain Review 1-8*, *Olson/Melville: A Study in Affinity*, by Ann Charters, *Numbers*, by Robert Creeley and Robert Indiana, *The First Decade: Selected Poems 1940-1950*, *Derivations: Selected Poems 1950-1956* and *Roots and Branches*, by Robert Duncan, and *Causal Mythology* and *Maximus Poems IV, V, VI*, by Charles Olson. Collected: *SS*, 242-51. Excerpted [Creeley, Duncan, and Olson sections only]: *Contemporary Literary Criticism* 2 (1974): 106, 122-23, 327. Excerpted [Creeley section only]: B43.

C154 "Shooting Blanks." *Nation* 211.17 (23 November 1970): [536]-537. Review of *The Dick*, by Bruce Jay Friedman. Uncollected.

C155 Untitled memoir of Edward Dahlberg. *TriQuarterly* 19 (Fall 1970): 90-91. Collected under the title, "A Memoir": *SS*, 98-99.
NOTE: The entire issue of *TriQuarterly* 19 (Fall 1970) was reprinted as *Edward Dahlberg: A Tribute*. See B12.

C156 " 'Art Is a Country by Itself.' " *Nation* 211 (14 December 1970): 635-36. Review of *A Voyage to Pagany*, by William Carlos Williams. Collected: *SS*, 20-22.

C157 "Billy McCoy." [poem] *Grosseteste Review* 3.3 (Winter 1970): 52. Collected: *WS*, 44; *SP*, 178.

C158 "Let's Call This." [poem] *Grosseteste Review* 3.3 (Winter 1970): 53. Collected: *WS*, 31; *SP*, 172.
4 Personally I can go back to the thirties] *line break introduced* Personally | I can go back to the thirties. *WS*+

C159 "New Programs." [poem] *Grosseteste Review* 3.3 (Winter 1970): 51. Collected: *WS*, 23.
13-15 I am coming through | on Channel 13, the educational | network.] *omitted*

C160 "Beautiful Soup." [poem] *Friendly Local Press* 1.6 (c. 1970): 4. Collected: *WS*, 9; *SP*, 165.
13-15 It is at least half true | that no adult | is beautiful] *omitted* *WS*+

C161 "Anatomy." [poem] *Friendly Local Press* 1.7 (c. 1970): 4. Collected: *CS*, 61; *SP*, 150.

C162 "1947 Blue Buick Convertible." [poem] *Friendly Local Press* 1.7 (c. 1970): 19. Collected: *CS*, 29.

C163 "A Poem for My Wife." [poem] *Friendly Local Press* 1.7 (c. 1970): 18. Collected: *CS*, 49; *SP*, 136.

C164 "Rum and Coca-Cola." [poem] *Friendly Local Press* 1.7 (c. 1970): 20. Collected: *CS*, 63.

1971

C165 "No Radical Chic in Brooklyn." [prose] *New York Times*, 16 January 1971: 29. Uncollected.
NOTE: An account of the working-class neighborhood in Brooklyn where GS grew up.

C166 "Captain Marvell." [poem] *Poetry Review* 62.3 (Autumn 1971): 257. Collected: *WS*, 34; *SP*, 163.

C167 "Lost in the Stars." [poem] *Poetry Review* 62.3 (Autumn 1971): [254]. Collected: *WS*, 33; *SP*, 164.

C168 "Miniature Gifts." [poem] *Poetry Review* 62.3 (Autumn 1971): 255. Collected: *WS*, 32.

C169 "They R in Season." [poem] *Poetry Review* 62.3 (Autumn 1971): [256]. Collected: *WS*, 42.
19-21 Last seen at a discussion | on the vaginal imagery | in the verse of a Great Brazilian] *omitted*

C170 "Fiction Roundups." *Modern Occasions* 1.4 (Fall 1971): 618-22. Review of *Flats*, by Rudolph Wurlitzer, *The Quest for Christa T.*, by Christa Wolf, and *Lame Duck*, by E. M. Beekman. Uncollected.

C171 "A Put-On?" [letter to the editors] *New York Review of Books*, 2 December 1971: 36. Uncollected.
NOTE: Discusses Roger Sale's "assault on *The Blood Oranges*" by John Hawkes, which appeared in *New York Review of Books*, 21 October 1971. Sale replies to GS's comments in a letter on the same page.

C172 "The Moon in Its Flight." [short story] *New American Review* 13 (1971): 153-63. Reprinted: B20 and B32. Uncollected.

1972

C172a " 'If one has never heard Bach, then Mantovani's fine.' " [critical article] *Crawdaddy,* 20 February 1972: 46. Uncollected.
NOTE: Discusses the New York Bohemia of the 1950s.

C173 "Newspapermen? Bushers." [fiction] *New York Times,* 31 May 1972: 41.
NOTE: An excerpt from *IQAT,* 142-43.

C174 " 'God Sweeten the Bitter Judgements of Our Lives.' " [critical essay] *Grosseteste Review* 5.1 (Spring 1972): 51-53. Collected: *SS,* 78-80.
NOTE: Discusses William Bronk.

C175 "The Assumption of Black Sambo." [poem] *Unmuzzled Ox* 1.3 (Summer 1972): 18. Collected: *WS,* 43.
8 accoutrement] accouterment

C176 "Cynical." [poem] *Unmuzzled Ox* 1.3 (Summer 1972): 17. Collected: *WS,* 15; *SP,* 160.
8-10 The American Spirit has not | disappeared, but is disguised | raised to the 10th power.] *omitted WS*+
11-14 In any park you may | descry citizens of Mars also | incognito, speaking tin pizza | and white port.] *transposed to become concluding stanza, 11.11-14 in WS*+
16 are defined] may be defined *WS*+
18-21 Movements and armies | spring from this trite figure | ritualized. Let's hear it | for the necessary war!] *omitted WS*+

C177 "Fiction Chronicle." *Modern Occasions* 2.1 (Winter 1972): 156-57. Review of *The Blood Oranges,* by John Hawkes. Collected: *SS,* 178-79. Reprinted: *Review of Contemporary Fiction* 3.3 (Fall 1983): 192-93.

C178 "The Various Isolated: W. C. Williams' Prose." [critical article] *New American Review* 15 (1972): 192-207. Collected: *SS,* 22-34.

1973

C179 "Poet of Absolute Inventions." *Nation* 216.2 (8 January 1973): 54-56. Review of *The Sorrows of Priapus,* by Edward Dahlberg. Collected: *SS,* 99-102.

C180 "Empty, Empty Promises, Promises." [prose] *New York Times,* 7 March 1973: 43. Collected: *SS,* 252-55. Reprinted: B19.
NOTE: One of a series of op-ed essays by different writers published under the title "Capitalism, for Better or Worse"; reader responses to the entire series, including two reactions to GS's piece, appeared 14 April 1971: 33.

C181 "Mosquitoes in New Jersey." [poem] *Mysterious Barricades* 3 (Spring 1973): 7. Collected: *WS*, 37; *SP*, 166.

C182 "Try to Write a Good Poem About Niagara Falls." [poem] *Mysterious Barricades* 3 (Spring 1973): 8. Collected: *WS*, 45.

C183 "Emerald on the Beach." *Parnassus* 1.2 (Spring/Summer 1973): 121-25. Review of *Selected Poems*, by John Wieners. Collected, with minor revisions: *SS*, 168-72. Excerpted: *Contemporary Literary Criticism* 7 (1977): 536-37.

C184 "Catechism." [fiction] *Chicago Review* 25.3 (1973): 19-31. Reprinted: *MS*, as entries in same sequence but different segments of "Lamont's Scrapbook," 19-21, 86-87, 144-46, 217-19, 289-93.

C185 "8 Sections from *Hotel Splendide*" [sic]. [prose] *Grosseteste Review* 6.1-4 (1973): 47-60. Reprinted, with minor changes: *S-H*, as sections B-D, F, H-I, L, and R, 9-14, 19-20, 23-26, 30-31, 42-43.

C186 "Fashion." [poem] *Grosseteste Review* 6.1-4 (1973): 85. Collected: *WS*, 24.

C187 "Gimlet." [poem] *Grosseteste Review* 6.1-4 (1973): 90. Collected: *WS*, 27; *SP*, 170.
5 brain!] brain. *WS*+

C188 "Loony Tune." [poem] *Grosseteste Review* 6.1-4 (1973): 87. Collected: *WS*, 38.

C189 "Paul Blackburn." [poem] *Unmuzzled Ox* 2.1-2 (1973): [22]. Collected: *WS*, 10.

C190 "The S. S. Sahara." [poem] *Grosseteste Review* 6.1-4 (1973): 89. Collected: *WS*, 28.
9 —inexplicable] inexplicable

C191 "A Silk Ascot for the Terrorist." [poem] *Grosseteste Review* 6.1-4 (1973): 86. Collected: *WS*, 25; *SP*, 161.
19-21 All the flags are flourished | or spat upon. Smoking rivers. | Bad music, fake art. Talking to myself.] *omitted* *WS*+

1974

C192 "Paul Blackburn (1926-1971)." [prose memoir] *Sixpack* 7-8 (Spring-Summer 1974): 242-44. Collected: *SS*, 111-13.

C193 "Cautious Circumspection Does Not Win the West." [poem] *Vort* 2.3

[also designated no. 6] (Fall 1974): 33. Collected: *WS*, 48-49; *SP*, 173-74.

C194 "Deluxe Assorted." [poem] *Vort* 2.3 [also designated no. 6] (Fall 1974): 35. Collected: *WS*, 13; *SP*, 176.

C195 "From Antony Lamont's Third Novel, *Rayon Violet.*" [fiction] *Vort* 2.3 [also designated no. 6] (Fall 1974): 36-37. Reprinted, under the title, "From *Rayon Violet;* pp. 109-112," as a part of "Lamont's Journal": *MS*, 331-34.

C196 "Glass Mind." [poem] *Vort* 2.3 [also designated no. 6] (Fall 1974): 34. Collected: *WS*, 30.

C197 "A Hit Album." [poem] *Vort* 2.3 [also designated no. 6] (Fall 1974): 32. Collected: *WS*, 18; *SP*, 180.
18 Oh] O *WS*+

C198 "A Library." *Vort* 2.3 [also designated no. 6] (Fall 1974): 38-40. Reprinted, under the heading, "Books," as part of "Halpin's Journal": *MS*, 31-34.

C199 Untitled statement about Donald Phelps. *Vort* 2.3 [also designated no. 6] (Fall 1974): 157.

C200 "You Are My Heart's Bouquet." [poem] *Vort* 2.3 [also designated no. 6] (Fall 1974): 31. Collected: *WS*, 29; *SP*, 171.

C201 "From *Splendide-Hôtel.*" [prose] *TriQuarterly* 29 (Winter 1974): 173-79. Reprints from *S-H* sections G, J, M, and W, 21-22, 27-28, 32-33, and 55-56.

C202 "Anonymous Sketch of the Writer." [fiction] *Partisan Review* 41.1 (1974): 24-29. Reprinted, under the heading "An Anonymous Sketch," as part of "Lamont's Notebook": *MS*, 259-63.

1975

C203 "Perfect Gifts." [fiction] *Seems* 6-7 [also designated 2.3] (Summer 1975): 94-[101]. Reprinted, with minor changes, as "Halpin's Journal": *MS*, 439-45.

C204 "Névtelen Vázlat az 'Iróról." [fiction, translated into Hungarian] *Nagy Világ* 20.8 (August 1975): 1160-[1164]. Translation by Tandori Dezsö of "An Anonymous Sketch," subsequently reprinted as part of "Lamont's Notebook": *MS*, 259-63.

C205 "The Late Jack Spicer's Work Is a Miraculous Thing." *Village Voice*, 13 October 1975: 83-84. Review of *The Collected Books of Jack Spicer*, ed. Robin Blaser. Collected: *SS*, 62-67.

C206 "The Notebooks of Antony Lamont." [fiction] *TriQuarterly* 34 (Fall 1975): 146-57. Reprinted as the chapter "A Bag of the Blues": *MS*, 278-88.

C207 "America, America." *Partisan Review* 42.3 (1975): 463-67. Review of *William Carlos Williams: The Knack of Survival in America*, by Robert Coles. Collected: *SS*, 34-39. Extensively quoted: Brogunier, Joseph. "An Annotated Bibliography of Works about William Carlos Williams." In *William Carlos Williams: Man and the Poet.* Ed. Carroll F. Terrell. Orono: National Poetry Foundation, University of Maine at Orono, 1983, [453]-585, esp. 480-81.

C208 "*Art Futures* Interview of the Month: Barnett Tete." [fiction] *New Directions in Prose and Poetry* 30 (1975): 12-28. Reprinted, without introductory note: *MS*, 339-53.

C209 "She is the Queenly Pearl." [fiction] *Partisan Review* 42.4 (1975): [535]-549. Reprinted with minor revisions and preceded by two prefatory paragraphs: *MS*, 226-39.

C210 Untitled critical note on David Antin. *Vort* 3.1 (1975): 55. Uncollected.

C211 Contribution to the column "Writers' Choice." *Partisan Review* 42.3 (1975): [475].
NOTE: Brief critical comments on *The Embodiment of Knowledge*, by William Carlos Williams, *Sheeper*, by Irving Rosenthal, and *The Poor Mouth*, by Flann O'Brien. Uncollected.

1976

C212 "What Is an Aardvark?" [prose] *New York Times*, 6 April 1976: 35.
NOTE: List of fifty questions "for aspirants to elected office" designed to test "general, as against specialized knowledge." Uncollected.

C213 "The Poetry of Louis Zukofsky: The Handles Are Missing." [critical article] *Village Voice*, 7 June 1976: 77-78. Collected: *SS*, 68-75. Excerpted: *Contemporary Literary Criticism* 7 (1977): 563.

C214 "Singing, Virtuoso." *Parnassus* 4.2 (Spring-Summer 1976): 57-67. Review of *The Journals*, by Paul Blackburn, ed. Robert Kelly. Collected, with minor factual revision: *SS*, 103-11. Excerpted: *Contemporary Literary Criticism* 9 (1978): 99-100.

C215 "The New York School, continued." *New York Times Book Review*, 19 September 1976: 8. Review of *Hush*, by David St. John, *Toujours L'Amour*, by Ron Padgett, and *Leaping Clear and Other Poems*, by Irving Feldman. Uncollected.

C216 "Verbal Color." *Bookletter* 3.5 (25 October 1976): 8. Review of *On Being Blue: A Philosophical Inquiry*, by William Gass. Collected under the title "Blue Gass": *SS*, 190-92.

C217 "Contemporary Grotesque." *Bookletter* 3.7 (22 November 1976): 12. Review of *The Autumn of the Patriarch*, by Gabriel García Márquez, translated by Gregory Rabassa. Collected under the title "García Márquez's Monster": *SS*, 193-95.

C218 "Being a Poet and Making a Pot." *New York Times Book Review*, 28 November 1976: [37]. Review of *Talking at the Boundaries*, by David Antin. Collected as "David Antin Talking": *SS*, 196-97.

C219 "A Garland of Impresions and Beliefes Culled from a Lifetime, by E.B., A Disappointed Author." [fiction] *Chicago Review* 27.3 (Winter 1975-76): 25-29. Reprinted, with minor changes in spelling: *MS*, 242-46.

C220 "Magic Composer." [poem] *Sun & Moon* 1 (Winter 1976): 4. Uncollected.

C221 "Orange Sonnet." [poem] *Sun & Moon* 1 (Winter 1976): 5. Collected: *WS*, 47; *O*, 51.
Orange Sonnet] Orange Sonnet: Seminar *WS*
Orange Sonnet] Seminar *O*
2 oranges] orange *WS*+

C222 "Never on Sunday." *Partisan Review* 43.1 (1976): [119]-121. Review of *A Month of Sundays*, by John Updike. Collected: *SS*, 187-89. Reprinted: *Critical Essays on John Updike.* Ed. William R. Macnaughton. Boston: G.K. Hall, 1982, 77-79.

C223 "Lost Lives." *Partisan Review* 43.4 (1976): [613]-616. Review of *J R*, by William Gaddis. Collected: *SS*, 180-83. Excerpted: *Contemporary Literary Criticism* 8 (1978): 227-28.

C224 Review of *Beyond the Bedroom Wall*, by Larry Woiwode. *Partisan Review* 43.4 (1976): 616-18.

C225 "Orange Sonnets." [suite of eight poems, numbered 1-8] *New Directions in Prose and Poetry* 32 (1976): 46-50.
CONTENTS:
"1939 World's Fair." Collected: *WS*, 40; *O*, 3; *SP*, 183.
1939 World's Fair] Orange Sonnet: 1939 World's Fair *WS*

"Across this water sits a shore." Collected: *WS*, 58; *O*, 24; *SP*, 188.
untitled] Orange Sonnet *WS*
10 china] China *WS*
"In Memoriam P. B." Collected: *WS*, 35; *O*, 25; *SP*, 192.
In Memoriam P. B.] Orange Sonnet | *In Memoriam P. B.* *WS*
3 by] By *WS*
10 Un sombrero] *Un sombrero* *WS*
"Now. Tell me how much I am to respect." Collected: *WS*, 57; *O*, 48.
untitled] Orange Sonnet *WS*
2 the Prince] The Prince *WS*
15 fellows] fellows. *WS*
"Broadway! Broadway!" Collected: *WS*, 56; *O*, 21; *SP*, 208.
Broadway! Broadway!] Orange Sonnet: Broadway! Broadway! *WS*
5 à la] *à la* *WS*
12-13 *stanza break*] *no stanza break* *O*+
"She was all in black. A statement." Collected: *WS*, 21; *O*, 31; *SP*, 201.
untitled] Orange Sonnet *WS*
10 *crème*] crème *O*+
"She whom no one ever found." Collected: *WS*, 12; *O*, 19; *SP*, 185.
untitled] "Orange Sonnet" *WS*
7 *crème glacée*] crème glacée *O*+
"Canta Naranja." Collected: *WS*, 51; *O*, 26; *SP*, 189.
Canta Naranja] Orange Sonnet: Canta Naranja *WS*

C226 "Tips for Writers." [prose] *WIP* 7 (1976): [1], [32]. Uncollected.

C227 Contribution to the column "Writers' Choice." [prose] *Partisan Review* 43.1 (1976): [145].
NOTE: Brief critical comment on *Langrishe, Go Down* and *Balcony on Europe*, by Aidan Higgins. Uncollected.

1977

C228 "Three Orange Sonnets." [poems] *Text* [1] (Winter 1976-1977): 38-40.
CONTENTS:
"Saying the Beads." Collected: *O*, 5.
14 Rhodonia] Rhodōnia
"Nadie come naranjas." Collected: *O*, 34.
NOTE: In its original periodical appearance, a misprinting in which the poem's first two stanzas were conflated so that 11. 1-8 emerged in a single stanza containing 11. 1, 6-8, was canceled by pasting a corrected version over the erroneous one.
"Homage to Arnaut." Collected: *O*, 29; *SP*, 206.

C229 "Like Sappho." *New York Times Book Review*, 13 February 1977: 27. Review of *Blue Chicory*, by Lorine Niedecker. Collected, with minor factual revision: *SS*, 88-90. Excerpted: *Contemporary Literary Criticism*

42 (1987): 295-96.

C230 "De pré est vénéneux mais jolie en automne." [poem] *Parnassus* 5.2 (Spring-Summer 1977): 62. Collected: *SP*, 243.
(after Apollinaire)] *omitted*

C231 "The Game That Exists Outside of Time." [prose] *New York Times*, 19 July 1977: 35. Uncollected.
NOTE: An essay on baseball.

C232 "Decades." [short story] *Esquire* 88.2 (August 1977): 95-96, 138-40. Reprinted: B25. Uncollected.

C233 "Land of Cotton." [short story] *Harper's* 255 (November 1977); 73-76. Uncollected.

C234 "Five Orange Sonnets." *Canto* 1.3 (Fall 1977): 127-29.
CONTENTS:
"Annie from Miami." Collected: *O*, 45; *SP*, 197.
"Variations 3." Collected: *O*, 41; *SP*, 191.
"Mr. America last seen crossing the road." Collected: *O*, 27; *SP*, 187.
"At twenty love disintegrates." Collected: *O*, 75; *SP*, 200.
"Je connais gens de toutes sortes." Collected: *O*, 56; *SP*, 211.

C235 "Orange Sonnet." ["The white rockers on the porch"] *Columbia, A Magazine of Poetry and Prose* 1 (Fall 1977): 14. Collected: *O*, 57.
"Orange Sonnet"] untitled

C236 "O'Mara of no fixed abode." [fiction] *TriQuarterly* 38 (Winter 1977): 179-90.
NOTE: This entire issue of *TriQuarterly* was later published as *In the Wake of the Wake*. See B27.
Reprinted under the heading " 'O'Mara' ": *MS*, 66-75.

C237 "Ten Orange Sonnets." *New Directions in Prose and Poetry* 35 (1977): 74-79.
CONTENTS:
"One Negative Vote." Collected: *O*, 23.
"Footnote." Collected: *O*, 61.
10 and fill] they fill
"Variations 1." Collected: *O*, 32.
"The Mansion of the Moon." Collected: *O*, 16.
"Variations 2." Collected: *O*, 39; *SP*, 190.
"White moons are blank. Blank moons." Collected: *O*, 30.
"That the mouth speak not daggers." Collected: *O*, 38.
"To Sulpicia." Collected: *O*, 70.
"Lone Star." Collected: *O*, 12.
"The Oranges Returned." Collected: *O*, 55; *SP*, 210.

1978

C238 "Perverse Story." *New York Times Book Review*, 1 January 1978: 6, 29. Review of *Too Much Flesh and Jabez*, by Coleman Dowell. Collected: *SS*, 132-33.

C239 "Baseball Announcers." [prose] *TV Guide* 26.18 (6 May 1978): 44. Uncollected.
NOTE: Discusses the television broadcasting of baseball games.

C240 "Mort Lucks." [critical article] *Arts Magazine* 53.2 (October 1978): 6. Collected: *SS*, 258-59.

C241 "*Neon*, *Kulchur*, Etc." [critical article] *TriQuarterly* 43 (Fall 1978): [298]-316. Uncollected.
NOTE: This entire issue of *TriQuarterly* was also published as *The Little Magazine in America: A Modern Documentary History*. See B28.

C242 "Louis Zukofsky." [critical article] *Paideuma* 7.3 (Winter 1978): 401-2. Collected under the title "A Word on Zukofsky": *SS*, 75-76.

C243 "Crool Time." [poem] *Partisan Review* 45.2 (1978): [275]. Collected: *SP*, 241.

1979

C244 "Chats With the Real McCoy." [fiction] *Atlantic Monthly* 243.3 (March 1979): 123-26. Reprinted, with minor revisions: *MS*, 36-43.

C245 "Miss and Hit." [poem] *Mississippi Review* 22-23 [also cited as 8.1-2] (Winter-Spring 1979): 37. Collected: *SP*, 248.
15 purples] purples.

C246 "Post-Modernism Explained." [poem] *Mississippi Review* 22-23 [also cited as 8.1-2] (Winter-Spring 1979): 36.

C247 "The Iceman, Again." [poem] *Atlantic Review* n.s. 1 (Spring 1979): 66. Collected: *SP*, 242.
10 cliches.] clichés.

C248 "Ou Sont Ilz, Ou, Vierge Souvrain?" [sic] [poem] *Atlantic Review* n.s. 1 (Spring 1979): 67. Collected: *SP*, 250.
title] "Où Sont Ils, Où, Vierge Souvrain?"

C249 "Good Night." [poem] *Fusta* 4.1-2 (Spring-Fall 1979): 175. Collected: *SP*, 249.

C250 "Raw Statistics." [poem] *Fusta* 4.1-2 (Spring-Fall 1979): 174. Uncollected.

C251 "Verlaine's Innocents." [poem] *Fusta* 4.1-2 (Spring-Fall 1979): 176. Collected: *SP*, 244.

C252 "From the Notebooks and Scrapbooks of Antony Lamont, Novelist." [fiction] *Chronicle of Higher Education*, 23 July 1979, "Books & Arts" sec.: R5. Reprints eleven passages selected nonsequentially from *MS;* in the order of their appearance, the passages appear on pages 5, 20 (two passages), 21, 291-92, 21, 86, 86, 144, 149-50, 293.

C253 "Twelve Études for Voice and Kazoo." [poems] *Sun & Moon* 8 (Fall 1979): 81-96.
CONTENTS:
"Huge Man in Tights Pants." Collected: *SP*, 225.
"Some Sap Sings a Poor Pantoum." Collected: *SP*, 226.
"Waltz of the Empty Roadhouse." Collected: *SP*, 227.
"Man in Old Blue Suit at the Plaza." Collected: *SP*, 228.
20 past.] past
"Ultima Despedida del Príncipe Poniatowski de Su Familia." Collected: *SP*, 229-30.
Title Ultima] 'Ultima
"Impromptu Solo on a Balcony." Collected: *SP*, 231-32.
"Jaime Valeroso y Borracho Consults His Journal." Collected: *SP*, 223.
"Woman Irritable Because of Her Menses." Collected: *SP*, 234-35.
Title Because] because
"Girl at Sixteen with Lightning." Collected: *SP*, 236.
15 touched] untouched
"Le Bateau d' Amour Descried on the Briny." Collected: *SP*, 237-38.
"Solitary Man Discovered in a Field of Daisies." Collected: *SP*, 239.
"In Which There is Nothing Up the Sleeve." Collected: *SP*, 240.
Title is] Is

C254 Contribution to "Some Outstanding Fictions 1970-1979." *Sun & Moon* 6-7 (Winter 1979): 192-95, esp. 195. Uncollected.
NOTE: A list of novels recommended by GS.

C255 "A Celebration of Sorts." [poem] *Scranton Literary Review* [unnumbered] (1979): 22. Collected: *SP*, 246.
8 la français] le français

C256 "For Colonel Williams on His Tenth Lustrum." [prose] *Truck* 21 (1979): [110-11]. Collected: *SS*, 94-95.
NOTE: A tribute to Jonathan Williams.

1980

C257 "From the Journal of Immutable Truths." [poem] *Invisible City* 26-27 (August 1980): 3. Collected: *SP*, 257.
4 ideas.] ideas
16 tombstones] tombstone

C258 "Mysteries Sacred and Profane." [poem] *Invisible City* 26-27 (August 1980): 3. Collected: *SP*, 255.
10 the ones] those

C259 "Everything Is a Still-Life." [poem] *South West Review* 9 (November 1980): 4. Collected: *SP*, 253.

C260 Contribution to "A Writers' Forum on Moral Fiction." *Fiction International* 12 (1980): [5]-25, esp. 21. Uncollected.

C261 "Zachodzacy ksiezyc." [short story, translated into Polish] *Literatura na Swiecie* 9 (113) (1980): [250]-261. Translation with critical notes by Jerzy Durczak of "The Moon in Its Flight," C172.

1981

C262 " 'Look, Up in the Sky.' " *Washington Post Book World*, 1 February 1981: 9. Review of *The Further Adventures of Halley's Comet*, by John Calvin Batchelor. Uncollected. Reprinted as "Shooting Down *Halley's Comet*": *New York Daily News*, 20 February 1981: M8.

C263 "The Frenetic Pulse of Puerto Rico." *Washington Post Book World*, 8 February 1981: 3. Review of *Macho Camacho's Beat*, by Luis Rafael Sanchez, translated by Gregory Rabassa. Collected as "La Guaracha": *SS*, 207-9. Excerpted: *Contemporary Literary Criticism* 23 (1983): 383-84.

C264 "Ninety-Nine Ways to Sew on a Button." *Washington Post Book World*, 8 March 1981: 6. Review of *Exercises in Style*, by Raymond Queneau, translated by Barbara Wright. Collected as "Le Style de Queneau": *SS*, 198-200.

C265 Contribution to "What I'm Writing, What I'm Reading." *New York Times Book Review*, 31 May 1981: 3, 44, esp. 44. Uncollected.
NOTE: List of books GS intends to read during the summer.

C266 "The Act of Creation and Its Artifact." [critical article] *Review of Contemporary Fiction* 1.1 (Spring 1981): 28-34. Collected: *SS*, 3-12.

C267 "From Work-in-Progress, *Blue Pastoral*." [fiction] *Review of Contem-*

porary Fiction 1.1 (Spring 1981): 35-47.
CONTENTS:
"In Which Blue Discovers Marys-londe and Is Given Advice." Reprinted as chapter 15: *BP*, 64-68.
"Supper at the Kind Brown Mill: A Country Drama. By Joanne Bungalow." Reprinted as chapter 16, "The Gavottes Read a Country Drama to Lift Their Spirits": *BP*, 69-75.
"Elegy for Jacques-Paul Surreale." Reprinted as chapter 27: *BP*, 123-27.
NOTE: Christopher Cox, discussing this issue of the *Review of Contemporary Fiction* in his column "Going Soft," *Soho Weekly News*, 11-15 August 1981, remarks that this section of *BP* is "strange stuff," seeming "to have been torn from the notebooks of an offspring of Chaucer and Joyce."

C268 "George Oppen: Smallness of Cause." [critical article] *Paideuma* 10.1 (Spring 1981): 23-24. Collected: *SS*, 173-74.

C269 "Reading Over the Writer's Shoulder." *Washington Post Book World*, 7 June 1981: 1-2. Review of *If on a winter's night a traveler*, by Italo Calvino, translated by William Weaver. Collected as "Travels with Calvino": *SS*, 201-3. Excerpted: *Contemporary Literary Criticism* 22 (1982): 94.

C270 "From the Journal of Immutable Truths." [poem] *Cervo Volante* 6 (June 1981): [5]. Reprinted from C257, with an Italian translation, "Dal diario delle verita 'immutabili," by Paul Vangelisti, also on [5].

C271 "Paul Bowles: The Clash of Cultures." *Washington Post Book World*, 2 August 1981: 3, 6. Review of *Midnight Mass*, by Paul Bowles. Collected: *SS*, 204-6.

C272 "Addenda 1981: After *Last Exit to Brooklyn*." [critical article] *Review of Contemporary Fiction* 1.2 (Summer 1981): 346-48. Collected: *SS*, 128-31.

C273 Excerpt from chapter 65, "Space and Time," of *CV*, included in: Collins, Glenn. "Metropolitan Diary." *New York Times*, 4 November 1981: C2.

C274 "In the Modernist Grain." *New York Times Book Review*, 22 November 1981: 1, 34-36. Review of *William Carlos Williams: A New World Naked*, by Paul Mariani. Collected: *SS*, 39-44.
NOTES: Letters in reaction to this review appeared in the *New York Times Book Review*, 27 December 1981: 2, including Michael Milburn's objections to GS's comments on Robert Frost and Randall Jarrell.

This review is extensively quoted by Joseph Brogunier in his "An Annotated Bibliography of Works About William Carlos Williams." In *William Carlos Williams: Man and Poet.* Ed. Carroll F. Terrell. Orono: National Poetry Foundation, Univ. of Maine at Orono, 1983, [453]-585, esp. 275-77.

C275 Letter from GS to Frederick Morgan. In Morgan's "Setting It Straight." *American Scholar* 50 (Autumn 1981): 367-70, esp. 568-69.
NOTE: GS's letter responds to a letter Morgan wrote to the *Partisan Review* objecting to GS's comments in E7 about the culturally conservative editorial policy of the *Hudson Review*.

C276 "The Disappearance of Oilcloth." [poem] *Partisan Review* 48.3 (1981): [461]. Collected: *SP*, 256.
19-20 White. White. White. | A chiming laughter. No bananas today. Tomatoes in love.] White. White. | White. A chiming laughter. No bananas today. | Tomatoes in love.
Reprinted, from *SP*: *Invisible City* 28 (December 1981): [2].

C277 "The Interesting Glass." [poem] *Bad Henry Review* (1981): 17. Collected: *SP*, 264.

C278 "The Open Boat." [poem] *Bad Henry Review* (1981): 16. Collected: *SP*, 265.
17 Any damn fool knows that but what finally do you] Any damn fool knows that you find out | As you find out but what finally do you

C279 "Poetic Coherence." [prose] *O.ARS* 1 (1981): 25. Uncollected.

1982

C280 "Blarney Spalpeen on the True Meaning of St. Patrick's Day." [fiction] *Conjunctions* 1 (Winter 1981-1982): 30-39. Reprinted as chapter 34, " 'Blarney Spalpeen' Gives a Speech on St. Patrick's Day": *BP*, 149-57.

C281 "Doc Dubuque's Idyll, or, Ah, Nature!" [fiction] *Conjunctions* 2 (Spring-Summer 1982): 186-89. Reprinted as chapter 32: *BP*, 143-46.

C282 Review of *Eternal Curse on the Reader of These Pages*, by Manuel Puig. *Washington Post Book World*, 1 August 1982: 1, 2. Collected as "The Ending Is Wanting": *SS*, 210-12. Excerpted: *Contemporary Literary Criticism* 28 (1984): 374-75.
NOTE: Published under the collective title, "South American Fantasy, Obsession and Soap Opera."

C283 "Some Remarks on *Island People*." [critical article] *Review of Contemporary Fiction* 2.3 (Fall 1982): 122-23. Collected: *SS*, 133-35.

C284 "In Which the Desert Sands Become a Colorful Riot." [fiction] *Conjunctions* 3 (1982): 89-96. Reprinted as chapter 58: *BP*, 274-80.

C285 "The Joli Corner." [poem] *William and Mary Review* 20 (1981-1982): 62. Uncollected.

1983

C286 Contribution to "Brooklyn, Borough of Writers." [prose] *New York Times Book Review*, 8 May 1983: 12-13, 31, esp. 31. Uncollected.
NOTE: A statement about Brooklyn's significance to GS.

C287 "Dr. Bone Shows the Lab to the Gavottes; with Learned Commentary." *Chicago Review* 33.3 (Winter 1983): 19-22. Reprinted as chapter 24: *BP*, 108-12.

1984

C288 "Rediscoveries: A Novel as Cold and Brilliant as Ice." [critical article] *Washington Post Book World*, 17 June 1984: 8. Uncollected.
NOTE: Essay on *Poil de Carotte*, by Jules Renard.

C289 "Een open boot." [poem, translated into Dutch] *De Volkskrant*, 2 October 1984. Translation by Peter Nijmeijer of "The Open Boat," *SP*, 265.

C290 "Zinken, zwemmen." [poem translated into Dutch] *De Volkskrant*, 2 October 1984. Translation by Peter Nijmeijer of "Sinking, Swimming," *SP*, 39.

C291 "A Dose of Strong Medicine." *New York Times Book Review*, 21 October 1984: 9. Review of *The Doctor Stories*, by William Carlos Williams. Uncollected. Excerpted: *Contemporary Literary Criticism* 42 (1987): 458.

C292 "Fictional Infinities." [critical article] *Review of Contemporary Fiction* 4.3 (Fall 1984): 145-50. Uncollected.
NOTE: Essay on "infinity in fiction," with particular reference to Joyce's *Finnegans Wake*, Flann O'Brien's *At Swim-Two-Birds* and *The Third Policeman*, and Beckett's *Molloy*.

C293 "El acto de la creación y su artefacto." [critical prose, translated into Spanish] *Syntaxis* 4 (Winter 1984): 31-39. Translation by Pablo Dominguez of C266.

C294 " 'For my day had passed.' " [critical article] *Adrift* 2 (Winter 1983-1984): 19. Collected: *SS*, 219-20.
NOTE: Essay on the novel *Cadenza*, by Ralph Cusack.

C295 "Bigos totalny." [fiction, translated into Polish] *Literatura na Swiecie* 158 (1984): 280-[322]. Translation by Jolanta Kozak of excerpts from *MS*, [i-v], 1-21, 25-27.

C296 "Twelve Poems." *Ninth Decade* 3 (1984): 3-10.
CONTENTS:
"Calafawnya."
"A Recasting of 'Apollinaire' by Walter Lowenfels."
"It Rains in Jersey. Another Lake."
"Picture."
"The Institute Doesn't Answer."
"Boring Tale."
"After Reading the Phrase 'Vital to Remember.'"
"On the Square."
"Interviewer: Really? (Laughter)."
"East St. Louis Tout a L'Heure."
"It."
"Sonnet Sonnet If I Say So."
All uncollected.

1985

C297 "Italo Calvino: The Play of the Imagination." *Washington Post Book World*, 22 September 1985: 5. Review of *Mr. Palomar*, by Italo Calvino, translated by William Weaver. Uncollected.

C298 "The Bathed Came and Out Moon Period All in Silver." [poem] *Brooklyn Review* 2 (1985): 49. Uncollected.

C299 "A Beehive Arranged on Humane Principles." [fiction] *Conjunctions* 7 (1985): 189-96. Reprints A22.

C300 "'The poem supreme, addressed to/emptiness' (Creeley)." [prose tribute to Basil Bunting] *Conjunctions* 8 (1985): 151-52. Uncollected.

1986

C301 "*Stahlwerk*." [fiction, translated into German] *Schreibheft* 27 (April 1986): 107-12. Translation by Bernd Klähn of selected sections of *SW*.
CONTENTS:
"1946 | Ziggy | Der Angriff" (*SW*, 70-71)
"1946 | Monte, der Graf | Die Taufe" (*SW*, 76-78)
"1951 | Monte, der Graf | Der letze Auftritt" (*SW*, 84-85)
"1949 | Pat Glade | Frohe Weihnachten" (*SW*, 97-99)
"1943 | Der schwarze Tom | Tot" (*SW*, 113-14)
"1949 | Das Mißverständnis" (*SW*, 127-29)
"1947 | Pepper | In der Sonne" (*SW*, 133-35)

C302 "Language—Lying and Treacherous." *New York Times Book Review*, 25 May 1986: 23. Review of *Death Sentence, When the Time Comes, The*

Madness of the Day, Vicious Circles, and *The Gaze of Orpheus,* by Maurice Blanchot. Uncollected.

C303 "Fighting a Losing Battle—and Proud of It: A Decade of *CoEvolution Quarterly.*" *California* 11.5 (May 1986): 36-[38]. Review of *News That Stayed News: Ten Years of CoEvolution Quarterly,* ed. Stewart Brand and Art Kleiner. Uncollected.

C304 "Two Mose Bankes." [fiction] *Review of Contemporary Fiction* 6.1 (Spring 1986): 87-98. Reprinted, without opening epigraph: *RT,* 44-57.

C305 "A Chrestomathy for a Personal Investigation of Jack Spicer." *Ironwood* 28 (1986): 196-201. Uncollected.

1987

C306 "*Ungerade Zahl.*" [fiction, translated into German] *Schreibheft* 29 (May 1987): 135-42. Translation of two passages from *ON,* pp. [3]-11 and pp. [59]-62, by Werner Schmitz.

C307 "Further Explorations in Fiction." *Washington Post Book World,* 11 October 1987: 8. Review of *Forty Stories,* by Donald Barthelme. Uncollected.

C308 "Recapitulations: First Series." [poems] *Dirty Bum* 2 (Winter 1987-1988): 30-[32].
CONTENTS:
"Once, when we were younger."
"Fifteen years ago, I, in tie."
"And jacket, you in black dress."
"We took the wrong train."
"And had to run in a . . . Cruel."
"Sun flaming, reddish."
All uncollected.

C309 "Beacon." [prose fiction] *PsychCritique* 2.2 (1987): 185-89. Reprinted: *RT,* 69-75.

C310 "Chayne of dragons." [fiction] *Conjunctions* 10 (1987): 85-90. Reprinted: *RT,* 7-12.

C311 "Snapshot from Copenhagen." [poem] *Sequoia* 31.1 (1987): 76. Uncollected.

1988

C312 Untitled letter to the editor. *New York Times*, 17 January 1988: H 12. Uncollected.
NOTE: Responds to "Clashing Views Reshape Art History," by Grace Glueck, *New York Times*, 20 December 1987.

C313 "Six Recapitulative Sonnets." [poems] *Boulevard: Journal of Contemporary Writing* 3.1 (Spring 1988): 129-32.
CONTENTS:
"Blue Carillons."
"Scent of Candida."
"Black Query."
"Jersey City News."
"Love in Persia."
"The Trip Forgotten."
All uncollected.

C314 "Defying the Controllers." *New York Times Book Review*, 13 November 1988: 12-13. Review of *Literary Outlaw: The Life and Times of William S. Burroughs*, by Ted Morgan. Uncollected.

C315 "Writing and Writers: *Disjecta Membra*." [critical essay] *Review of Contemporary Fiction* 8.3 (Fall 1988): 25-35. Uncollected.

C316 "Lost Songs." *Columbia, A Magazine of Poetry and Prose* 13 (1988): 167-68. Uncollected.
NOTE: This is a list of song titles submitted by GS in response to the editors' request for passages or titles that have been cut from or not included in his published work.

C317 "Scenes from *Bouquet Rag*." [prose fiction] *Conjunctions* 12 (1988): 267-76. Reprinted, with minor revisions: *M*, 79-89.

1989

C318 "from *Misterioso*." [prose fiction] *Stanford Humanities Review* 1.1 (Spring 1989): [98]-109. Reprinted: *M*, 7-20.

C319 "Seven Gaudy Poems." *Talisman: A Journal of Contemporary Poetry and Poetics* 2 (Spring 1989): 11-17.
CONTENTS:
"A wanting, a desire."
"The current cant is 'needs.' "
"What does one need."
"To live."
"Ah, but what does one—?"

"Desire? Submerge the ego."
"In the image of a knight."
All uncollected.
NOTE: GS dedicates the sequence of poems to William Bronk.

C320 "Days." [poem] *Screens and Tasted Parallels* 1 (1989): 162. Uncollected.

C321 "New Attachment." [poem] *Screens and Tasted Parallels* 1 (1989): 162. Uncollected.

C322 "Dark Discovery." [poem] *Screens and Tasted Parallels* 1 (1989): 163. Uncollected.

1990

C323 "Four Orange Crushes." [poems] *VIA: Voices in Italian Americana* 1 (Spring 1990): [133]-135. Uncollected.

C324 "The Sea, Caught in Roses." [fiction] *Zyzzyva* 6.2 (Summer 1990): 75-79. Uncollected.

D. DUST JACKET COPY AND BOOK BLURBS

Unsigned Dust Jacket Copy

D1 Selby, Hubert. *Last Exit to Brooklyn.* New York: Grove, 1964. Five-paragraph description of the novel on inside flaps of dust jacket, concluding with a quotation from C81, from which the entire description is adapted; also, a one-paragraph biographical statement about Selby on the rear of the dust jacket. The Evergreen/Black Cat paperback edition abbreviates GS's original copy.

D2 *New American Story.* Ed. Donald Allen and Robert Creeley, with an introduction by Warren Tallman. New York: Grove Press, 1965. Four-paragraph description of the anthology on inside flaps and rear of dust jacket; also brief biographical statements about Allen, Creeley, and Tallman on rear of dust jacket. The Evergreen/Black Cat paperback edition (1965) abbreviates GS's description and biographical statements on rear cover.

D3 Heckstall-Smith, Anthony. *The Consort: A Romantic Fantasy.* New York: Grove Press, 1965. Three-paragraph description of the novel and two-paragraph biographical statement about Heckstall-Smith on inside flaps of dust jacket. The Zebra paperback edition (1966) abbreviates and revises GS's original description of the book.

D4 Schneck, Stephen. *The Nightclerk: Being His Perfectly True Confession.* New York: Grove Press, 1965. Three-paragraph description of book and three-paragraph statement about the novel's receiving the Formentor Prize on inside flaps of dust jacket. Paperback edition (1966) includes a brief description on rear cover that is different from GS's original description.

D5 Esfandiary, F. M. *Identity Card.* New York: Grove Press, 1966. Four-paragraph description of the novel on inside flaps of dust jacket.

D6 Kerouac, Jack. *Satori in Paris.* New York: Grove Press, 1966. Five-paragraph description of book on inside flaps of dust jacket and one-paragraph biographical statement about Kerouac on back cover of jacket. GS did not write the copy for the Black Cat paperback edition.

D7 Osborne, John. *Plays for England: I. The Blood of the Bambergs, II. Under Plain Cover; The World of Paul Slickey.* New York: Grove Press, 1966. The Evergreen/Black Cat paperback edition (1966) includes GS's one-paragraph description of the book and brief biographical statement about Osborne.

D8 *Heirs to Freud: Essays in Freudian Psychology.* Ed. Hendrik M. Ruitenbeek, Ph.D. New York: Grove Press, 1966.
Three-paragraph description of book and one-paragraph biographical statement about Ruitenbeek on inside flaps of dust jacket.

D9 Vargas Llosa, Mario. *The Time of the Hero.* Translated by Lysander Kemp. New York: Grove Press, 1966.
Four-paragraph description of novel on inside flaps of dust jacket. One-paragraph biographical statement about Vargas Llosa on rear of dust jacket. Editorial revisions were made in GS's text.

D10 *The Book of Grass: An Anthology on Indian Hemp.* Ed. George Andrews and Simon Vinkenoog. New York: Grove Press, 1967.
Four-paragraph description of book on inside flaps of dust jacket. GS did not contribute to the wrapper copy of the Black Cat paperback edition (1968).

D11 Anonymous. *Harriet Marwood, Governess.* New York: Grove Press, 1967.
Five-paragraph description of book and one-paragraph statement about its putative authorship on inside flaps of dust jacket.

D12 Beardsley, Aubrey, and John Glassco. *Under the Hill.* New York: Grove Press, [1967].
Four-paragraph description of book on inside flaps of dust jacket and biographical statements about Beardsley and Glassco on rear of dust jacket.

D13 Blackburn, Paul. *The Cities.* New York: Grove Press, 1967.
Two-paragraph description of book and one-paragraph biographical statement about Blackburn on rear cover. An Evergreen Original paperback book.

D14 Borges, Jorge Luis. *A Personal Anthology.* Ed. Anthony Kerrigan. New York: Grove Press, 1967.
Three-paragraph description of book on front flap of dust jacket and two-paragraph biographical statement about Borges on back flap.

D15 Gombrowicz, Witold. *Pornografia.* Translated by Alastair Hamilton. New York: Grove Press, 1967.
Six-paragraph description of novel on inside flaps of dust jacket. Two-paragraph biographical statement about Gombrowicz on rear of dust jacket.

D16 Goytisolo, Juan. *The Party's Over: Four Attempts to Define a Love Story.* Translated by José Yglesias. New York: Grove Press, 1967.
Three-paragraph description of book on inside flaps of dust jacket. One-paragraph biographical statement about Goytisolo on rear of dust jacket.

D17 Higgins, Aidan. *Langrishe, Go Down.* New York: Grove Press, 1967.
Two-paragraph description of novel on front flap of dust jacket. One-paragraph biographical statement about Higgins on rear of dust jacket.

D18 Jones, LeRoi. *The Baptism & The Toilet.* New York: Grove Press, 1967.
One-paragraph description of plays on back cover. One-paragraph biographical statement about Jones included in preliminary pages of the book. An Evergreen paperback original.

D19 ———. *Tales.* New York: Grove Press, 1967.
Five-paragraph description of collection and one-paragraph biographical statement about Jones on inside flaps of dust jacket. GS did not contribute to the copy for the Evergreen paperback edition (1968).

D20 Noone, John. *The Man with the Chocolate Egg.* New York: Grove Press, 1967.
Three-paragraph description of novel and one-paragraph biographical statement about Noone on inside flaps of dust jacket. Editorial revisions were made in GS's text.

D21 Olson, Charles. *Human Universe and Other Essays.* New York: Grove Press, 1967.
Five-paragraph description of the book on inside flaps and one-paragraph biographical statement about Olson on the rear of the dust jacket. The Evergreen paperback edition abbreviates GS's original copy.

D22 Perec, Georges. *Les Choses: A Story of the Sixties.* Translated by Helen R. Lane. New York: Grove Press, 1967.
Four-paragraph description of the book on inside flaps and one-paragraph biographical statement about Perec on the rear of the dust jacket.

D23 Pinget, Robert. *The Inquisitory.* Translated by Donald Watson. New York: Grove Press, 1967.
Five-paragraph description of novel on inside flaps of dust jacket and one-paragraph biographical statement about Pinget on rear of dust jacket.

D24 Rosenthal, Irving. *Sheeper.* New York: Grove Press, 1967.
Four-paragraph description of book and one-paragraph biographical statement on inside flaps of dust jacket. Black Cat paperback edition (1968) reproduces GS's biographical statement on a preliminary page.

D25 Rumaker, Michael. *Gringos and Other Stories.* New York: Grove Press, 1967.
One-paragraph description of book on front flap of dust jacket and one-paragraph biographical statement about Rumaker on rear of dust jacket.

D26 Sherwood, James. *Stradella.* Revised edition. New York: Grove Press, 1967.

Three-paragraph description of novel on inside flaps of dust jacket and one-paragraph biographical statement about Sherwood on rear of dust jacket.

D27 Williams, Heathcote. *The Speakers.* New York: Grove Press, 1967.
Four-paragraph description of novel on inside flaps of dust jacket. GS did not contribute to the copy for the Black Cat paperback issue.

D28 Kandel, Lenore. *Word Alchemy.* New York: Grove Press, 1968.
Three-paragraph description of book and one-paragraph biographical statement about Kandel on rear of dust jacket.

D29 Vallejo, César. *Poemas Humanos Human Poems.* Translated by Clayton Eshleman. New York: Grove Press, 1968.
Four-paragraph description of the book and one-paragraph biographical statements about Vallejo and Eshleman on inside flaps of dust jacket. GS did not write the cover copy for the Evergreen paperback issue.

D30 Vian, Boris. *Mood Indigo.* Translated by John Sturrock. New York: Grove Press, 1968.
Three-paragraph description of novel and one-paragraph biographical statement about Vian on inside flaps. GS did not write the cover copy for the Evergreen paperback issue.

D31 Carim, Enver. *The Golden City.* New York: Grove Press, 1969.
Four-paragraph description of novel on inside flaps of dust jacket and one-paragraph biographical statement about Carim on rear of dust jacket.

D32 Goytisolo, Juan. *Marks of Identity.* Translated by Gregory Rabassa. New York: Grove Press, 1969.
Two-paragraph description of novel and one-paragraph biographical statements on Goytisolo and Rabassa on inside flaps of dust jacket.

D33 Guare, John. *Three Plays by John Guare: Cop-out, Muzeeka, Home Fires.* New York: Grove Press, 1969.
Three-paragraph description of book and one-paragraph biographical statement about Guare on rear of dust jacket.

D34 Beckett, Samuel. *Collected Works of Samuel Beckett.* 16 vols. New York: Grove Press, 1970.
GS was responsible only for the two-paragraph bio-critical statement that appears on each volume's end flap.

D35 Kenner, Martin, and James Petras, eds. *Fidel Castro Speaks.* New York: Grove Press, 1970.
Description lacking because no copy of dust jacket was located.

D36 McClure, Michael. *Star.* New York: Grove Press, 1970.
One-paragraph description of book and one-paragraph biographical statement on rear cover of Evergreen Original edition.

D37 Sanders, Ed. *Shards of God.* New York: Grove Press, 1970.
Five-paragraph description of novel and one-paragraph biographical statement about Sanders on inside flaps of dust jacket.

D38 *Showcase I: Plays from the Eugene O'Neill Foundation.* Introd. by John Lahr. New York: Grove Press, 1970.
Description lacking because no copy of dust jacket was located.

D39 Tindall, Kenneth. *Great Heads.* New York: Grove Press, 1970.
Four-paragraph description of novel and one-paragraph biographical statement about Tindall on inside flaps of dust jacket. Evergreen Black Cat paperback edition includes one paragraph description on back cover drawn from the original Grove edition.

D40 Burroughs, William S. *The Wild Boys: A Book of the Dead.* New York: Grove Press, 1971.
Four-paragraph description of the novel on the inside flaps and a one-paragraph biographical statement about Burroughs on the rear of dust jacket.

D41 Cleef, Monique van, and Joseph Liss. *Domination for Hire: The Story of Monique van Cleef.* New York: Grove Press, 1971.
Description lacking because no copy of dust jacket was located.

D42 Levy, Howard, and David Miller. *Going to Jail: The Political Prisoner.* New York: Grove Press, 1971.
Four-paragraph description of the book on the inside flaps of the dust jacket and one-paragraph biographical statements about the authors on the back of the jacket.

D43 Selby, Hubert, Jr. *The Room.* New York: Crove Press, 1971.
Four-paragraph description of novel and one-paragraph biographical statement about Selby on inside flaps of dust jacket.

Signed Book Blurbs

D44 Oppen, George. *This in Which* [poetry]. New York: New Directions/San Francisco Review, 1965.
25w statement on back cover of dust jacket of the clothbound edition and the back cover of the wrapper of the paperbound issue, excerpted from C64.

D45 Reznikoff, Charles. *Testimony: The United States (1885-1890) Recitative* [poetry]. New York: New Directions/San Francisco Review, 1965.
32w statement on inside front flap of dust jacket.

D46 Zukofsky, Louis. *All: The Collected Short Poems 1923-1958.* New York: Norton, 1965.
90w statement on back cover of dust jacket, excerpted from C94.

D47 Williams, Jonathan. *An Ear in Bartram's Tree* [prose]. Chapel Hill: Univ. of North Carolina Press, 1969.
7w statement on inside front flap of dust jacket.

D48 Selby, Hubert, Jr. *The Room.* New York: Grove Press, 1971.
40w statement on back of the dust jacket, excerpted from C81.

D49 Feld, Ross. *Plum Poems.* Jargon 71. New York: Jargon Society, 1972.
225w statement on front flap of wrapper. Reprinted as "Ross Feld's Plums": *SS*, 167. Excerpted in Jonathan Williams's *Uncle Gus Flaubert Rates The Jargon Society in One Hundred One Laconic Présalé Sage Sentences.* Chapel Hill: Hanes Foundation, Rare Book Collection, University Library, Univ. of North Carolina at Chapel Hill, 1989, 24.

D50 Duncan, Robert. *The Opening of the Field* [poetry]. New York: New Directions, 1973.
49w statement on back cover of the wrapper of paperback issue, excerpted from C153.

D51 Stephens, Michael Gregory. *Paragraphs* [fiction]. Amherst, MA: Mulch Press, 1974.
20w statement on back cover.

D52 Dowell, Coleman. *Island People* [novel]. New York: New Directions, 1976.
20w statement on back of dust jacket.

D53 Carter, Angela. *The Bloody Chamber* [short stories]. New York: Harper & Row, 1979. First American edition.
12w statement on back of dust jacket.

D54 Fleisher, Michael L. *Chasing Hairy* [novel]. New York: St. Martin's, 1979.
75w statement on back of dust jacket.

D55 Dowell, Coleman. *The Silver Swanne* [short story]. New York: Grenfell Press, 1983.
45w statement included in the promotional brochure for *The Silver Swanne* issued by Grenfell Press prior to publication.

D56 ———. *White on Black on White* [novel]. Woodstock, VT: Countryman Press, 1983.

15w statement on back cover of dust jacket about Dowell's *Too Much Flesh and Jabez*, excerpted from C238.

D57 Duncan, Robert. *Ground Work* [poetry]. New York: New Directions, 1984.
15w statement on rear flap of the dust jacket of the cloth edition and on the back cover of the paperbound edition, excerpted from C153.

D58 Carter, Angela. *Nights at the Circus* [novel]. New York: Viking, 1985. First American edition.
12w statement on back of dust jacket; identical to D53.

D59 Powers, Richard. *Three Farmers on Their Way to a Dance* [novel]. New York: Beech Tree Books, 1985.
35w statement on back of dust jacket.

D60 Acker, Kathy. *Literal Madness: Kathy Goes to Haiti, My Death My Life by Pier Paolo Pasolini, and Florida* [novels]. New York: Grove Press, 1987.
90w statement on back of dust jacket.

D61 Dowell, Coleman. *The Houses of Children: Collected Stories.* New York: Weidenfeld & Nicolson, 1987.
5w statement on front of dust jacket.

D62 ———. *Too Much Flesh and Jabez* [novel]. Elmwood Park, IL: Dalkey Archive, 1987.
15w statement on back cover of book's wrapper, excerpted from C238.

D63 Mathews, Harry. *Cigarettes* [novel]. New York: Weidenfeld & Nicolson, 1987.
45w statement on back of dust jacket. Statement reprinted in first preliminary page of the paperback edition issued by Collier Books, Macmillan Publishing Company, New York, 1987.

D64 Rexroth, Kenneth. *World Outside the Window: The Selected Essays of Kenneth Rexroth.* Ed. Bradford Morrow. New York: New Directions, 1987.
25w statement on the back flap of the dust jacket, excerpted from C78.

D65 Tindall, Kenneth. *The Banks of the Sea.* Elmwood Park, IL: Dalkey Archive, 1987.
70w statement on back cover of dust jacket.

D66 Blanchot, Maurice. *Thomas the Obscure.* Barrytown, NY: Station Hill, 1988.
30w statement on back of the dust jacket, excerpted from C301.

D67 ———. *Death Sentence.* Barrytown, NY: Station Hill, 1988.
40w statement on the back of the dust jacket, excerpted from C301.

D68 ———. *The Unavowable Community.* Barrytown, NY: Station Hill, 1988.
30w statement on the back of the dust jacket, excerpted from C301.

D69 Ellis, Trey. *Platitudes* [novel]. New York: Random House, 1988.
25w statement on preliminary page [1].

D70 Powers, Richard. *Prisoner's Dilemma* [novel]. New York: Beech Tree Books/William Morrow, 1988.
5w statement about Powers's *Three Farmers on Their Way to a Dance* on the back of the dust jacket, excerpted from D59.

D71 Dahlberg, Edward. *Samuel Beckett's Wake and Other Uncollected Prose.* Ed. Steven Moore. Elmwood Park, IL: Dalkey Archive, 1989.
70w statement on the back of the dust jacket, excerpted from C179.

E. INTERVIEWS AND RECORDINGS

E1 Ossman, David. "Gilbert Sorrentino." In *The Sullen Art: Interviews with Modern American Poets.* New York: Corinth, 1963, 46-55.
Conducted in early 1960 and subsequently broadcast over the radio stations of the Pacifica Foundation of Los Angeles, this interview concentrates on the American poetic scene in the late 1950s. GS discusses his editing of *Neon* and the magazine's limited audience; he also explains the nature of Robert Creeley's influence on his poetry and describes his own conception of poetry and methods of composition. Other topics treated include the importance of Pound and Olson to GS's generation, and GS's attitude toward Allen Ginsberg and the Beats.

E2 O'Brien, John. "Imaginative Qualities of Gilbert Sorrentino: An Interview." *Grosseteste Review* 6.1-4 (1973): 69-84. Rev. version subsequently published as the first part of "An Interview with Gilbert Sorrentino," *Review of Contemporary Fiction* 1 (Spring 1981): 5-27.
Conducted in 1971-72, this interview begins with general topics: the relation between GS's prose and poetry; his use of the innovations in prose techniques of Joyce, Flann O'Brien, Wyndham Lewis, and William Carlos Williams; GS's conception of writing as neither representation of fact nor expression of feeling but the creation of perfect beauty. Also included are lengthy discussions of his first three novels, focusing on the darkness of *SC*, GS's motive for the narrative discontinuities of *SW*, and the satiric rationale of *IQAT*.

E3 Alpert, Barry. "Gilbert Sorrentino—An Interview Conducted by Barry Alpert, Westbeth, New York City, April 7, 1974." *Vort* 6 [also cited as 2.3] (Fall 1974): 3-30.
Topics range widely over GS's career from the late 1940s into the early stages of *MS*. Substantial biographical material about GS's connections with the 1950s New York literary scene, including his ties to William Carlos Williams, Hubert Selby, Jonathan Williams, LeRoi Jones, Robert Creeley, and Joel Oppenheimer as well as his involvement with *Neon*, *Yugen*, *Kulchur*, and Grove Press. Detailed discussions of GS's poetic practice along with accounts of the individual collections *DSU*, *BW*, *PF*, and *CS*. Also covers GS's development of nonrepresentational fiction, including lengthy discussions of *SC*, *SW*, and *IQAT*.

E4 Coburn, Randy Sue. "Sorrentino's 'Stew' Starts to Bubble." *Washington Star*, 21 June 1979: C5, C10.
Conducted in New York at the Grove Press office shortly after publication of *MS* in 1979, the interview incorporated in this article focuses on the commercialism of the New York publishing scene in connection with GS's difficulties in placing *MS*, GS's admiration for Joyce and Flann O'Brien, his conception of the writer's relation to audience, and on *MS* itself, including its private jokes and deliberate misspellings.

E5 McCullough, David W. "Eye on Books." *Book of the Month Club News*, Fall 1979: 12. Reprinted as "Gilbert Sorrentino" in McCullough's *People, Books & Book People* (New York: Harmony Books, 1981), 165-66.
In the quotations embedded in this short article, GS emphasizes the bookish quality of *MS* and briefly notes his interest in trashy best-sellers, his admiration for Henry James, Algernon Blackwood, and Flann O'Brien, and his increasing disillusionment with commercial publishing.

E6 O'Brien, John. "An Interview with Gilbert Sorrentino." *Review of Contemporary Fiction* 1.1 (Spring 1981): 5-27.
First part conducted in fall of 1971 and originally published as E2. The second part, conducted by mail in 1979, concentrates on the conception, composition, and aesthetics of *MS.* GS discusses his handling of fictive voice, his use of lists to remove the impedimenta of life from narrative, and his efforts to push the novel toward the condition of total artifice. GS also comments on his approach to poetry, with specific reference to *O.*

E7 Barone, Dennis. "An Interview with Gilbert Sorrentino." *Partisan Review* 48.2 (1981): 236-46.
GS comments on the avant-garde New York artistic scene during the 1950s and early 1960s. His discussion ranges widely over such topics as the socioeconomics of literature and publishing during those decades, Pound's crucial role in promoting new literature, the social importance of the Cedar Bar, the critical neglect of William Carlos Williams and Louis Zukofsky as symptomatic of the fate of serious American writers, the production of *Neon*, and GS's own interest in Robert Creeley, Edward Dahlberg, and Paul Goodman. Interview does not address GS's own work or writing practices.

Barone comments: "I interviewed Gilbert Sorrentino one afternoon in September 1976 for approximately three hours at his apartment in Manhattan. Through several drafts, I reduced this material to twenty single-spaced pages. William Phillips of the *Partisan Review* reduced the interview to eight single-spaced pages. Among the comments omitted by Mr. Phillips are ones such as that which describes Robert Bly as 'Lorca with a corncob.' Mr. Phillips cut entire passages on the deep imagists; William Gaddis; Ford Maddox Ford; Barney Rosset; Edward Dorn; the end of *Neon* and the *Neon Obit;* the Beats, poetry readings, and mass media; the conservatism of the 1960s; and a passage about the *Hudson Review*. . . . Longer passages on Robert Creeley and Hubert Selby, Jr. were shortened. The taped interview and all correspondence relating to it can be found at the Contemporary Culture Collection, Samuel Paley Library, Temple University, Philadelphia, Pennsylvania" (letter to William McPheron, 22 April 1990; TLS at CSt).

In "Setting It Straight," *American Scholar* 50 (Autumn 1981): 567-70, Frederick Morgan, editor of the *Hudson Review*, objects to GS's comment in this interview that his magazine was unreceptive to innovative American writing in the 1950s. Morgan registers his complaints by printing correspondence exchanged with both the *Partisan Review* and GS (C275).

E8 Vangelisti, Paul. [Untitled excerpt from an unpublished interview.] *Invisible City* 28 (December 1981): [2].
In this brief excerpt from an otherwise untranscribed interview conducted April 1979, GS comments on Paul Blackburn's poems, contrasting them with the closed form of his own poetry.

E9 "A Moveable Feast." [Reading and interview, hosted by Tom Vitale, conducted in New York in 1982.] 30 min. tape cassette.
GS reads from *CV:* chapter 5, "Macy's San Francisco," 16-18; "A Description of the Photograph" section from chapter 22, "Willing Suspension of Disbelief," 81-83; and chapter 27, "Mottoes," 96-98. GS also discusses the nature of fiction, emphasizing art's independence from both politics and moral wisdom.

E10 Reading at the Poetry Center, San Francisco State University, 10 February 1983. 48 min. videotape.
GS reads the poems "Crool Time" (*SP*, 241), "The Iceman, Again" (*SP*, 243), "Verlaine's Innocents" (*SP*, 244), "A Celebration of Sorts" (*SP*, 246), "The Lemonade Panel" (*SP*, 247), "Good Night!" (*SP*, 249), "Miss and Hit" (*SP*, 248), "Everything Is a Still-Life" (*SP*, 253), "Mysteries Sacred and Profane" (*SP*, 255), "The Disappearance of Oilcloth" (*SP*, 256), "Evils of the City" (*SP*, 259), "Barely Aware of the Insistent Loud Roars" (*SP*, 260), and "Razzmatazz" (*SP*, 266-67); GS also reads "Elegy for Jacques-Paul Surreale," chapter 27 of *BP*, 123-27.

E11 Trueheart, Charles. "PW Interviews Gilbert Sorrentino." *Publishers Weekly* 223.21 (27 May 1983): 70-71.
Occasioned by the publication of *BP*, the interviewer intersperses critical observations about the novel with GS's comments on the aesthetics of his fiction, the audience for his books, and his attitude toward John Barth, Robert Pinget, and Jack Kerouac. GS's remarks emphasize the generative power of form.

E12 Gray, Lynn. "Interview: Gilbert Sorrentino." *Fiction Monthly*, December 1984: 3, 10.
Interviewer's questions provoke GS into important statements about the theory of writing as well as his own individual practice. GS elaborates his twin principles that true artists inhabit a world of forms, which alone generate content. GS rejects writers who regard language as a conveyor of information for purposes of communication, arguing instead that it should be seen as a substance shaped by the writer's obsessions into artifacts, not manipulated by his ideas into messages. GS's discussion of specific works locates the governing intent of *MS* not in parody but erasure of the author, of *AS* in the rehearsal of high-modernist techniques, and of *BP* in the restoration of the author through the presentation of a battered, syntactically insane language that can be attributed to GS himself. GS concludes by insisting that the writer is outside society, obliged only to serve his own obsessions and that to make salable products for waiting audiences is to be

trapped by other people's aesthetic desires and lose the artist's proper freedom.

E13 Ross, Jean W. "C[ontemporary] A[uthors] Interview." *Contemporary Authors.* New Revision Series, vol. 14. Detroit: Gale Research, 1985: 454-56.
Conducted by mail in June 1984, this interview ranges widely, touching on GS's teenage reading of the social protest novelists James T. Farrell, Theodore Dreiser, and John Dos Passos, his interest in jazz, his editorial work at Grove Press, his attitude toward teaching, and his approach to structure in fiction.

E14 Myers, George, Jr. "Starting Where Joyce Ended." *Columbus Dispatch,* 6 December 1987: 9C.
Intersperses critical comments about *RT* with excerpts from a mail interview occasioned by the book's publication. GS explains that *RT* is an exploration of the nature of information as facts are affected by memory and prejudice through different levels of telling. Since all the facts are malleable, labile, suspect, GS explains, the reader is caught in an endless process of contradiction.

E15 Gontarski, S. E. "Working at Grove: An Interview with Gilbert Sorrentino." *Review of Contemporary Fiction* 10.3 (Fall 1990): 97-110.
In this interview, conducted by mail during 1989, GS discusses in detail the editorial temper and daily operations of Grove Press during his tenure there. Topics covered include the role played by Barney Rosset's literary and political tastes in determining Grove's publishing program, the nature of editorial work at Grove and its difference from more commercial houses, the importance of Donald Allen's *The New American Poetry 1945-1960,* and the significance of Selby's *Last Exit to Brooklyn.* GS also discusses the most notable books published by Grove and comments on how *MS* came to Rosset.

F. REVIEWS OF SORRENTINO'S BOOKS

The Darkness Surrounds Us (1960)

F1 Levertov, Denise. "Poets of a Given Ground." *Nation* 193 (14 October 1961): 251-53, esp. 251-52.
Though GS has not yet achieved his own variation within the tradition that William Carlos Williams and Ezra Pound established and Charles Olson and Robert Creeley have extended, *DSU* abundantly evidences his virtuosity, moral force, and noble intelligence. GS promises to be one of the best poets of his time. (250w) Excerpted: *Contemporary Literary Criticism* 22 (1982): 391.

F2 Stanley, George. *Yugen* 8 (1962): 34.
Contrary to GS's claim that poetry engenders unsure thinking, the poem is properly absolute predicate, tracking not uncertainty but necessity. (150w)

Black and White (1964)

F3 Clark, Thomas. "The Gestures of Deliberation." *Poetry* 107.2 (November 1965): 121-24, esp. 121-22.
BW registers a specifically urban mode of life, deliberately emptying the physical world of all but conventional significance and then exploiting this familiarity. Though sometimes crabbed in tone, many of *BW*'s poems are forms successfully driven out of the routine mass of language and act. (200w)

F4 Howard, Richard. "Two Against Chaos." *Nation* 200 (15 March 1965): 289-90.
BW marks the end of GS's apprenticeship to Robert Creeley. Using poetry as an instrument to create the self, GS's centripetal verse accommodates experience accurately and coherently. Though the edges of his world are tinged with doom, GS's invention of selfhood has produced a number of beautiful lyrics, of which "Maytime" is the book's best. (400w)

F5 Malanga, Gerard. *Kulchur* 19 (Autumn 1965): 99.
A poetry of sensation derived from William Carlos Williams's theories, *BW* suffers from GS's failure to convert the noise of very complex word-groups into music. (200w)

The Sky Changes (1966)

F6 Anon. *Bookbuyer's Guide*, March 1966.
SC is the story of a desperate man on an unfulfilled quest. (25w)

F7 ——. *Chapel Hill* [NC] *Weekly*, 10 April 1966.
SC gives evidence that it was written by a poet who knows how to play upon various aspects of sexual love. (75w)

F8 ——. *Choice* 3.11 (January 1967): 1018.
A good poet with a distinctive voice, GS has written a taut novel whose form is more original than its ideas. Enacting the contemporary fictional syndrome of isolated, suffering egos, *SC* is distinguished by its compressed and tortured style, which captures the characters' pain. (150w)

F9 ——. *Virginia Kirkus Service* 34.5 (1 March 1966): 267-68.
Disclosing a world of rotten people and situations, *SC* is not the glad, mad trip of Kerouac's *On the Road* but a bitter, more adult insight into hip America. (175w)

F10 ——. *Washington Post Book World*, 6 April 1986: 12.
Composed with dazzling and precise verbal dexterity, *SC* is replete with sadness for lost love and despair over a cheapened American culture. (100w)

F11 ——. *World Progress* [Chicago], Spring 1966: 74.
SC is written with more elegance than is usually found in hardboiled tales of its type. (35w)

F12 Brooks, Gwendolyn. "Storm Clouds." *Book Week*, 8 May 1966: 8.
GS is a poet, and *SC* is poetry influenced by an insight both agitated and clear. (225w)

F13 Carroll, John M. *Library Journal* 93.5 (1 March 1966): 1248.
GS's literary devices of no names, no inhibitions, and no continuity make *SC* a repetitive, tiresome, clinical prolongation of a psychological case study of a bad marriage. (175w)

F14 Douthit, Peter L. "Book Finds Raw Truth in Travels." *Fort Worth Star-Telegram*, 27 March 1966, sec. 6: 5.
A brilliant, beautiful book, *SC* strips the disguises from our misery and meanness, disclosing life to be a constant but fascinating dance of pain. (275w)

F15 Elman, Richard. "Critics' Choices for Christmas." *Commonweal* 91 (5 December 1969): 311-14, esp. 314.
A deeply moving, even shattering experience, *SC* is the best divorce novel in recent years. Also shaped by strongly felt, honest feelings, GS's poems are similarly distinguished, their power and language virtually unique in his generation. (150w)

F16 Howard, Richard. "Interior Landscapes." *New Leader* 49 (9 May 1966): 24-25.

GS is primarily concerned with form's ability to render a life fully accountable. By seizing on the metaphorical possibilities of the American landscape to accommodate chaos, *SC* shows art's power to transform pain and weakness into joy and beauty. While thematically a night journey into unholy places, stylistically *SC* literally embodies the mind's process of change by making every detail become an incarnation of the reality presented. (1250w)

F17 Hunter, Charles. "Compelling Story of Hunt for Life." *Evening Post* [Charleston, SC], 22 April 1966.
Explicit in detail yet sparingly written, *SC* is a tragic tale of man's futile search for life's meaning. (175w)

F18 Monsky, Susan. "Sjhoort Takes." *Boston Globe*, 11 May 1986: 92.
SC captures the breakup of a marriage with brutal, arresting precision. (100w)

F19 Moore, Steven. *Review of Contemporary Fiction* 8.2 (Summer 1988): 313.
The revised edition perfects *SC*'s pitch, rendering it a triumphant exercise in tone and color. The novel's fierce writing and unrelieved bleakness separate it from more exuberant road books of the 1950s as well as from realistic fiction. (225w) This review also treats *MS*.

F20 Raksin, Alex. "Now in Paperback." *Los Angeles Times Book Review*, 20 April 1986: 12.
Though its tone is dominated by despair and disillusionment, *SC* also offers the pleasures of GS's intense concentration and the poignancy of those few moments when redemption seems possible. (125w)

F21 Schlueter, Paul. "Sex, But No Satisfaction in Two New Novels." *Daily Egyptian* [Carbondale, IL], 24 August 1966: 4.
SC is a boring and trite book, though in the hands of a more practiced and sensitive writer, its subject matter could have become art. (225w)

F22 Sward, Robert. "Poets at Novels." *Poetry* 112.5 (August 1968): 353-56, esp. 353-54.
Moving with the urgency of poetry, *SC* possesses an integrity of style that justifies its extreme self-preoccupation. (250w)

The Perfect Fiction (1968)

F23 Anon. *Kirkus Reviews* 36 (15 January 1968): 95.
A central emptiness infuses *PF*, shattering all forms of reality and denying any coherent vision of life. This formlessness reflects GS's deliberate abdication of the artist's traditional role and is at once honest and unsettling. (150w)

F24 Burns, Gerald. "Poets and Anthologies." *Southwest Review* 53.3 (Summer 1968): 332-36, esp. 334-35.
PF is haunted by Wallace Stevens and Robert Creeley, the two most abstract poets of our century. But GS cannot handle abstractions above the cocktail-party level, so the volume is a letdown. (325w)

F25 Dawson, Fielding. *Noose* 5 (1 June 1968): [11], [13]; review completed in *Noose* 7 (27 July 1968): [1].
PF shows GS in his finest voice but also provokes resentment. The latter springs from GS's need to draw conclusions and make abstract remarks, a maneuver that reveals GS's anxiety and robs him of his real power. Stated differently, *PF* imposes a single voice on double or multiple perspectives, a dangerous tactic that triggers the control of consciousness and alienates GS's poetry from its true substance in the unconscious. (725w)

F26 Early, Joe. *Noose* 5 (1 June 1968): [13].
PF is a significant book that continues the thrust of *SC.* (25w)

F27 E[shleman], C[layton]. *Caterpillar* 7 (1969): 246-47.
A book of great adamancy, *PF* explores the delusion that we can change our lives. It is empowered by GS's bitter conviction that change itself is fiction and that possession of the object of desire is literally impossible. (350w)

F28 Feld, Ross. "Something Plus Something Does Not Make One Thing." *Promethean* 15.2 (1967-1968): 19-24.
PF serves as a corrective to poetry that glibly mixes art and the world in order to ameliorate life. The great force and beauty of GS's poems occurs, in fact, exactly at those moments when art and the world are revealed to be "separate but equal." The poems are hard, often bitter, and painfully personal, recalling Spicer's unsentimental understanding of the writer's fate, but they also achieve undeniable beauty. (1900w)

F29 Grigsby, Gordon K. *Per/Se* 3.3 (Fall 1968): 75-76, esp. 75.
The styles of Wallace Stevens and William Carlos Williams almost overpower GS's voice in *PF.* Though GS's speech is poignant, witty, and refreshingly unpretentious, his subject matter is too familiar. (225w)

F30 Howard, Richard. "Masters and Friends." *Poetry* 113.5 (February 1969): 338-60, esp. 346-47.
A grim book caught in the deathgrip of pain, *PF* dedicates its Creeley-esque poems to their own collapse and emptiness. Abandoning his earlier commitment to sensuous experience, GS here projects a persona detached from seeing and feeling. (250w)

F31 Phelps, Donald. *Noose* 8 (15 September 1968): [1], [3].
PF represents a triumph over the contradiction between the immediacy of reality and hierarchic values that stalemates GS's earlier work, including

SC. The same solicitude for one's hidden, irreducible self remains, but in *PF* GS achieves autonomy of mind and renders language the vehicle of his contention with experience. GS's emphasis on validating art as behavior contrasts with Fielding Dawson's concern with autobiography and accounts for Dawson's reservations about *PF* (see F25). (500w)

F32 Schneider, Duane B. *Library Journal* 93.4 (15 February 1968): 757-58.
GS taps the cliché and relies on banality to express in *PF* a painful, heartfelt lament for the drabness and darkness of reality. (150w) Excerpted: *Contemporary Literary Criticism* 22 (1982): 391.

Steelwork (1970)

F33 Anon. *Antioch Review* 31.1 (Spring 1971): 132.
SW is a dreadful novel whose sadism and sexuality parody sentimental versions of urban America. (100w)

F34 ———. *Herald American* [Palm Springs, CA], 10 December 1970.
A human, funny, intelligent novel, *SW* moves as the memory does, tracing the corruption of decent people by easy wartime money. (100w)

F35 ———. *Kirkus Reviews* 38 (1 August 1970): 826.
SW is a kinetic scrapbook whose brilliant individual pieces mute the novel's bitterness at the tragic erosion of the American dream. GS's ethnic and period distinctions are subtle, strengthening interest in his characters' soured, impoverished lives. (180w)

F36 ———. *Long Beach* [CA] *Independent*, 18 November 1970.
SW is a fine novel, with vividly drawn vignettes. (25w)

F37 ———. *Publishers Weekly* 198.3 (20 July 1970): 69.
Though GS's talent for converting firsthand experience into memorable characters is considerable, *SW* fails to achieve coherent form and remains an unsatisfying fragment. (175w)

F38 Alpert, Barry. "Local Turf." *Caterpillar* 15-16 (April-July 1971): 284-86.
Reprinted: *Vort* 2.3 [also designated no. 6] (Fall 1974): 59-61.
Extending the geographical delineation of Hubert Selby's *Last Exit to Brooklyn*, *SW* definitely maps GS's own Brooklyn neighborhood. Curiously inverting the structure of *SC*, *SW* deliberately blurs temporal relations to focus attention on the connection of events to the physical area. GS's geographic art lacks, however, Selby's ability to communicate moral judgments without direct comment. The character Gibby is GS's persona in the novel. (1000w)

F39 Keyishian, Harry. "Dead Ends." *Book World*, 8 November 1970: 8.
SW's powerful rendition of lower-class despair suffers badly from the

absence of a coherent narrative consciousness. (200w)

F40 Klinkowitz, Jerome. *Village Voice Literary Supplement*, 22 November 1973: 27-28, esp. 28.
A spatial portrait of a Brooklyn neighborhood, *SW* consists of a collage of past moments, each infused by the sense of loss. (150w) This review also treats *IQAT* and *S-H*.

Revised version published as "A Capsule Review," a section of "Gilbert Sorrentino's Super-Fiction," *Chicago Review* 25.4 (1974): 77-89, esp. 86-88, reprinted in Klinkowitz's *The Life of Fiction*. Urbana: Univ. of Illinois Press, 1977, 14-15, and excerpted in *Contemporary Literary Criticism* 22 (1982): 392-94.

F41 Levin, Martin. "Reader's Report." *New York Times Book Review*, 8 November 1970: 52.
Powerfully evocative, *SW* exhibits a surprisingly wide range of tones, from nostalgia to disgust. (165w)

F42 O'Connell, Shaun. "Just What Grows in Brooklyn." *Nation* 212 (21 June 1971): 790-92.
The scrambled chronology and arbitrary jumpcuts of GS's method succeed in formally expressing *SW*'s themes of despair and senselessness. Though sharing Hubert Selby's vision of frustration and violence, the novel also achieves moments of personal release. Ultimately GS's style redeems the work. (1750w) Excerpted: *Contemporary Literary Criticism* 7 (1977): 447-48.

F43 Selby, Hubert, Jr. "A Neighborhood of Changing People." *Los Angeles Times*, 1 November 1970, Calendar sec.: 52.
SW is a beautiful but deceptively simple book, its surface clarity opening onto profound depths that change the reader's perception of reality. An artist not an entertainer, GS shows the changes that slowly overtake a neighborhood inhabited not by weirdos but real people. *SW* teaches about the simple day-by-day survival of man in his own world. (1300w)

F44 Warner, Jon M. *Library Journal* 95.16 (15 September 1970): 2936.
SW successfully captures the poetry and beauty as well as the squalor and pettiness of Brooklyn life. (100w)

Corrosive Sublimate (1971)

F45 Anon. *Choice* 9.3 (May 1972): 371.
Though providing thematic variety and occasional brilliance of image and phrase, *CS* is more typically characterized by parched wit and anticlimax. The spirit of Robert Creeley broods over these poems, which are often deliberately inarticulate. (125w)

F46 Guimond, James. "Moving Heaven and Earth." *Parnassus* 1.1 (Fall-Winter 1972): 106-15, esp. 109-11.
Reflecting the strong tastes and dislikes of GS's intensely urban sensibility, *CS*'s excellent poems move from illusion to clarity. GS's hard-edged imagery and crisp tone unsentimentally expose pain, pleasure, and their frequent mixture. "Coast of Texas" is the volume's best piece. (850w) Excerpted: *Contemporary Literary Criticism* 3 (1975): 461.

F47 Katz, Bill. "Little Presses." *Library Journal* 97.16 (15 September 1972): 2846-47, esp. 2846.
A mature, able poet, GS offers in *CS* a definite political and moral stance about urban America. (75w)

F48 Levendosky, Charles. "Poet's Review." *Casper* [WY] *Star Tribune*, 28 October 1972: 9A.
The poems in *CS* are like sharp prisms that reflect man's destruction of himself and his planet. Their bitterness derives from thwarted idealism. GS's clear vision is too rooted in reality to allow any comfort. (250w)

Imaginative Qualities of Actual Things (1971)

F49 Anon. *Antioch Review* 31.3 (Fall 1971): 440.
IQAT is a first-rate novel that redeems GS's promise as a seriocomic writer. (110w)

F50 ———. *Booklist* 68.6 (15 November 1971): 274.
Blending sex and sycophancy, *IQAT* offers cardboard characters in a book that is essentially a digression from a novel. (50w)

F51 ———. *Kirkus Reviews* 39 (15 August 1971): 895.
IQAT is not a fictional recreation of a real time and place but a savant hip parody, an antinovel full of lists and author interpolations. (250w)

F52 ———. *Publishers Weekly* 200.6 (9 August 1971): 41.
IQAT is a startling, savage novel about human destruction that tempers its fury with both compassion and a fresh writing style. (180w)

F53 Christianson, Virgil. "Wise Guy?: Novelist Sends Reader a Letter." *Atlanta Journal and Constitution*, 19 December 1971: 8C.
Failing to adhere to traditional standards of both plot and characterization, *IQAT* is less a novel than a letter, which most readers will refuse. GS does, however, have a great ear for dialogue. (400w)

F54 De Feo, Ronald. *Modern Occasions* 2 (Winter 1972): 148-52, esp. 150-51.
Less a novel than a series of asides on "Stupidity in the Arts Today," *IQAT* is lively and funny satire but not as deeply felt as *SW*. GS's gratuitous use of the clichéd devices of self-reflexive fiction defeats his own purposes,

discouraging the reader's serious interest in his characters. (1000w) Excerpted: *Contemporary Literary Criticism* 3 (1975): 461-62.

F55 Graver, Lawrence. *New York Times Book Review*, 2 July 1972: 6-7.
Instead of the austere antinovel the book's self-consciousness promises, *IQAT* is a conventional satire in which GS's malicious wit too easily depletes his subject. (340w) Excerpted: *Contemporary Literary Criticism* 22 (1982): 392.

F56 Halliday, Mark. "Not 'Just Another.'" *Providence* [RI] *Journal*, 30 January 1972, "Leisure" sec.: H8.
Following no dried-up formula for traditional excitement, *IQAT* wittily and provocatively challenges fiction's conventions to remind readers that the chief character of any novel is always the novelist. Empowering *IQAT* is GS's bitter resentment of untalented writers and disgust at bad books, negative feelings that threaten to undermine GS's own art. (750w)

F57 Hannigan, Paul. *Ploughshares* 1.4 (Spring 1973): 92-94.
Not a realistic novel but a parody that combines a roman-à-clef and Augustan scourge, *IQAT* is a funny book. Underlying GS's virtuosity as a prose stylist is bitter contempt for both the subjects of his satire and for narrative fiction generally. This spite extends to the reader, finally revealing GS's mind to be common and sentimental, a Charles Bukowski manqué. (725w)

F58 Klinkowitz, Jerome. *Village Voice Literary Supplement*, 22 November 1973: 27-28.
IQAT channels GS's hatred for New York publishers into a striking novelistic innovation. Though GS despises conventional narrative art, his non-illusionistic focus on words ironically succeeds in producing brilliantly conceived characters. (840w) This review also treats *SW* and *S-H*.
Revised version published as "A Capsule Review," a section of "Gilbert Sorrentino's Super-Fiction," *Chicago Review* 25.4 (1974): 77-89, esp. 86-88, reprinted in Klinkowitz's *The Life of Fiction*. Urbana: Univ. of Illinois Press, 1977, 14-15, and excerpted in *Contemporary Literary Criticism* 22 (1982): 392-94.

F59 Lipsius, Frank. "3 Novels: Indifference and Conventionality." *Philadelphia Inquirer*, 21 November 1971: 6H.
IQAT succeeds despite GS's good-natured indifference to the novel, including his neglect of plot. The book works because GS writes so well and engages the reader in interesting questions like what is entailed in suspending belief when nothing is believable. (175w)

F60 Lopez, Eddie. *Fresno* [CA] *Bee*, 7 November 1971.
GS is very crude. His bag is satire, written in a style reminiscent of Kerouac and Henry Miller. (75w)

F61 Powers, Ed. "Read It and Laugh—Perhaps at Yourself." *Cleveland Press*, 26 November 1971.
IQAT is a perceptively funny book that does a job on the dilettantish losers of the hip art community. GS's zany manipulation of language and footnotes softens the satire and makes his bitterness bearable. (150w)

F62 Rabassa, Gregory. "There Goes the Neighborhood." *Nation* 215 (21 August 1972): 123-24.
Exhibiting affinities with Cortázar's experimentalism, *IQAT* offers a dystopian vision of the aimless 1950s that combats the decade's fraudulence with GS's own artistic integrity. (1200w) Excerpted: *Contemporary Literary Criticism* 22 (1982): 392.

F63 Scholes, Robert. *Saturday Review* 54 (23 October 1971): 88.
IQAT is a bitter, funny, and moving novel about the contemporary world of art and letters. Through energetically realized characters, the novel articulates its anguish at the cultural forces that suppress authenticity. *IQAT*'s stylistic self-consciousness also counters these forces by subverting clichés. (725w)

F64 Theroux, Paul. *Book World*, 7 November 1971: 2.
GS's truculent intelligence lends power to *IQAT*, which otherwise suffers from artistic posturing similar to the pretensions it venomously attacks. (400w) Excerpted: *Contemporary Literary Criticism* 22 (1982): 391-92.

F65 Warner, Jon M. *Library Journal* 96.15 (1 September 1971): 2672.
In clean, hard prose *IQAT* expresses with caustic humor GS's theories on writing and the sham of American cultural values. (225w)

Splendide-Hôtel (1973)

F66 Anon. *Antioch Review* 34.1-2 (Fall-Winter 1975-76): 244-45.
Sardonically countering the plasticity of American culture with the poet's passionate grasp of particulars, *S-H* both bristles with Orwellian indignation and vibrates with lively details. Though many of GS's inventions are wonderful, the antiacademic tirades are gratuitous. (300w) Excerpted: *Contemporary Literary Criticism* 7 (1977): 452.

F67 ———. *Publishers Weekly* 204.11 (10 September 1973): 57.
These baroque prose poems pay deliberate homage to Rimbaud and Baudelaire. (40w)

F68 ———. *Washington Post Book World*, 3 June 1984: 12.
GS's wit, irony, and effortless invention create prose of rare deliciousness that also offers a philosophy and critique of contemporary writing. (120w)

F69 Carruth, Hayden. "Levertov." *Hudson Review* 27.3 (Autumn 1974): [475]-480, esp. [475]-476.
Though *S-H* is a work of originality and imagination, GS's view of the poet as a superior person exempt from practicality and capable of managing the real world through the creation of a super- or antireality is dangerous and antiquated. Denise Levertov's contrary conception of the artist's relation to history offers a perfect answer to GS. (250w) Excerpted: *Contemporary Literary Criticism* 7 (1977): 448.

F70 Fawcett, Sharon. "Colors." *Open Letter* 3rd ser. 5 (Summer 1976): 97-99.
GS's homage to Rimbaud and William Carlos Williams, *S-H* is a defense of poetry which returns to the primary constructs of words in order to recover primary meanings and images. (750w) Excerpted: *Contemporary Literary Criticism* 14 (1980): 498.

F71 Gillespie, Adrienne. *Library Journal* 99.4 (15 February 1974): 492.
Precise language and synesthetic style transform this apocalyptic meditation on the exile of the heart into a genuine vision. (100w)

F72 Henkin, Bill. *City* [San Francisco], 4 December 1973: 39.
S-H abounds in some of GS's best prose. (75w)

F73 Klinkowitz, Jerome. *Village Voice Literary Supplement*, 22 November 1973: 27-28, esp. 28.
Refusing to confuse fiction with the world, GS chooses a completely artificial structure for *S-H*, which keeps attention on the page itself. Neither a dull parahistorical record nor a bland metafiction recounting a second-order story, GS's fiction is instead something made, its substance controlled by its method. (550w) This review also treats *SW* and *IQAT*.
Revised version published as "A Capsule Review," a section of "Gilbert Sorrentino's Super-Fiction," *Chicago Review* 25.4 (1974): 77-89, esp. 86-88, reprinted in Klinkowitz's *The Life of Fiction*. Urbana: Univ. of Illinois Press, 1977, 14-15, and excerpted in *Contemporary Literary Criticism* 22 (1982): 392-94.

F74 Lewis, Harry. *Valley Advocate* [Amherst, MA], 26 December 1973.
Bitterly focused on the sores of life and the failures of joy, *S-H* is a book without hope, neglecting art's duty to open onto life. (250w)

F75 McLellan, Joseph. *Washington Post Book World*, 18 November 1973: 5.
Reflecting Rimbaud, these brilliant prose poems feature visions of cataclysm. (45w)

F76 Sciborski, Rod. *Independent Press-Telegram* [Long Beach, CA], 19 December 1973.
Though *S-H* is intense, often frenzied, and bursting with flashes of poetic association, GS's tribute to Rimbaud and William Carlos Williams remains anomalous because of its arbitrary structure and indifference to audience.

Its drone of esoteric artistry makes *S-H* difficult to appreciate. (275w)

F77 Zinnes, Harriet. "Polar Night of America." *Parnassus* 3.1 (1974): 204-9. Though constructed as a bulwark against the devastation of philistine America, *S-H* neglects the aesthetic principle that form extends from content; it also laments art's debasement only by debasing it further. Meditating on both Rimbaud and William Carlos Williams, *S-H* radically diminishes their visions and substitutes tinsel for their art. Though GS's prose is sometimes vigorous and there is amusement in identifying his allusions, *S-H* finally disappoints. (2250w)

Flawless Play Restored (1975)

F78 Myers, Paul. *Library Journal* 100.8 (1 April 1975): 688.
As drama *FP* is unactable and as literature it is unreadable. (75w)

F79 O'Brien, John. [written for] *Chicago Sun-Times*, March 1975.
Recreating the biting satire, ribald comedy, and brilliant linguistic play of Ben Jonson's masque, *FP* attacks the menagerie of American types created by the depraved imaginations of Hollywood, Madison Avenue, bad literature, and pop culture. All share in corrupting language, but GS's own inventiveness and style transform this gross material into hard, pure art. (500w)

The *Chicago Sun-Times* sent proof copy of this review to Black Sparrow Press in late March, but actual publication of the review has not been confirmed.

White Sail (1977)

F80 Anon. *Choice* 14.11 (January 1978): 1500.
A pleasant volume that lacks, however, a clear intellectual superstructure, *WS* is distinguished by GS's famously antithetical orange sonnets, which playfully undermine conventional poetic organization. GS's aesthetic concentrates on the absolute integrity of unique experience. (225w)

F81 J[acob], J[ohn]. *Booklist* 74.8 (15 December 1977): 664.
Less an analytical poet than a lyricist, GS does not involve himself intensely with his subject matter but concentrates instead on craft and meaning. (50w)

The Orangery (1978)

F82 Anon. *Choice* 15.7 (September 1978): 875.
A rewarding divertissement that blends the serious and the humorous, *O* avoids the failure that usually attends a writer's decision to pursue exhaustively a single concept. (75w)

F83 Booth, Martin. "The Dated, the Demanding, the Daunting." *Tribune* [London], 8 June 1979: 7.
Exhibiting the knowledge of the authoritarian poet, GS successfully expands the simple into a vast panorama of feeling. With its terse, implication-dense language, the poetry of *O* requires concentrated attention. (125w) Excerpted: *Contemporary Literary Criticism* 14 (1980): 500.

F84 Finkelstein, Norman. "Magic in Emporia." *Daimon* 11 (Winter 1978-1979): unpaginated.
GS's best book of poems to date, *O* fulfills the promise of *CS* and *S-H*, converting their bitterness and rage into perfectly rendered form. His devotion to image enables GS to transform the junk in the attic of the American mind into strangely plangent art. In *O*, the poet is himself a performer, masking his alternate moods of nostalgia and bitterness with bravura linguistic games. Though the diction is outrageous and the rhymes absurd, the emotion is painfully genuine. GS's handling of the sonnet recalls William Bronk. (725w)

F85 Geddie, Tom. "Orange Is the Color of My True Love's Poems." *Dallas Times Herald*, 12 March 1978: 4G.
By believing completely in his words, GS creates in *O* a stark work exclusively of his own invention. (325w)

F86 Grealish, Gerard. *Best Sellers* 38.10 (January 1979): 327-28.
O is a beautiful book that suspends reason to create a world where experience is absolutely what it is. GS repeats a network of words through different contexts to weave an emotive fabric that intimates an elusive female figure, whose presence resonates throughout the volume. (450w) Excerpted: *Contemporary Literary Criticism* 14 (1980): 498-99.

F87 H[all], J[oan] J[offe]. "Almost-Round Book Full of Special Fruit." *Houston Post*, 4 June 1978: 5AA.
Working within strict limitations, GS achieves a delightful tour de force. (200w)

F88 J[acob], J[ohn]. *Booklist* 74.19 (1 June 1978): 1535.
GS's poetry continues to be a unique American event. *O* uses the random occurrence of the word "orange" to lend thematic coherence to otherwise unrelated materials. (50w)

F89 Kart, Larry. "Poets Who Speak with Authority." *Chicago Tribune Book World*, 14 May 1978: 2.
In *O* GS pushes authority toward personal authoritarianism, insisting not only on the power to make literary rules but also to enforce them. His elitist quest is antipoetic, seeking to destroy conventional beauty. (200w)

F90 Lefcowitz, Barbara F. *Washington Book Review*, June 1979.

Despite its gimmicks and fancy French allusions, *O* startles attention into fresh perceptions, especially by its dazzling images of daffy-sad America. In part an elegy for lost American dreamers, *O* also demonstrates how formal conventions can serve innovative purposes. (650w)

F91 Sale, Richard. *Texas Writers Newsletter* 20 (June 1979): 3-5.
A sad voice haunted by the loss of youth and intimacy dominates *O*. But this solemn gloom is tempered by GS's wit and technical skill, which transform verbal games and literary clichés into revelation. (500w)

F92 T., M. *Kliatt Young Adult Paperback Book Guide*, Spring 1978: 17-18.
An exercise book based on the sonnet form, *O* is an extraordinary poetic sleight of hand that creates simultaneous impressions of visual brightness, vaudeville, and radical linguistic displacement. (100w)

F93 Trueblood, Valerie. *American Poetry Review* 8.1 (January-February 1979): 29.
Dazzling and fierce, *O* is an elegiac series in which anger plays contrapuntally against grief and memory. The best poem-of-America during the year, *O* expresses GS's sense of the American artist's strain to see the nation whole without repudiating it. (425w) Excerpted: *Contemporary Literary Criticism* 14 (1980): 499.

Mulligan Stew (1979)

F94 Anon. *Kirkus Reviews* 47 (15 February 1979): 219.
MS revives the sixteenth-century tradition of literary pamphleteering, wildly attacking the current publishing world and its moribund modes. Though GS's coyness sometimes becomes smug, *MS* is a genuinely hilarious avalanche of vaudeville, parody, obsessive junk, and literary homage. (325w)

F95 ———. *Manchester Evening News*, 21 October 1982.
MS is an indescribable parody novel that displays GS's vicious humor and is an entertainment throughout. (55w)

F96 ———. *Publishers Weekly* 215.10 (5 March 1979): 100.
An extraordinary work that some will find irresistable and many others unreadable, *MS* is brilliantly clever, extremely funny, and controlled by a delicate irony. (175w)

F97 ———. *QPB* [Quality Paperback Book Club] *Review*, December 1979: 17.
A hilarious tour de force, *MS* is a highly original novel. (45w)

F98 ———. *Time Out* [London], 30 May 1980.
Though an echo of what better authors have done, *MS* is so good-humored about its narcissism and its sloppy excesses are so idiosyncratically

persistent that the book transcends the tradition of which it is probably the last example. (125w)

F99 Anderson, Elliott. "Two Novels as Funhouse Mirrors." *Chicago Tribune Book World*, 24 June 1979: 5.
Though a significant literary achievement, *MS* is not new but rather follows the tradition of the self-conscious novel whose conventions are evident in Flann O'Brien, James Joyce, and John Barth. A book about the narrative imagination, *MS* is truly comic. (550w)

F100 Atchity, Kenneth John. "Kettle of Kitsch." *San Francisco Review of Books* 5.3 (September 1979): 15-16.
A comic masterpiece whose stylistic exuberance registers delight in life's super-abundant excess, *MS* marks a cultural watershed by incorporating the Irish perspectives of Joyce and Flann O'Brien into American culture and leavening horror with laughter. *MS* proceeds along three methodologically marked strands, incorporating numerous varieties of bad writing. Though aimed at an audience that has read everything, it escapes being pedantic because it is so hilarious. (1700w)

F101 ———. "Mirth, Madness in a Magical Mix of Literary Leftovers." *Los Angeles Times Book Review*, 8 July 1979: 1, 14.
A masterpiece in the history of wit and imagination, *MS* murders the self-reflexive novel. Its complex but clearly labeled, three-part structure forces the audience to reassess the act of reading. Like the work of Rabelais, Sterne, Joyce, and Flann O'Brien, GS's novel occupies an anamolous literary space that is, however, unique within the American tradition. (800w)

This review also appeared as: "Sorrentino's Potlach: Literary Leftovers," *St. Louis Globe-Democrat*, 14 July 1979; "The Printed Word: 'Mulligan Stew,'" *Tucson Daily Citizen*, 14 July 1979; "Everyone Will Love 'Mulligan,'" *Atlantic City Press*, 22 July 1979; and "Sorrentino's 'Stew' Masterpiece," *Indianapolis*, 22 July 1979.

F102 Auerbach, Michael. "Sorrentino's 'Mulligan Stew': Bare Bones and Leftovers." *UCLA Daily Bruin*, 26 July 1979.
MS is one of the most amazingly self-destructive novels ever written. Though obscure, obtuse, and self-indulgent, *MS* has a recognizable structure, many sublimely comic moments, and a nihilistic point of view that allows GS to juggle his characters with mad frivolity. More interesting than GS's many allusions are his methods of skirting around conventional narrative and creating his story through fragments. (450w)

F103 Bailey, Hilary. "A Masque for Faking." *Guardian* [London], 29 May 1980: 16.
MS is genuinely anarchic and impressively fertile-minded. A book about books within books, it is a light show of talent and verbal ingenuity that upends conventional fiction. (175w)

F104 Billings, Jim. "Sorrentino's Stew." *Springfield* [MO] *News and Leader*, 25 August 1979.
If GS's purpose in *MS* is to satirize writers in general and avant-garde novelists in particular, he has succeeded in hilarious fashion. (150w)

F105 Bradbury, Malcolm. "Writing Mocking Writing." *New York Times Book Review*, 26 August 1979: 9, 18.
Raising experiment to the level of high intellectual comedy, *MS* deserves unstinting acclaim for its success in displacing the whole idea of perfect literature. Grounded in the conviction that language generates everything—and nothing—GS's neo-Joycean concoction endlessly animates meaning's comic self-contradictions. *MS* both mocks and thrives on language's power to create and deny structures of significance. (600w)
Excerpted: "A Selection of the Best Books of 1979." *New York Times Book Review*, 25 November 1979: 58, and *Contemporary Literary Criticism* 14 (1980): 501.

F106 Braverman, Millicent. "A Word on Books." [radio script, broadcast 12 September 1979 on KFAC-FM, Los Angeles]
A wildly funny modernization of Joyce that will appeal to anyone who revels in the experience of reading, *MS* relentlessly parodies great styles and great masters. (225w)

F107 B[utscher], E[dward]. *Booklist* 75.20 (15 June 1979): 1521.
MS provides howls of pure pleasure by satirizing a literary scene that is forever confusing success with quality. But beneath the comedy lies the bruised heart of a creator. (125w)

F108 Casey, Kevin. *Hibernia* [Dublin], 17 April 1980: 19.
MS is a brilliantly funny stew, with wonderful chunks of pure pastiche. Though GS draws on Joyce and Flann O'Brien, *MS* shows much native talent and originality. (200w)

F109 ———. "Dazzling Melange." *Hibernia* [Dublin], 8 May 1980: 28.
Bookish but never boring, *MS* is an investigation of the nature of the creative process and of the reality and value of fiction. A non-traditional writer, GS deserves the greater attention that *MS* ought to bring him. (800w)

F110 Clark, Jeff. *Library Journal* 104.8 (15 April 1979): 977.
A distinguished addition to contemporary postrealistic fiction, *MS* is an awesomely multistoried verbal construct about a creative mind's paranoid breakdown. (100w)

F111 Cockshutt, Rod. "Slogging Through a Literary Theme Park." *Observer* [Charlotte, NC], 10 June 1979.
MS defies explication. In the very funny microcosmos it creates, the center does not hold, but GS also makes his readers wonder why they even should care whether it does or not. (300w)

F112 Dirda, Michael. "The Far Side of Parodies." *Washington Post Book World*, 17 June 1979: 1, 6.
A dazzling display of linguistic virtuosity and literary parody, *MS* controls its chaos of language through three interrelated narratives that are sustained by S. J. Perelman-like humor and Rabelaisian bawdiness. (1400w) Excerpted: *Contemporary Literary Criticism* 14 (1980): 500.
MS entered among the "Current and Choice," *Washington Post Book World*, 24 June and 1 July 1979.

F113 Edwards, Thomas R. "Feeding on Fantasy." *New York Review of Books* 26.12 (19 July 1979): 41-42, esp. 42.
A wonderful book of literary parody, *MS* merges critical and creative imagination in its comic exploration of language's power to appropriate life. For GS, the predicament that reality is almost wholly constructed of—and disabled by—words is an occasion not for philosophizing but fun. (600w) Excerpted: *Contemporary Literary Criticism* 14 (1980): 500-501.

F114 Entsminger, Gary. "Writing about . . . Writing." *Roanoke* [VA] *Times and World-News*, 10 February 1980: F4.
An exuberant, hilarious novel about the art of writing, *MS* emulates Joyce and Nabokov in its exploration of the artist and the creative process. Parodying most literary styles and genres, *MS* momentarily but successfully penetrates the facade of art. (500w)

F115 Epps, Garrett. *Saturday Review* 6 (26 May 1979): 68-69.
Intended to be the American equivalent of *At Swim-Two-Birds*, *MS* cannot match Flann O'Brien's skill. But GS does possess a painfully clear vision of the petty paranoia of the literary life that is too accurate to be funny. (260w)

F116 Evans, Stuart. *Times* [London], 24 April 1980: 10.
MS is hallucinogenic broth. Though GS is sometimes self-indulgent, his zestful invention, hilarity, and irreverence make *MS* a special book. (350w)

F117 Feinstein, Elaine. *Times* [London], 18 June 1981: 17.
An inordinately clever book, *MS* adopts the manners and modes of avant-garde fiction and fashionable critical theory to both satirize and impress academic readers. This review also treats *AS*. (400w)

F118 Frakes, James R. "A Tasty Literary Bouillabaise That Numbs and Blows the Mind." *Plain Dealer* [Cleveland], 22 July 1979, sec. 4: 18.
A thick stew of parody, puns, literary in-jokes, and every fashionable fictional mode, *MS* attacks the reader from all sides with a pyrotechnical display that threatens to turn into a day of uproarious doom. (425w)

F119 Frank, Katherine. "A Literary Parlor Game or a Serious Novel?" *Miami*

Herald, 19 August 1979: 7E.
A brilliant, eclectic mélange of nearly every conceivable literary genre, *MS* is relentlessly bookish. Though its self-conscious cleverness sometimes verges on silliness, *MS* is finally a glorious celebration of the imagination. (750w)

F120 Gingher, Robert. "Sorrentino!" *Greensboro* [NC] *Daily News*, 15 July 1979: G5.
MS parodies contemporary experimental fiction and satirizes today's publishing industry. Oblivious to commercial formulas, it is unpredictable and daringly inventive, delightfully quickening the imagination despite its self-indulgences and length. (1000w)

F121 Goodspeed, John. *Critics' Place* [television script produced for the Maryland Center for Public Broadcasting, aired 6 September 1979].
Sly, tricky, amusing, occasionally irritating, *MS* is more like late Nabokov than Joyce's *Ulysses*. GS is a first-rate writer, especially of parody. (150w)

F122 Green, Geoffrey. *American Book Review* 2.2 (October 1979): 16.
One of the funniest books of recent years, *MS* recycles established styles, plots, scenes, and characters both to satirize the contemporary literary and publishing worlds and to question the possibility of artistic originality. A literary descendent of Flann O'Brien's *At Swim-Two-Birds*, *MS* is an ingenious self-reflexive novel organized on the principle that we are all referential beings subjectively interacting with a world we only partially understand. By refusing to mold his imagination in the image of reality, GS wrests vital literary art from an imagination otherwise buried in conventional language. (1300w)

F123 Grumbach, Doris. "All the Fictions for a Seasonal Feast." *Washington Post Book World*, 9 December 1979: 1, 8-9, esp. 8.
While judged by some critics to be the year's best book, *MS*—though often very funny—grows tiresome before its end. (40w)

F124 Harmon, Gary L. *Magill's Literary Annual* (1980): 544-49.
A confection of language about a novelist's descent into madness, *MS* places GS among the masters of self-reflexive fiction. Rejecting the mimetic techniques and moral vision advocated by such modernist novelists as John Gardner, GS joins other experimental writers like Ronald Sukenick in redefining the purpose of fiction. In *MS* GS transforms the worlds of middle-America and middle-brow realistic literature into a wholly verbal universe that humorously absorbs the environment we call our own. This is accomplished through a variety of techniques, most notably GS's inventive use of lists. (2700w)

F125 Kamenetz, Rodger. "Stew Be or Not Stew Be." *Sun* [Baltimore], 2 September 1979: D5.
Drawing on the techniques of Joyce and Raymond Queneau, *MS* is a

bitter, hilarious novel that is marred by passages of tortuous boredom. GS's self-indulgence and bitterness are typical—but unnecessary—excesses of the avant-garde novel. GS's allusiveness does, however, evoke a wonderful sense of literature as a collective effort. (600w)

F126 Kast, Rick. "Hall of Mirrors: Writer's Characters Take on Lives of Own." *News Leader* [Richmond, VA], 9 January 1980.
MS is a wacky prose work about the pitfalls, even the impossibility of the modern novel. Reflecting a relative universe where we are reduced to repeated images of ourselves, *MS* is a hall of mirrors within which GS is hilarious, perverse, self-indulgent, and entertaining. (500w)

F127 Kenner, Hugh. "The Traffic in Words: No Place for the Avant-Garde." *Harper's* 258 (June 1979): 83-84, 88-90.
MS is a contour map of the Reading Public that was created by a publishing industry more concerned with profit than the life of the mind. GS's novel, typically American in its reliance on sheer energy instead of style, is also a send-up of the Schlock avant-garde, which is as factitious as the Reading Public created by the economic necessities of mass production. *MS* is subversive in its frank recognition of big-time word-merchandising. (3600w)
Rpt. in *Historical Fictions.* San Francisco: North Point, 1990, 256-65.

F128 Kirby, Martin. *New Orleans Review* 8.1 (Winter 1981): 111-12.
GS is a determinedly avant-garde writer, and *MS* is a hardcore avant-garde work that closely follows that literary school's single-minded commitment to novelty of form. Though the avant-garde's efforts to discover new formal devices are now bankrupt, *MS* is still worth the intelligent reader's time, for GS's sense of the outrageous partly offsets *MS*'s abundance of literary clichés and erudite bookishness. (1200w)

F129 Kisor, Henry. "New and Readable." *Chicago Sun-Times,* 17 June 1979, "Book Week" in "Showcase" sec.
MS is a marvelous stew of literary hijinks. (10w)

F130 ———. "Fiction's 10 Best, 1979: It Was a Year for the Old Pros." *Chicago Sun-Times,* 16 December 1979, "Book Week" in "Showcase" sec.: 15.
A neglected writer more concerned with form than reality, GS has created a gloriously successful stew of literary parodies that pushes language to its hilarious limits. (75w)

This review also appeared as: "A Good Fiction Year, and That's a Fact," *Cleveland Press,* 27 December 1979; "1979: Year of Big Names," *Huntsville* [AL] *Times,* 23 December 1979; "The Year's Best: Men Dominate Fiction," *St. Paul Pioneer Press and Dispatch,* 22 December 1979; and "The 'Ten Best' for 1979 Picked by a Fiction Critic," *Times-Picayune* [New Orleans], 23 December 1979.

F131 Lacy, Allen. "Take One Rejection Slip, Add Water, and Stir: Sorrentino's Fictional Recipe is Highly Seasoned." *Chronicle of Higher Education,*

23 July 1979, "Books & Arts" sec.: R4.
A work of comic genius that illuminates the processes of artistic creation, *MS* is a literary curiosity that fits no standard genre. While GS's droll humor stands in contrast to the ennui of much avant-garde literature, his work nonetheless demands a learned reader with a taste for verbal pyrotechnics. (1050w) Excerpted: "A Packful of 1979's Best Books," *Chronicle of Higher Education*, 7 December 1979, "Books & Arts" sec.: 14, and *Contemporary Literary Criticism* 14 (1980): 501.

F132 Larsen, Ernest. "Colonel Mustard in the Study with the Smith-Corona." *Village Voice*, 28 May 1979: 81.
Exploiting the avant-garde's vapid cliché of the novelist writing a novel, *MS* is a hoax whose overabundance of playfulness exhibits neither wit nor appetite but sheer self-indulgence. Only occasional narrative threads save the reader from despair amid the multiple layers of gamesmanship that void all authenticity. *MS* parodies even the creative process of writing, which it satirically reduces to an egoistic sham. (1450w) Excerpted: *Contemporary Literary Criticism* 14 (1980): 499-500.

F133 Lask, Thomas. "Publishing: Capital Made of Washington Life." *New York Times*, 9 March 1979: C22.
An exacting and severe critic of poetry, GS appears to be taking on the publishing establishment in his forthcoming novel, *MS*. (150w)

F134 Lauzen, Sarah. "Prose: New Characters." *Antioch Review* 38.2 (Spring 1980): 251-54.
A self-proclaimed member of the "Schlock" avant-garde, GS directs *MS*'s satire not only at the publishing industry's commercialism but also at the real travesty of mistaking the fictional world for the natural world. *MS* questions the reality we invest in words. (1300w)

F135 Leader, Zachary. "Irrealist Deconstruction." *Times Literary Supplement*, 2 May 1980: 486.
Derived from Flann O'Brien and postmodernist notions of text production, *MS* is a parody of avant-garde fiction and its familiar conventions. Despite funny passages—especially those springing from GS's uncanny ear for bad writing—the novel is often murderously boring. (1100w)

F136 Leonard, John. *New York Times*, 24 May 1979: C21.
Neither the avant-garde novel nor the New York publishing scene may survive *MS*, which combines parody, complaint, paranoia, and pop-absurdism into a suicide-kit of modernism. Hilariously raging against the packagers and merchandisers of the sensibility as commodity, GS is a writer of extreme and alarming seriousness—both very angry and quite clever. (700w)

This review reprinted in *Books of the Times* 2.5 (July 1979): 244-45, and also appeared as: "A 'Stew' Full of Parody and Rage," *San Francisco Examiner & Chronicle*, 8 July 1979; " 'Mulligan Stew': Recipe Parody of

Modern Fiction," *Herald-Times* [Bloomington, IN], 3 June 1979. Review excerpted: *Contemporary Literary Criticism* 14 (1980): 499.

F137 Lewis, Peter. "The Artiness of Fiction." *Stand* 23.1 (1981): 51-57, esp. 53-54.
A virtuoso exercise in postmodern fictionality, *MS* attempts to deflect criticism of its monstrous inflation and self-indulgence by parodying its own procedures. (330w)

F138 Long, Robert Emmet. "Experimental Novel Turns on its Creator—and Reader." *Christian Science Monitor*, 17 May 1979: 14.
A staggeringly ambitious novel driven by comic exuberance and excess, *MS* is both bawdy and literary, everywhere haunted by the ghosts of such experimental novelists as Joyce and Gide. Verbosity sometimes overpowers technical brilliance. (580w)

F139 Magrinat, Gustave. "Literature as an Inside Joke." *St. Louis Post-Dispatch*, 15 July 1979: 4C.
Though GS's talents are enormous and *MS* is flawlessly organized, this satire on writers and publishers suffers from narrowness of vision. GS refuses to define the difference between authentic and fake writers. He also refuses to extend his literary debunking to the antirealist devices his own work employs. By not parodying this tradition, *MS* leaves out of range most of contemporary literature and reduces itself to a superior academic exercise. (250w)

F140 Maguire, Patrick. "Seven Types of Hilarity." *Literary Review* [Edinburgh] 2.39 (August 1981): 3.
MS takes apart the literary world with hilarious invention and blistering parodic skills. GS's gift for burlesque ruthlessly deflates the overwritten and underimagined as they appear in countless genres. *MS* is sufficiently fine to earn forgiveness for its confessed sin of bookishness. (450w)

F141 Massie, Allan. "A Fate Worse Than Dearth." *Scotsman*, 26 April 1980: 3.
MS is a brilliant, witty exploration of the dilemma of the creative artist who sees his fictional characters assume a life of their own. GS is a fecund master of parody who "can not only write the hind leg off a donkey but sew it on again." (800w)

F142 McDonald, William. "Life Is a Juice." *Lone Star Review* [monthly supplement to *Austin American-Statesman*, *Dallas Times Herald*, and *Houston Chronicle*].
Delicately humorous, awesomely complex, and sometimes brilliant, *MS* may possibly mark the end of the neo-modernist movement in literature begun by Joyce. With its highly self-reflexive techniques emphasizing the difficulty in determining ultimate reality, *MS* both re-creates and parodies the neo-modernist experience of madness and existential despair. As the novel slips on wide-eyed relativity, the reader experiences

not only GS's skill but also the wild, hallucinogenic tremors of a writer's deepest private and professional lusts, anxieties, and schizophrenia. (800w)

F143 McMahan, Allan. "Paperback News." *Journal-Gazette* [Fort Wayne, IN], 17 June 1979.
MS is a collection of literary parodies of such diverse subjects as erotic poetry and astrology charts, written by as many well-known authors. (35w)

F144 Mellors, John. "Star War." *Listener* 103 (22 May 1980): 660-61, esp. 661.
Energetically wielding parody and pastiche, *MS* purveys some large dollops of entertainment. But unfortunately, GS has neither self-discipline nor regard for his audience's discrimination, so that the reader feels conned by much of *MS*'s jokey fantasy. (250w)

F145 Messerli, Douglas. *Washington Review* [Washington, DC], February-March 1980: 28.
Though paying homage to Joyce, *MS* is basically a reaction against the avant-garde tradition and represents a radically different sensibility. Satirizing literary fools incapable of transcending clichés, *MS* is actually closer to Flaubert's *Bouvard et Pecucet:* both are anatomies that dissect and classify cultural reality, exposing the tendency of any society to confuse knowledge and experience with pedantry. *MS* reveals how the abuse of language and the confusion of knowledge with information has made it impossible to distinguish between truth and sham. (600w)

F146 Miner, Tom. *Sacramento Bee*, 17 June 1979.
MS is not a cookbook, though a cookbook would make better reading. (75w)

F147 Moore, Steven. *Review of Contemporary Fiction* 8.2 (Summer 1988): 313.
MS is one of the few truly significant novels of the '70s, required reading for anyone interested in modern literature. (75w) This review also treats *SC*.

F148 Morrison, Blake. "Catholic Dispensations." *Observer*, 27 April 1980: 39.
MS pursues its highly self-conscious and allusive course with typical American excess. Though it is too rambling and diverse to achieve unity, the work wears its postmodernism lightly and offers some hilarious moments. (330w)

F149 Nouryeh, Christopher. *World Literature Today* 54.1 (Winter 1980): 108-9.
MS focuses on the struggle between what reality offers GS and what he tries to make of it, finally arguing that truth in life and truth in a fiction are not identical. A realist who uses the form of life but not its substance, GS presents his audience less with a zesty, exhilarating novel than an intricate book that demands work to read. (550w)

F150 O'Connell, Shaun. "Who Put the Overalls in Mrs. Murphy's Chowder?" *Boston Globe,* 19 August 1979: A9.
While *SW* balances form and function, *MS* offers only formal play. Predicated on the literary cliché that realistic representation is phony, *MS* suffers from serious doubts about the nature and purpose of fiction. GS's insistence that the novel ought neither express the self nor mirror reality damages his talent. (900w)

F151 Olson, Clarence E. "1979, A Vintage Year for Fiction." *St. Louis Post-Dispatch,* 2 December 1979: F1-2, esp. 2.
An amazing display of GS's talent, *MS* is an intricate inside joke about the way fiction is written. (35w)

F152 Pachoda, Elizabeth. *Nation* 229 (29 December 1979): 697.
MS revives the old-fashioned pleasure in the deliberately avant-garde. (20w)

F153 Rudman, Frank. *Spectator* 244 (24 May 1980): 21.
MS is less a novel than an audacious celebration of GS's linguistic and literary inventiveness. (250w)

F154 Saltzman, Arthur M. "'Wordy Tombs.'" *Chicago Review* 31.4 (Spring 1980): 95-99.
A potpourri of literary parody, vaudeville comedy, and the general discharge of an obsessive mind, *MS* is an impressive example of meta-fiction and formal experimentation. Though it will frustrate readers who require verisimilitude, chronological structure, empathy, and other traditional means of entering a novel, *MS* possesses a startling vitality that delights even as it mocks conventional expectations. Greatly indebted to *At Swim-Two-Birds, MS* follows closely the set of rules for fiction that Flann O'Brien prescribes in his self-reflexive novel. Like Joyce, GS is fascinated by the magnitude of life and art's power to reconstitute its details. *MS*'s numerous inventories thus not only represent the dead weight of the cultural past but also record GS's capacity to reinvigorate language. (2250w)

F155 Seymour-Smith, Martin. "On the Ropes." *Financial Times* [London], 12 July 1980: 12.
GS is one of those American writers who say exactly what they want without reference to structure or sense, and *MS* is typical of his unorganized work. (150w)

F156 Somerville-Large, Gillian. "Novels of the Week: Rambling On." *Irish Times,* 10 May 1980.
Never ceasing to be funny and exuberant, *MS* is a huge, rambling novel where fashionable literary styles are imitated and joined together in an intricate patchwork with a brilliant pattern all its own. (450w)

F157 Spearman, Walter. "The Literary Lantern." *Durham* [NC] *Sun*, 4 August 1979: 15A.
A mixture of parody, pornography, and black comedy, *MS* brilliantly and hilariously satirizes contemporary literature and publishing. Though providing an abundance of both mental puzzlement and belly laughs, the novel is also self-indulgent, over-written, and too long. (450w)
Spearman's column also appeared in five other North Carolina newspapers as well as in the *Danville* [VA] *Register.*

F158 Speary, Willard. "A Taste for Parody." *Los Angeles Herald Examiner*, 28 August 1979: B4.
MS is a unique literary hash that GS concocts by parodying—with impeccable taste—nearly all forms of writing, from love letters to baseball scorecards. Constantly mocking the contemporary world, *MS* remains readable because of GS's wit and style. (375w)

F159 Stille, Alexander. "Ulysses Stew." *Soho Weekly News*, 27 September 1979: 61-62.
Though *MS* contains some marvelous comic writing, too often experiment is a mask for self-indulgence. *MS*'s umbrella format includes disparate pieces of writing that allow GS to use his gift for impersonating many voices and his wonderful ear for parody. In contrast to the fun and excitement of these tangential bursts of comic writing are *MS*'s experimental fragments, which are embarrassing and tedious imitations. GS's attempt to write a modernist masterpiece works against the originality of his own talent. (550w)

F160 Strang, Steven. "Sorrentino's Wild and Funny Novel of Avant-Gardism." *Providence* [RI] *Journal*, 1 July 1979: F16.
A major, wildly comic novel, *MS* is a witty examination of contemporary American culture. It parodies the paraphernalia of modern fiction, using the technique of making lists to especially good satiric effect. Though paying extensive homage to such other writers as Joyce and Nabokov, *MS* is finally GS's own work. (550w)

F161 Templeton, Wayne. *West Coast Review* 15.1 (June 1980): 54-57.
Though perhaps intended to be read as a statement against pseudo-innovative fiction, *MS* self-destructs, defeated by its own affectations. The novel's devices for defusing this negative judgment cannot deny GS's ultimate responsibility for all of *MS*'s overly self-indulgent, often immature narrative voices. The most successful portion of *MS* is its least experimental sections. (1750w)

F162 Vincent, Sally. *Punch* 281 (18 November 1981): 926.
A book that forces the reader to work, *MS* seems constructed from bits of text randomly torn from GS's compulsive habit of constant composition. (325w)

F163 Waters, Greg. "'Mulligan Stew'—Tasty Writing Seeking a Cult." *Flint* [MI] *Journal*, 4 November 1979: H4.
An imaginative and remarkable novel that relies on puns, parodies, and put-ons, *MS* tells a story of literary creation and self-destruction in the metanovelistic mode of Kurt Vonnegut, John Barth, and Thomas Pynchon. Despite its strong notes of despair, *MS* is a comedy because of GS's madcap sense of humor. (950w)

F164 Weston, John. [Radio script, broadcast 1 August 1979 on KUSC-FM, Los Angeles.]
A virtuoso performance, *MS* is a farce constructed of a mad cacophony of bits and pieces, from which a novel does eventually emerge. Though proceeding in bursts and starts without any sustained direction, *MS* nonetheless offers a sure intelligence and a finely honed cynicism. GS is best at parody, which is wonderful but often overdone. (700w)

F165 Zochert, Donald. "A Glorious Stew of Literary Hijinks." *Chicago Sun-Times*, 27 May 1979, "Book Week" in "Showcase" sec.: 10.
An inventive, seriocomic writer with an enviable ability to draw desperate laughter out of everyday life, GS is preoccupied with the forms of fiction and the disorder of reality. *MS* is a virtuoso performance, a barroom brawl of thoughts about the anguish and exhilaration of writing, a blunderbuss of literary parodies. Investigating the flip side of the imagination, GS's novel sends up many disparate literary forms, which he somehow makes hang together. (800w)

Aberration of Starlight (1980)

F166 Anon. *Evening Post* [Charleston, SC], 5 December 1980: 5C.
GS's battery of literary devices operates to disclose the complexity of ordinary events in ordinary people's lives. (75w)

F167 ———. *Kirkus Reviews* 48 (1 June 1980): 736.
Another literary-games-playing product similar to GS's other brittle books, *AS* sets up a desperately ordinary story and then deliberately fires the characters flat into pasteboard. By self-consciously jellying itself in cliché, the novel destroys its best and truest aspects. (300w)

F168 ———. *Providence* [RI] *Journal*, 18 January 1981.
Experimental narrative techniques and literary pretentiousness render completely flat a potentially highly provocative story. (120w)

F169 ———. *Publishers Weekly* 217.23 (13 June 1980): 67.
GS's lyrical prose and daring format excite compassionate interest in characters otherwise distinguished by their ugliness, bigotry, and hatreds. (125w)

F170 ——. *Publishers Weekly* 219 (10 April 1981): 68.
AS bares the realities behind its characters' lives. (50w)

F171 [Adams, Phoebe-Lou]. *Atlantic* 246.2 (August 1980): 83.
GS's impressive technical skills are artfully applied to delineate a world where convention thwarts desire. So successfully does GS's brilliant language expose the characters' banality and brutality, that style unfortunately emerges as the novel's only truly engaging element. (250w)
Excerpted: *Contemporary Literary Criticism* 22 (1982): 394.

F172 Balitas, Vincent D. "Faulkner Under Starlight." *America* 144.19 (16 May 1981): 410.
Though basically realistic, *AS* remains quite innovative in its techniques. Effectively conveying a sense of its local setting and time, the novel portrays characters enmeshed in the motion of history who lack any stable sense of identity. GS examines the processes by which we construct fictions that organize daily life. (500w)

F173 Braverman, Millicent. "A Word on Books." [radio script, broadcast 21 May 1981 on KFAC-FM, Los Angeles]
An experimental, innovative novel of real depth and dimension, *AS* proves that literature is more than a story, that it is imagination as delightfully complex as the human mind itself. (225w)

F174 B[rosnahan], J[ohn]. *Booklist* 77.1 (1 September 1980): 34.
GS employs his usual stylistic tricks to transform a conventional story into an extravaganza of wit and contradiction that remains, however, under his inventive control. (90w)

F175 Campbell, McCoy C. "Compassionate Story of Four Lost Souls." *Chattanooga* [TN] *Times*, 30 August 1980: B4.
GS's unique narrative approach lays bare the secret fantasy worlds of his characters and compassionately exposes the futility of their efforts to escape the intolerable loneliness of reality. Though some sequences are almost pornographic, GS's stylistic skill lends them literary merit. (300w)

F176 Carpenter, Lucas. "A Subtle Craftsman's Evocation of the 1930s." *Newsday* [Melville, NY], 10 August 1980, Ideas sec.: 20.
An imaginative experimentalist free from avant-garde obscurantism and intellectual self-indulgence, GS typically meshes innovative techniques with unlikely subjects to produce novels at once comic and mysterious. A subtly crafted work, *AS* shows GS at his best, creating an illusion of the absolute essence of life. (600w)

F177 Clark, Jeff. *Library Journal* 105.18 (15 October 1980): 2234-35.
Composed with incisive detail, *AS* is profoundly moving. GS is one of our best writers, and in this novel he is at the top of his form. (100w)

F178 Cole, William. "Citronella Summer." *Prime Time* 1.9 (September 1980): 81.
Less wild and experimental than *MS*, *AS* is a milder, more likable novel, distinguished by the accuracy of its historical re-creation and the simplicity of its characters. (300w)

F179 Davenport, Guy. "In Late Eclectic Modern." *New York Times Book Review*, 10 August 1980: 15.
A fashionable study in nostalgia that beautifully re-creates the tone of Depression America, *AS* also exemplifies GS's stylistic boldness, which resides in his frank borrowing of techniques from such innovative writers as Joyce, Flann O'Brien, and E. L. Doctorow. Though *AS*'s plot is a tacky love story and its characters hardly more than stereotypes, GS refreshes this conventional material through the rigor of his modernity. GS is that rare exception in experimental writing, an author free of pretension and dullness. (750w) Excerpted: "Notable Books of the Year." *New York Times Book Review*, 30 November 1980: 38; "Paperbacks: New and Noteworthy." *New York Times Book Review*, 31 May 1981: 55; *Contemporary Literary Criticism* 22 (1982): 394.

F180 DeMarco, Charles. *Best Sellers* 40.8 (November 1980): 278.
AS's disorienting techniques and clichéd plot interfere with the reader's sympathy for the characters GS otherwise labors mightily to enliven. This confusing experimentalism is needlessly complicated, for it only serves to enforce the overworked principle that every human being's perception is different. (250w)

F181 Dirda, Michael. "Sorrentino's 'Starlight' Is a Many-faceted 'Rashomon.' " *Plain Dealer* [Cleveland], 31 August 1980: 8C.
Quieter than *MS*'s send-up of the contemporary literary world, *AS* returns to the character sketches of *SW* and *IQAT*. The novel's interest lies not in its banal plot but the technique of its telling. Mad about elaborate narrative structures, GS exercises his modernist style to elevate this family romance into a tale about terrible loneliness. (750w)

F182 Donovan, Laurence. "Keeping Modernism Alive and Well." *Miami Herald*, 5 October 1980: 7E.
A gentle spin-off from the Joycean mayhem of *MS*, *AS* is a sad, yet joyously comic novel that captures the quotidian world of ordinary people without any elitist deflection. Though its simple tale is told in unrelentingly banal language that hovers on parody, GS's use of cliché finally transcends satire to reveal humans tragically imprisoned by their own inarticulateness. Though his characters are enfeebled by verbal convention, GS's narrative structure demonstrates the mystery of their lives and leaves GS in contention as the major fabulist of the 1970s. (950w)

F183 Dowell, Coleman. " 'Starlight': Laughter and Brilliance." *Courier-Journal* [Louisville], 31 August 1980: D5.

AS is a book of great loveliness, strength, and brilliance. Its laughter is earth-size, in contrast to *MS*'s cosmic and cruel humor. *AS*'s genius lies in its endlessly inventive narration. Telling and retelling a simple plot, it reveals the lives of its central characters to be funny and shameful and shocking and piteous, often all at the same time. This is quite peculiar for GS, who is the practitioner nonpareil of literature that constantly keeps the reader aware of writing qua writing. (850w)

F184 Dybek, Stuart. "A Lucid Modernist Wields a Pen of Acid." *Detroit News*, 24 August 1980, "Lively Arts" sec.: 2F.
AS demonstrates GS's special ability to blend modernist techniques with clarity, humor, and anger at the meanness of human affairs. The novel's richness resides not in its simple plot but in its theme-and-variation approach to narrative structure as well as in its resonant language. The flow of slang, cliché, and other pulp verbiage is especially important, for it turns language into landscape and reveals how words fuel the repression that dominates the characters' lives. (750w)

F185 Ely, Hank. "Sorrentino Novel Is Impressive: Disparity of Perspectives Equals Power and Insight." *Winston-Salem* [NC] *Journal*, 31 August 1980.
GS's strategy of refracting a simple plot through complex narrative techniques enables *AS* to probe the disparate nature of its characters fully. The result combines the pleasures of writing skills and a powerful story into an exceptional novel. (400w)

F186 Entsminger, Gary. "A Round-Robin of a Tale of 1939." *Roanoke* [VA] *Times and World-News*, 7 December 1980.
AS concerns itself with the reliability and relativity of perception. Though GS is very sensitive to language and its intellectual implications, his characters are driven only by emotions. This discrepancy between GS's omniscient narrative voice and his characters' limited perspectives governs *AS*. (600w)

F187 Epps, Carrett. "Book Bricfs." *Saturday Review* 7 (August 1980): 62.
In contrast to the overstuffed, aggressively avant-garde *MS*, *AS* is a tightly focused novel about the spiritual devastation of life's compromises. *AS* does, however, retain GS's characteristic formal pyrotechnics as well as his unsentimental compassion for the self-deceptive daydreams of ordinary Americans. (275w)

A condensed version of this review appeared in the column, "SR Recommends," *Saturday Review* 7 (September 1980): 107. Review excerpted: *Contemporary Literary Criticism* 22 (1982): 394.

F188 Evans, Stuart. *Times* [London], 24 June 1982: 10.
A splendid technical achievement as well as a very moving story, *AS* possesses a superb structure, writing that is supple, subtle, and precise, and characters who are infuriatingly credible and human. (250w)

F189 Feinstein, Elaine. *Times* [London], 18 June 1981: 17.
AS is similar in its collage technique to *MS* but with greater narrative drive. It rises to tragic heights in the consciousness of the repressive father, in whose warped, deprived, and xenophobic spirit the whole filthy waste of the American Depression is focused. This review also treats *MS.* (300w)

F190 Flower, Dean. "Fiction Chronicle." *Hudson Review* 34.1 (Spring 1981): [105]-116, esp. 106-7.
Despite the excessive artiness GS derives from Joyce, *AS* succeeds quite wonderfully at the level of documentary and psychological realism. (190w)

F191 Gerchick, Ruth. "Novelist Turns Cliché into Poetry." *Scarsdale* [NY] *Inquirer,* 18 September 1980: 7.
AS succeeds in engaging readers in the trivial lives of ordinary people through its skillful revelation of character. Purposefully composed of clichés, the novel also transforms its overused popular vocabulary into poetry. (450w)

F192 Gray, Francine du Plessix. *Commonweal* 107 (5 December 1980): 696-97.
Unlike *MS*'s didactic commitment to postmodernist techniques, *AS* vibrates with a precise rendition of the social reality of working-class Americans. The marvelous tension between the prosaic facts of GS's plot and the pyrotechnics of his style makes *AS* a masterpiece of current fiction. (180w)

F193 Greenwell, Bill. "Novels for Contortionists." *New Statesman* 102 (17 July 1981): 21-22, esp. 21.
GS is a formalist hell-bent on experiment. In *AS* he merges the raw realism of James M. Cain with the fantasy of Robert Coover but retains the virtues of neither. GS's technical somersaults exceed his subject matter. (375w)

F194 Hall, Joan Joffe. "Desire, Fantasy, Hypocrisy in 'A Little Masterpiece.'" *Houston Post,* 31 August 1980: 15AA.
A little masterpiece about sexual desire, fantasy, and hypocrisy, *AS* owes much to Joyce but never allows its characters to become ponderous or symbolic. GS's experimental style is seldom distracting. (300w)

F195 Harmon, Gary L. *Magill's Literary Annual* (1981): 1-4.
Rejecting the conventions and wisdom of realistic fiction, *AS* continues GS's efforts to create a separate world that dominates the imagination like life itself. Beginning with a cliché from popular romance novels, GS deftly accumulates thousands of fascinating, superficial details to reveal the complex humanity of four ordinary characters. Though the world *AS* discloses is soured by suffering and loneliness, GS succeeds in couching these hard truths in a sparkling range of entertaining scenes and language. (2100w)

F196 Harris, Roger. "Star Quality." *Star Ledger* [Newark, NJ], 14 September 1980.
Contrary to GS's avant-gardist reputation, *AS* is an extremely good but thoroughly old-fashioned, realistic novel. (200w)

F197 Higgins, Fitzgerald. *Grand Rapids* [MI] *Press*, 7 September 1980.
Uniting sympathetic insight and technical virtuosity into a rich and moving novel, *AS* focuses on the distortion of human relations caused by people's imprisonment in their own and each others' desires. *AS*'s method employs highly conventionalized, even hackneyed language, to create a montage at once fantastic and ordinary that closely parallels the commonplace lives of the novel's characters. (400w)

F198 Jarecke, George W. "Seven Contemporary Novels—A Review Essay." *Southern Humanities Review* 16.2 (Spring 1982): 155-64, esp. 159-60.
AS's completely believable characters earn the reader's total sympathy. But GS's self-conscious use of modernist devices, especially the catechism borrowed from Joyce, distracts attention from his careful depiction of an era and a people. (350w)

F199 Kline, Betsy. "Rounding Out Your Holiday Gift List." *Kansas City Star*, 14 December 1980.
AS tells a story in which love is always distorted by sour motives. (20w)

F200 Koenig, Rhoda. "The Book Bag: Paperbacks for a Season in the Sun." *New York*, 6-13 July 1981: 88-89.
AS is a giddy, funny, sexy, not-quite-love story. (100w)

F201 Labberton, Melissa. "Sorrentino Uses a Variety of Literary Devices to Create His Characters." *Seattle Times*, 28 December 1980.
GS is more stylist than storyteller. A literary exercise that fails to truly tax his talents, *AS* is about human needs and the distortions in perception they cause. GS's narrative method makes the novel like a puzzle, in which the pieces make sense only at the end. (550w)

F202 Lauzen, Sarah E. "The Quiddity at the Breakfast Table." *New York Arts Journal* 22 (1981): 18-19.
A self-appointed modernist watchdog who continually questions the reality we invest in words, GS has devoted himself to maintaining standards for the self-reflexive novel. While *AS* is a modular text whose expressive form fully communicates GS's central theme, the novel also shifts our perception of modernism by incorporating once experimental techniques into the standard practice of character and event. This anti-nostalgic Depression story finally remains memorable less for its plot than its exercise of technique, especially the controlling narrative voice which disrupts any illusion of simple representation. (2500w)

F203 LeClair, Thomas. *New Republic* 183 (30 August 1980): 34-35.

Muting the ironic voice and stylistic invention of *MS*, *AS* is an anachronism in GS's career. Scrupulously limited to the words and thoughts of common people, the novel achieves a depth of emotional participation new to GS's work. *AS* exposes its characters as victims of both the banality of conventionalized language and of the petty cruelty of religious piety. A disciplined novel, *AS* may be GS's best, but it nonetheless fails to engage his talents fully. (950w)

F204 Lodge, David. "The Sad Heart at the Carnival." *Times Literary Supplement*, 10 July 1981: 774.
While *MS* successfully "carnivalized" literary conventions in a postmodernist mode, *AS* retreats to the early modernist preoccupation with the unsharable nature of experience. Though GS's shifting of narrative discourses foregrounds form, *AS* is only superficially experimental and remains essentially a sentimental story about thwarted desire. Unlike Joyce's practice in *Ulysses*, GS's use of debased rhetorical manners is not stylized but mimetic, causing the reader only embarrassment and lowering his spirits. (1500w)

Two letters, responding to Lodge's review and commenting on *AS*'s setting, were published in the *Times Literary Supplement:* 14 August 1981: 934; 11 September 1981: 1037.

F205 Logan, William. "Experiments in Terror, Isolation, Self-Delusion." *Chicago Tribune Book World*, 28 September 1980: 6.
Though a witty evocation of the sexual desires of its characters, *AS* is too superficial to support GS's formal experiments. GS believes too strongly in the organizing power of these narrative strategies, which he applies too cooly and mechanically to his banal subject matter. (275w)

F206 McInerney, Jay. "Jersey Rashomon." *Village Voice*, 24-30 September 1980: 41-42.
AS integrates the metafictional play of *MS* with the gritty realism of *SW*. This tension between postmodernist devices and the documentary urge generates powerful insight into the brave beauty of characters caught in the fierce mechanism of fate. GS's historically specific language effectively captures their late-Depression purgatory, in which clichés seem the only defense against frustration. *AS* is a funny, bitter, wistful poem of endurance. (450w)

F207 Mellors, John. "Holiday Homes." *Listener* 106 (30 July 1981): 89.
Though displaying GS's usual technical virtuosity, *AS* stresses competence at the expense of experimentalism. The novel successfully depicts sexual tensions, but the rigid repetition of its narrative pattern ultimately renders *AS* too predictable. (400w)

F208 Montrose, David. *New Statesman* 104 (6 August 1982): 24.
By recounting the same events from different perspectives, GS takes the reader inside his characters' heads to reveal their motivations. (60w)

F209 Morse, John. "Gilbert Sorrentino's *Aberration of Starlight.*" *Chicago Review* 32.2 (Autumn 1980): 112-14.
Disciplined and decorous in comparison with *MS*'s wild lampooning of literary convention, *AS* initially appears to be an example of traditional realism. But the deliberate banality of GS's characters prevents sustained interest at this level; rather what engages the reader's attention is the novel's formal challenge, GS's strictly structured rehearsal of the disparate elements of the modernist style. In fact, GS reverses the expectation that stylistic innovations should serve plot and instead uses the traditional story to clarify the strengths and weaknesses of experimental techniques. But these modernist ploys are as dated and clichéd as his characters, suggesting that in both subject matter and style *AS* is an exercise in amused nostalgia, a gentle requiem for both social and literary manners. (2200w) Excerpted: *Contemporary Literary Criticism* 22 (1982): 395-96.

F210 Murphy, Marese. "Novels of the Week: Conundrums." *Irish Times,* 12 June 1982: 12.
With an easy prose style, *AS* is cogently designed and compelling in its sad insight. (200w) Also reviews *CV.*

F211 Nesbitt, W. J. "Lyrical Love." *Northern Echo* [Darlington, England], 26 June 1981.
Using techniques that derive from the Irish tradition of the novel, *AS* creates a powerful sense of actuality and despair. (150w)

F212 Nye, Robert. "Moorcock's Progress: New Fiction." *Guardian* [London], 2 July 1981: 14.
Underneath its surface of avant-garde tricks, *AS* is a pretty banal book. GS's furious modernism cannot conceal his simple lack of imagination. (90w)

F213 O'Brien, John. "Sorrentino: The Illusions of the 1930s." *Chicago Sun-Times,* 3 August 1980, "Book Week" in "Showcase" sec.: 13.
Exposing the romantic illusions of Depression America, *AS* is a brilliant novel that compassionately depicts the unglamorous dimension of human loss. *AS*'s richly complex insights into the inconsistencies and contradictions of its characters stem from GS's highly structured narrative, which rotates four different styles through closely parallel techniques. (500w)

F214 O[krent], N[eil]. *West Coast Review of Books* 6.6 (November 1980): 37.
Disjunctive narrative style distracts from graphically erotic scenes that are intended to enliven this otherwise conventional family saga. (300w)

F215 O'Leary, Theodore M. "Novel Studies Minutes of Truth Frozen in Time." *Kansas City Star,* 17 August 1980.
AS provides insight into the insecurities, fears, and lusts of its characters through the narrative's circular view of events. But except for the experimental devices employed to achieve these shifting perspectives, *AS* is not

avant-garde but rather a realistic portrayal of mainstream human conduct. (650w)

F216 Ratner, Rochelle. "Points of View." *Soho News* [NY], 27 August 1980: 13.
An experimental novel predicated on characterization as the basis of fiction, *AS* bridges the gap between avant-garde and traditional narrative. But while GS successfully reveals the loneliness of his characters and perfectly captures their language, *AS* nonetheless suffers from an absence of external action, which threatens most readers' interest. (625w)

F217 Rubins, Josh. "Balancing Act." *New York Review of Books*, 18 December 1980: 63-64.
After *SW* and *IQAT* shrewdly subverted the conventions of the novel and *MS* repudiated the genre's very premises, *AS* appears to be a reversion to traditional narrative in which GS self-indulgently overwhelms his sad, simple tale with experimental literary devices. But in fact, *AS* is a complex balancing act. The novel's terminally hip authorial persona is the book's central figure and proves to be as much a victim of shackling circumstances as the characters whose story he tells. The risks GS takes are, perhaps, too great for his fragile story, but the attempt is insidiously affecting. (1800w) Excerpted: *Contemporary Literary Criticism* 22 (1982): 396-97.

F218 Sage, Lorna. "The Cold Breath of Autumn." *Observer*, 30 August 1981: 20.
Emulating Flann O'Brien's sentimental side, *AS* is a comparatively cosy novel that turns the acrobatics of the antinovel into parlor games. (150w)

F219 Scambray, Kenneth. "Recent Publications on 'Matters Italian.'" *Italo-Americano* [Los Angeles], 23 July 1981: 12.
Bringing together Irish and Italian Catholic cultures, *AS* dramatizes the fading of traditional values that once bound families together. The furious pace and lack of chronology in GS's narrative technique parallels his characters' lack of moral equilibrium. (300w)

F220 Sebak, Richard. "Details Give Book Life." *State* [Columbia, SC], 21 September 1980: 12B.
What truly distinguishes *AS* is neither its flashy techniques nor multiplicity of points of view but GS's wonderful ability to distill potent images. (425w)

F221 Seib, Philip. "There Is No Sameness in the Works of Sorrentino." *Dallas Times Herald*, 3 August 1980: 4G.
GS is not satisfied with the novel's conventional format. In *AS* he rejects straightforward narrative for a mixture of styles that expresses the imprecision of his characters' lives. The great strength of GS's writing is evidenced by the interest *AS* generates in the novel's essentially unattractive characters. (650w)

F222 Smith, Cassandra L. "A Textual Variant." *Los Angeles Herald Examiner*, 7 September 1980: F5-F6.
AS vibrates with imagination and virtuosity as GS employs a variety of avant-garde literary devices to reveal the humanity lurking behind his central characters. With its lyrical prose radiating with magic, *AS* is the kind of masterpiece of style and impeccable rhythm that is only evoked by a true artist. (525w)

F223 Solomon, Carl. *American Book Review* 3.2 (January-February 1981): 5.
AS is a pleasantly nostalgic reconstruction of American ethnic types, whose behavior is governed by clichés, shallow religion, steamy sex, and anti-Semitism. Though GS's language anachronistically mixes diction from different historical eras and his accounts of sex scenes lack subtlety, the descriptions of nature are lyrical. (600w)

F224 Somerville-Large, Gillian. "Novels of the Week: Stew Again?" *Irish Times*, 11 July 1981: 13.
In *AS* GS continues the parody of Joycean techniques that he began in *MS*. Though some critics might object that this is repetitive and that GS should develop his own style, Joyce's method remains vital and GS uses it very successfully. [The review is written as a mock interview.] (300w)

F225 Starn, Frances. "Moving Melodrama of American Life." *Independent and Gazette* [CA], 14 September 1980, Sunday Magazine sec.: 26.
AS performs the most difficult trick of novel writing, the successful grafting of a moving story onto an artificial framework so that depth and integrity are achieved and gimmickry avoided. Thematically concerned with the grim realities of family life, *AS* captures the flavor of working-class Brooklyn. (325w)

F226 Steensma, Robert C. "Marginal People." *Chronicles of Culture* (March-April 1981): 16-17, esp. 17.
A formless, tasteless antinovel about the sexual hangups of spiritually marginal people, *AS* is pretentious as fiction and bankrupt as moral statement. Its trendy literary horseplay serves only to satirize characters of no intrinsic interest or use. (600w)

F227 Stokes, Geoffrey. "Remainderama." *Village Voice Literary Supplement* 32 (February 1985): 19.
A delicate work, *AS* is GS's most sustained conventional novel. (20w)

F228 Toppman, Lawrence. *News* [Charlotte, NC].
AS's changing points of view recall Faulkner's technique in *The Sound and the Fury*. As *AS* progresses, the narrators stand forth but the events recede from sight. Each perspective is true to the character who narrates it, and that makes the people true to the reader. (200w)

F229 Wellejus, Ed. "Bookshelf." *Erie* [PA] *Times-News*, 23 November 1980.

AS is a compassionate and delightful novel about the torments and pleasures of family, romance, and sex. (75w)

F230 West, Michael. "The Old Artificer Is Up to His Flashy Tricks Again." *Sun* [Baltimore], 21 September 1980: D5.
A wizard in wordcraft who is committed to experimental techniques, GS subordinates the tale to its telling in *AS*. Though a well-made, rational, even dazzling book, *AS* rarely comes to life because of GS's emphasis on hi-tech style. (500w)

F231 West, Paul. "Charting the Course of Star-Crossed Lovers." *Washington Post Book World*, 31 August 1980: 4.
An ungratifying tease, *AS* involves the procrastinated seduction of a banal woman by a bore. GS chooses to document these lives on their own terms, instead of imaginatively articulating them through a more sensitive narrative voice. Because of this willful ventriloquism, *AS* is a lazy book that demonstrates how empty American realism has become. (800w) Excerpted: *Contemporary Literary Criticism* 22 (1982): 394-95.

F232 Wheeler, Elizabeth. "A Moment in Human Time Made Tender, True." *Los Angeles Times Book Review*, 14 September 1980: 4.
Though its narrative method may seem cute and contrived, *AS* successfully transforms an obvious emotional situation into a novel that is funny and poignant, tender and sad. It shows how good intentions create meanness. (675w)

F233 Wood, Steve. *Tulsa World*, 16 November 1980: F5.
AS has a broader appeal than *MS* because it is highly readable and stable. Though GS's style at first seems merely an imitation of Joyce, as *AS* develops, the style becomes a sincere attempt to tell a story and create characters. (250w)

F234 Zamora, Lois Parkinson. "Sorrentino: Goodbye Newtonian Stability." *Houston Chronicle*, 12 October 1980, "Zest" sec.: 17.
Though GS is a literary iconoclast who abandons narrative stability for the dislocations of multiple points of view, *AS*'s true strengths lie in those traditional elements of interesting characters and effective settings. While many of GS's experimental techniques are self-indulgent, sometimes they enhance the reader's insight into life. (725w)

Crystal Vision (1981)

F235 Anon. *Kirkus Reviews* 49 (15 September 1981): 1176.
A companion-piece to *SW*, *CV* is a fluorescent, subtle book whose comedy is wonderfully broad. Always an irrepressible vaudevillian, GS also strives to reach beyond high modernist entertainment to produce literary correctives. Underlying *CV*'s laughs is a closely woven examination of the nature of symbols and illusion. (425w)

F236 ———. *Publishers Weekly* 220.17 (23 October 1981): 47.
CV's characters and their stories are neither compelling nor comic, their voices all absorbed in GS's monochromatic tone. (150w) Excerpted: *Publishers Weekly* 222.16 (15 October 1982): 64.

F237 ———. "Notes on Current Books." *Virginia Quarterly Review* 58.2 (Spring 1982): 43-63, esp. 53-54.
A cross between Studs Terkel and John Barth, GS is a major novelist whose *CV* seeks to realize the unrealized potential of its characters by transforming their neighborhood myths into art. (125w)

F238 Anderson, Roger K. "Sorrentino: Humanity Writ Small." *Houston Chronicle,* 18 April 1982, "Zest" sec.: 21.
Though uneven, *CV* is a small tour de force that takes life to be largely imagination and is unwilling to grant either linear time or Newtonian physics. Always partly about language and its limit, *CV* reads as if Salinger had written Hubert Selby's *Last Exit to Brooklyn.* (750w)

F239 Askins, John. " 'Crystal Vision' Is Clearly Different." *San Jose Mercury News,* 17 January 1982, "Tab" sec.: 16.
Refusing the well-wrought plot and memorable characterization of popular novels, *CV* deals in ideas and is oblique, teasing, and elusive. Though *CV* is a game GS plays against traditional fiction, the book, unlike most experimental work, is pleasurable reading. (500w)

F240 Bartlett, Jeffrey. *San Francisco Review of Books* 6.10 (January 1982): 11.
CV is GS's most extreme study of the human need to invent through language a fantasy life that compensates for the brutal tedium of daily life. With no plot and little narration, *CV* revives many characters from *SW* as it exposes the illusions we live by while also, rather sadly, accepting their necessity. GS is an experimental writer who refuses easy answers, and in *CV* he clearly affirms the flickering light imagination casts against the darkness of existence. (900w)

F241 B[rosnahan], J[ohn]. *Booklist* 78.6 (15 November 1981): 427.
CV uses dialogue perfectly located in time and place to recreate New York street life. (75w)

F242 Buckley, John. *Saturday Review* 8 (November 1981): 78.
A high-strung, hilarious comic romp, *CV* is a plotless, though poignant, grab bag of stories that reveals the characters' sources of misery. Though a secondary project for GS, *CV* is a remarkable achievement. (200w)

F243 B[yrne] J[ack]. *Review of Contemporary Fiction* 2.1 (Spring 1982): 186-87.
CV takes twenty-five of its characters directly from *SW*, but each has been completely metamorphosed. Thus, *CV* is not a sequel to *SW* but a further development of the fictionality of GS's characters, all of whom are endowed with the tools necessary for survival in the literary world. This

world, GS suggests, is parallel to Dante's Limbo, existing at the outskirts of both Heaven and Hell. (500w) Excerpted: *Contemporary Literary Criticism* 40 (1986): 386-87.

F244 Clark, Jeff. *Library Journal* 106.10 (15 November 1981): 2253-54.
CV is a hilarious novel that paradoxically both demolishes story and captures a moving perception of "real life." (120w)

F245 Cody, Fred. "A Joycean Flow in a Candy Store." *San Francisco Chronicle Review*, 29 November 1981: 12.
A marvelous mixture of slapstick and the sublime, *CV* is GS's defiant paean to the human spirit, celebrating its stubborn resilience in his own razzle-dazzle style. This empathy for his characters lends a new dimension to GS's linguistic extravagance and ransacking of American mass culture. (500w)

F246 Cryer, Dan. "When the Cheering Stops: Good Writers, Bad Novels." *Newsday* [Melville, NY], 20 December 1981, "Ideas" sec.: 20.
An exuberantly experimental novelist committed to exploring American culture, GS fails in *CV* to match *AS*'s achievement. In *CV* GS is so enamored of his own verbal skills that he forgets to tell a story. Though GS has been successful in teasing conventional formulations, in *CV* his virtuoso abilities only call attention to themselves. (500w)

This review also appeared as: "A Cloudy 'Vision' and a Pretentious 'Poppa,'" *News American* [Baltimore], 3 January 1982.

F247 Cunningham, Valentine. "Cock-and-Bull Storytelling in Hell." *Times Literary Supplement*, 4 December 1981: 1420.
CV sustains GS's tribute to the Anglo-Irish word-mongering giants Joyce, Beckett, and Flann O'Brien, not only by its allusions to their work but also by its nonstop storytelling. But these magical tales built on precedent fictions prove to be not delightful glosses on experience but lies that betray both the tellers and their audience. As dreams are disillusioned and playfulness becomes sinister, *CV* discloses a hellish world where all is make-believe, completely empty for endlessly echoing styles. (1825w)

A letter by Louis Mackey comments on Cunningham's review: *Times Literary Supplement*, 22 January 1982: 81.

F248 Donovan, Dianne C. *Midwest Book Review* [television script, broadcast on WYOU, Madison, Wisconsin].
Readers seeking a straightforward novel with a clear plot will be disappointed by *CV*'s rambling dialogue, changeable characters, and shifting scenes, but others who appreciate experimental writings and works reflecting the tone and depth of New York will be pleased. (150w)

F249 Donovan, Laurence. "Candy Visions Spun from Whole Cloth." *Miami Herald*, 17 January 1982: 7E.
CV displays not only GS's perfect ear for American banter, with its subversive humor and clichéd sentimentality, but also his artistic roots in

Joyce, Beckett, and Flann O'Brien. As *CV*'s time, place, and characters shift mysteriously, GS's irrepressible voice and his use of tarot symbolism lend unity to the novel. Despite its pleasures, *CV* leads ultimately to a gloomy appraisal of its characters' fates. (750w)

F250 Eisen, Eugen. "Art Spawned by the New Criticism." *Los Angeles Herald Examiner*, 10 January 1982: 6F.
Making no pretense to imitate reality, *CV* is a fiction about the making of fiction, a self-reflecting artifact. Though nothing happens in *CV* aside from the characters' conversations, the world GS creates, while unconventionally designed, is nonetheless shaped and meaningful. (300w)

F251 Evans, Stuart. *Times* [London], 24 June 1982: 10.
CV consists of a large cast of characters who participate in, edit, re-form, and argue about each other's lives, fictions, and fantasies. This elaborate mosaic, though it sounds anarchic and self-indulgent, possesses an intricate beauty, from which emerge both a coherent picture of humble urban people and a sardonic commentary on the fictionalist's craft. (250w)

F252 Feld, Ross. "The Year in Books." *Nation* 233 (26 December 1981): 712-14, esp. 712.
An elegantly orchestrated performance of fictional displacement, *CV* subverts metaphor and symbol beyond academic criticism's powers of retrieval. (50w)

F253 Gurewitsch, Matthew. "Kaleidoscopic Voices." *St. Louis Post-Dispatch*, 24 January 1982: 4F.
Offering neither plot nor character, *CV* instead consists of sharp, pointed, precise apparitions that collectively convey an overwhelming sense of the vanity of human endeavor. Unfortunately, the clarity of the parts only heightens the vagueness of the whole, which never achieves any stable order. (500w)

F254 Kart, Larry. "Candy Store Turned into an Inferno." *Chicago Tribune Book World*, 14 February 1982: 6.
A fiction of extreme density and strength, *CV* repays its extraordinary demands on the reader's attention with corresponding rewards. Reanimating the Brooklyn world of *SW*, *CV* precisely charts the spiritual death that occurs when the imagination tries and fails to meet the world. Though GS's rage may strike the average reader as sheer crankiness, it is the source of his power and endows *CV* with absolute value. (750w)

F255 LeClair, Thomas. "Street Corner Society: Voices from a Brooklyn Boyhood." *Washington Post Book World*, 20 December 1981: 6, 8.
In *CV* GS is a comic anthropologist, using the risky methods of experimental fiction to unearth the oral culture of presuburban Brooklyn. Displacing plot with anecdote, *CV* treats characters not as bourgeois personalities but as composites of street-corner civilization. Breaking

from the high literariness of *MS*, this ethnic experimentalism gives up the middle ground of probability to join the extremes of versisimilitude and artifice. (850w) Excerpted: *Contemporary Literary Criticism* 40 (1986): 384-85.

F256 Lee, Hermione. "At Spaghetti Junction." *Observer*, 30 May 1982: 31.
Teetering between magical success and pratfalls, *CV* dramatizes America's loss of pastoral innocence while also brilliantly subverting realistic fiction. GS's passion for the thingness of things redeems his art's tiresome self-absorption. (230w)

F257 Murphy, Marese. "Novels of the Week: Conundrums." *Irish Times*, 12 June 1982: 12.
The rambler in GS dominates *CV*, which quickly exhausts patience with its tediously meandering conversations among bizarre characters. (75w) Also reviews *AS*.

F258 Nesbitt, W. J. "The Crystal Set of Drinkers and Loafers." *Northern Echo* [Darlington, England], 28 May 1982.
While *AS* uses conventional narrative techniques to create a powerful sense of despair and actuality, *CV* consists entirely of fragments of talk, which are, however, lively and inventive. (125w)

F259 O'Brien, John. "Sorrentino's Newest Novel Demystifies the Mysterious Tarot." *Chicago Sun-Times*, 20 December 1981, "Book Week" in "Showcase" sec.: 30.
CV transforms the characters of *SW*, dropping them into a landscape constructed by literalizing the imagery of the tarot deck. Lacking both plot and setting, *CV* concentrates on language, its wacky dialogue setting the novel loose from the familiar world, while yet strangely echoing it. A genius whose work cannot be imitated, GS creates in *CV* a world that is both profoundly comic and pathetic. (750w)

This review also appeared as: "A Comic Genius Plays Around with the Tarot," *Honolulu Star Bulletin & Advertiser*, 17 January 1982.

F260 O'Hara, J. D. "Coteries and Poetries." *Nation* 234 (2-9 January 1982): 20-21.
GS continues to go his own way, independent of the 1960s literary coteries that he was associated with. *CV* itself gestures toward new directions in GS's fiction. The novel is consistent with the methods of his earlier works, including flat characters, borrowed and arbitrary forms, compulsive sex scenes, and self-conscious criticism. But *CV* also patronizes its characters instead of sneering at them and introduces as well a new sentimentalized nostalgia. (1200w) This review also treats *SP*. Excerpted: *Contemporary Literary Criticism* 40 (1986): 385-86.

F260a Pastore, Judith. *VIA: Voices in Italian Americana* 1 (Spring 1990): 178-79.
CV restructures the novel, mixing realism, fabliaux, and fantasy in a post-

modern mélange that problematizes character, plot, setting, and time. Despite its playful tricks and street-corner humor, *CV* is a Dantesque vision of the modern damned, evoking great sadness for its lost souls. (550w)

F261 Pritchard, William H. "Novel Discomforts and Delights." *Hudson Review* 35.1 (Spring 1982): 159-76, esp. 166.
GS's characteristic refusal of character and plot is unrelieved by any humor in *CV*, which is a real dud compared to his earlier novels. (120w)

F262 Reefer, Mary M. "Chips of Literary Brilliance Form Obscure Mosaic." *Kansas City Star*, 27 December 1981: 12F.
Living in a void reminiscent of Beckett's *Waiting for Godot*, the characters in *CV* talk in clichés and non sequiturs, their conversations nonsensically parodying pseudo-intellectuals and academics. Though some of *CV*'s highly polished chapters are very funny, even GS's brilliant writing cannot compensate for the novel's lack of focus and coherence. (850w)

F263 Saari, Jon. "Put Gilbert Sorrentino at the Top of the List." *Cincinnati Enquirer*, 14 February 1982: 1-11.
Uncorrupted by commercialism, GS is an original voice of contemporary American fiction who never repeats himself. While *AS* had stopped time to freeze an image of human frailty forever, *CV* abolishes the illusion of time. A fictional contradiction built on the marriage of street-corner wise guys and bookworms, *CV* re-establishes the oral tradition in American literature. (750w)

F264 Sabatini, Arthur J. "The Vision, Alas, Is Diffused." *Philadelphia Inquirer*, 19 December 1981: 6-A.
Though *MS*'s dazzling narrative outdid even Julio Cortázar's *Hopscotch*, *CV* is not a complete success. Proceeding with the logic of a street-corner bull session, *CV*'s numerous vignettes are written with such crispness and clarity that the prose style is itself a crystal vision. But finally the plot does not cohere. (575w)

This review also appeared as: "Slideshow of 50s," *Watertown* [NY] *Daily Times*, 28 December 1981.

F265 Seidenbaum, Art. "Non Sequiturs and Ne'er-Do-Wells." *Los Angeles Times*, 25 November 1981, sec. 5: 6.
CV is not a novel but a multiringed literary circus, whose arena holds, though some of its acts fail. Speaking constantly in both gutter and grandiloquent language, GS's characters offer a message—if memory does not sustain life, then invent the means to persist. (750w)

F266 Sullivan-Drury, Maureen. *Best Sellers* 41.11 (February 1982): 412-13.
Though struggling for language and techniques that communicate without the mediating mirror of fettered reality, *CV* is highly readable. (320w)

Selected Poems (1981)

F267 Creeley, Robert. "Poetry of Commitment." *Washington Post Book World*, 2 August 1981: 5-6, esp. 6.
SP revives the high modernist appetite for language and what words can make. The volume testifies to GS's delight in formal design and playful echoes of writers he admires. (250w) Excerpted: *Contemporary Literary Criticism* 40 (1986): 383-84.

F268 de Vries, Bart. *Prisma* [Voorburg] [In Dutch], 1983.
Though GS is better known for his prose than his poetry, the latter is as artful and interesting as the former. Grounded in William Carlos Williams and also drawing on Symbolist practice, GS's poetry successfully combines artifice with autobiographical detail. (200w)

F269 McNeil, Helen. "In the Line of the Image." *Times Literary Supplement*, 29 January 1982: 113.
In the post-Poundian style of imagery that abjures symbolism, GS attempts to distance his work from academic imitators of the avant-garde. But his assumption of ordinary reality's absolute validity and his arrogation to poetry of special prerogatives place GS closer to the mainstream writers he loathes. (250w) Excerpted: *Contemporary Literary Criticism* 40 (1986): 386.

F270 Middleton, Peter. "Fictional Memories." *Ninth Decade* 3 (1984): 10-17.
SP not only reflects GS's links to American poetry with antecedents in Williams and Pound but also declares his major differences from such figures as Charles Olson, Jack Spicer, and Amiri Baraka. Grounded in both the English and French lyric traditions, especially Baudelaire and Apollinaire, GS's poetry shudders with feelings of loss, and it heroically refuses the optimism of speculative ideas. Though disappointed enough in failed human possibilities to produce powerful elegies, GS's meditative memory moves not toward belief in any transcendent reality but toward the fictionality of art. Relentlessly skeptical, GS displaces romantic vision with fiction, which for him is absolutely powerless to affect anything. His poetry sings in a cosmic estrangement that denies any possible politics and passionately asserts an irretrievable damnation. (4200w)

F271 O'Hara, J. D. "Coteries and Poetries." *Nation* 234 (2-9 January 1982): 20-21, esp. 21.
Contrary to the long lists and sentences of his fiction, *SP* shows a different GS, using short lines and minimal vocabulary. Dominated by themes of his dead mother, lost women, love, and obsessive memories from the distant past, the poems are glum and very personal, though the nostalgia, wit, and more traditional form of GS's most recent pieces make them extremely pleasant reading. (500w) This review also treats *CV*. Excerpted: *Contemporary Literary Criticism* 40 (1986): 385-86.

F272 Seidman, Hugh. "Poems and Excitement." *New York Times Book Review*, 8 November 1981: 13, 32, 34-35.
An important and unique voice whose poetry possesses unassailable moral and artistic integrity, GS possesses a harsh edge that is clearly not intended to charm. Though he has raised cynicism to a high art, his poems are capable of great vulnerability and sentiment, especially through a nostalgia for an irredeemable past. Rigorously formal, GS tends toward clear, direct diction and disdains symbol, metaphor, and mythic reference, though for him the poem is a thing unto itself without need of external justification. (850w) Excerpted: *Contemporary Literary Criticism* 40 (1986): 384.
SP entered among the "Editors' Choice," *New York Times Book Review*, 15 and 22 November 1981.

F273 T[hesen], S[haron]. *Review of Contemporary Fiction* 2.3 (Fall 1982): 149-58.
SP successfully retains the spirit and integrity of the original volumes and proves the importance and vitality of GS's contribution to American poetry since the 1950s. GS's poetry is committed to the revelation of truth, grace, and beauty in the measures of language that resists the dominant culture's connection of language to power. Marked by GS's care for the opacity, materiality, and integrity of language, his poetry recognizes its vulnerability in a society that values counterfeit vitality, mechanized language, and easy art. One of the most notable aspects of his style is repetition, which serves variously as musical measure, structuring device, theme, and remembrance. Also remarkable is GS's ability to recapture the past's fantasy of itself and place it in the cells of the present imagination. GS has, in fact, a genius for articulating popular fantasies out of a magazine America that doesn't exist but exists everywhere. Particularly important poems include "(Sonnet with X's)," "Miss and Hit," "Coast of Texas," and "The Language Barrier." (2000w)

F274 Weinstein, Norman. *Sulfur* 5 (1983): 166-68.
Though a great American novelist who is revitalizing the form and spirit of the novel, GS is a much less innovative poet. Splenetic and bitter, the early poems in *SP* are extensions of Creeley's craft and posture, with tense, tightly focused lines expressing existential displacement through ironic detachment. While GS's verbal agility deepens in the later work, his psychological depth does not. His pathologizing produces a cynical carping relieved only by occasional bursts of romantic sensibility. (575w)

Blue Pastoral (1983)

F275 Anon. *Kirkus Reviews* 51 (15 March 1983): 335-36.
With Renaissance rhetoric and malapropisms galore, *BP* uses the journey format to demolish all varieties of Americana. A few sections are brilliant, proving again how stern a dazzler GS can be. But as a whole, *BP* is tired

and oppressive, mechanically recycling old devices. This is very minor, ultimately enervating entertainment. (300w)

F276 ———. *Publishers Weekly* 223.13 (1 April 1983): 51.
A picaresque romp sustained by a clever pastiche of traditional styles and literary genres, *BP* is an outrageously funny satire on American manners and mores. (125w)

F277 Adams, Phoebe-Lou. *Atlantic* 251.6 (June 1983): 105.
GS uses parody, misquotation, and hideous verse to demonstrate American folly, a revelation which is, however, inadequate to compensate for *BP*'s lack of the conventional pleasures of fiction. (50w)

F278 Becker, Alida. "The Bookshelf/Fiction." *Philadelphia Inquirer*, 21 August 1983: R7.
Not a novel but a demonstration of GS's considerable learning, *BP* displays GS's gift for capturing nuances of voice and his glee in parodying literary styles. Despite some glorious set pieces, the average reader will find *BP*'s artifice wearing and self-indulgent. (200w)

F279 B[rosnahan], J[ohn]. *Booklist* 79.15 (1 April 1983): 1016.
BP's dazzling wordplay and highly inventive humor may be too experimental for most general readers. (100w)

F280 Byrne, Jack. *Review of Contemporary Fiction* 5.1 (Spring 1985): 135-36.
Though very different from *SW*, *BP* nonetheless recalls elements of that earlier novel. Its humor derives from satires on a wide range of topics, including literary conventions, the academy, regionalism, and ethnic pomposities. (1100w)

F281 Buj, Lorenzo. "The Rise of the Guided Tour." *Lance* [University of Windsor] 46.26 (19 April 1984).
GS's latest wallop of labyrinthine farce, *BP* is so delightfully spun that its clever web of literacy does not so much disfigure reality as render it flexible. GS's wordplays hang on *BP*'s skeleton of a storyline with Joycean horseplay, but he never abuses either his artistic freedom or his readers. (475w)

F282 Clark, Jeff. *Library Journal* 108.7 (1 April 1983): 760-61.
A brutally hilarious parody of pop culture clichés, *BP* gives direction to the creative lunacy of *MS*. (75w)

F283 Clute, John. "Pastoral-Parodical." *Times Literary Supplement*, 2 August 1985: 855.
An American metafiction of bone-crushing rectitude and unremitting smugness, *BP* is motivated by scorn for American culture. Though its linguistic high jinks are banal, the novel occasionally batters the reader into laughter. (350w)

F284 Conarroe, Joel. "Characters on a Course." *New York Times Book Review*, 19 June 1983: 13, 25.
At once lavishly inventive and excessively cute, *BP* both exhilarates and exasperates, its dazzling satire alternating with sophomoric jokes. Governed by a dark Swiftian humor, *BP* democratically attacks American cultural follies, though GS's rage sometimes threatens to exceed the bounds of even bad taste. While particularly funny about academics, *BP* is itself a very bookish work, relying on literary references for its effects. (800w) Excerpted: "Notable Books of the Year," *New York Times Book Review*, 4 December 1983, and *Contemporary Literary Criticism* 40 (1986): 387-88.

F285 Cryer, Dan. "Sorrentino Gets Away with Murder." *Peninsula Herald* [Monterey, CA], 24 July 1983.
In *BP* GS toys with his readers, serving up an undisciplined hodgepodge of a book while heading off criticism with snide remarks about book reviewers. A work to delight academic interpreters of literature, *BP* can, however, be amusing, especially in its no-holds-barred satire of every ethnic group, profession, and region of America. (225w)

F286 Cunningham, Valentine. "Fictional Tricks." *Observer*, 28 October 1984: 25.
BP continues GS's demonstration that novels don't reflect reality but are only verbal structures. A ventriloquial tour of contemporary American rhetorics, *BP* is most successful when directly satirical. Otherwise, its literary self-consciousness is no more than tired, empty narcissism. (200w) Excerpted: *Contemporary Literary Criticism* 40 (1986): 389.

F287 D['Arcy], D[avid]. "Notebook." *In These Times* 7.31 (10-23 August 1983): 18-19.
A dazzling fiction improvisor, GS creates in *BP* a massive parody of the pastoral and picaresque literary traditions. *BP*'s ribald but overscholarly inventions show GS's superb ear for American English and his ecumenical irreverence. But despite GS's raucous energy and technical breadth, he has trouble sustaining *BP*'s humor. (300w)

F288 de Vries, Bart. *Prisma* [Voorburg] [In Dutch], 1984.
In *BP* imagination and reality are closely woven together by one of the most important modern American writers. This literary concert in various keys is suitable only for readers familiar with American literature and fully conversant with contemporary American idioms. (200w)

F289 Evans, Stuart. *Times* [London], 25 October 1984: 16.
A satirical fantasy of ebullient invention, *BP* is a sprawlingly comprehensive send-up of the pastoral form. Though GS's ruthless satire of almost every aspect and assumption of American life has immense energy and versatility, the novel's mannered mixture of archaic and foul demotic diction becomes finally very wearing. (225w)

F290 Ezell, Margaret. "Sorrentino: When the Narrator Drops His Guard . . ." *Houston Chronicle*, 31 July 1983, "Zest" sec.: 18.
A highly artificial, self-conscious, and literate comedy, *BP* constantly challenges the reader to get through the Slough of Language and to overcome its Cunning Narrator. The narrative itself is like a kaleidoscope, transforming bits of human nature into clever literary styles and patterns. But much of GS's artifice seems contrived and peevish; only when he revels in the powers of the English language does *BP*'s charm and comic power shine through. (550w)

F291 Lewis, Roger. "Ring of Words." *New Statesman* 108 (2 November 1984): 32.
A modern American *Candide*, *BP* offers a bedazzling picaresque journey across literary styles. The novel's irrepressible language and constantly transmogrifying form place demands on the reader's attention, but GS's literary references enrich rather than obtrude. (200w)

F292 Loprete, Nicholas J., Jr. *Best Sellers* 43.4 (July 1983): 168-69.
An overripe farrago of popular culture parodies and linguistic exercises, *BP* is defeated by its own cleverness. (200w)

F293 Masters, Stephen. "A Literary Bumper Crop." *Night Life*.
BP does for the pastoral novel what *Ulysses* does for the Greek epic. With great virtuosity and high comic effect, GS subverts pastoral conventions to his own ends. Subordinating plot and message to form and technique, *BP* exploits literature's artifice to create a very strange, very funny, very brilliant book. Though GS's vicious parodies can be disturbing, *BP*'s art is finally a foil to life's absurdity, serving more to celebrate than condemn the ridiculous. (850w)

F294 Mellors, John. "American Nightmare." *Listener* 112 (13 December 1984): 30.
An intellectual farce in the form of an odyssey across a variety of literary landscapes, *BP* succeeds through its fantastic humor and amusing parody. (250w)

F295 Middleton, Peter. *City Limits* [London], 16-22 November 1984: 87.
BP is metafiction that uses one of the oldest self-reflexive literary forms, the pastoral, to satirize the corruption of sophisticated life. *BP* consists of a series of knowing parodies of different kinds of American fiction, thus continuing GS's quarrel both with fiction's complacent assumption that narrative is a window onto the world and with its frequent acquiescence to ideology and stereotype. But *BP* is too passive in face of its materials and never gets beyond the terms of the self-centered exploitative society it attacks. GS has abandoned mimetic realism but not its underlying assumptions. (350w)

F296 Miner, Valerie. "Muse for a Musician and Mocking Themes." *Los Angeles*

Times Book Review, 7 August 1983: 12.
Garishly contrived and sophomoric in its artifice, *BP* exhibits more passion for showing off than communicating. But this literary braggadocio is less disturbing than GS's camp misanthropy. His derisive wit employs both sexist and racist epithets, unrelieved by any redeeming social vision. Though GS plays boldly with form and his language approaches Joycean wakefulness, this promise dissolves in jaded self-consciousness. (600w)
Excerpted: *Contemporary Literary Criticism* 40 (1986): 388.

F297 Moore, Dennis. " 'Pastoral' Revives Picaresque Novel." *Charlotte* [NC] *Observer*, 21 August 1983.
Always clever and sometimes exhilarating, *BP* continues GS's efforts to separate himself from conventional literature. Its multiplicity of voices is *BP*'s greatest strength. (175w)

F298 O'Brien, John. "Gilbert Sorrentino Tilts at Language." *Washington Post Book World*, 22 May 1983: 5.
BP merges the formal conventions of Renaissance pastoral with the geographical structure of *SC* to perform an anatomy of language. Each chapter demonstrates how language is abused, tortured, and rendered senseless by the various discourses of contemporary society. Hysterically glorifying this linguistic corruption to the point of utter chaos, *BP* ends with language gone mad. The comic brilliance of GS's achievement is awesome, pure, and perfectly executed. (750w)

Abbreviated, revised version: "Current & Choice," *Washington Post Book World*, 29 May 1983, and 5 June 1983. Excerpted: *Contemporary Literary Criticism* 40 (1986): 387.

F299 Riggenbach, Jeff. "A Jollie Sconce through Medled Greese." *San Jose Mercury News*, 14 August 1983, "Arts & Books" sec.: 23.
Taking its title, style, and structure from pastoral literature, *BP* features intricately detailed parodies of pastoral forms. Though there are compensating moments of inspired wordplay and satire, most readers will become totally indifferent to *BP*'s dense, allusive pages and GS's often intimidating art. (1000w)

F300 ——. *Berkeley Monthly* 13.12 (September 1983): 43-44.
An intimidatingly clever and demanding novel, *BP* is unfortunately too dense and allusive for most readers. Nonetheless, *BP* has its pleasures, especially the chapters that satirize nonliterary subjects. (1025w)

F301 Sawhill, Ray. "Some Kind of Hero." *Newsweek* 102 (4 July 1983): 73.
An experimentalist with the instinct of a showman, GS has always endowed literary contrivance with the improvisational excitement of jazz. But *BP*'s attempt at black comedy grows tedious, despite the fun of its numerous parodies. While GS's earlier novels used innovative techniques to magically reveal character, in *BP* these devices are only ornate excrescences. (325w)

F302 Skenazy, Paul. "An Author Who Can Walk on His Tongue." *San Francisco Chronicle Review*, 10 July 1983: 7.
BP continues GS's practice of writing novels about writing novels. Constantly reminding readers that novels are verbal constructions produced by untrustworthy authors, *BP* attacks social and cultural pretensions. Though GS's virtuoso bag of stylistic tricks creates great fun, *BP* is less a whole book than a collection of writing exercises. Despite its cleverness and comedy, *BP* is more exhausting than entertaining. (700w)

F303 Werner, Craig. *Magill's Literary Annual* (1984): 99-103.
GS is America's Brecht. In *BP* he attacks T. S. Eliot's elitist dichotomy between contemporary anarchy and mythic order by exposing all myths as fabricated conventions and refusing to promote any one version as an objective or correct way of ordering life. GS's revelation that all mediations of experience are arbitrary finally emphasizes less the impossibility of order than the potential for a shared comic consciousness. GS's profoundly pluralistic sensibility collapses conservative hierarchies and lays the foundation for a populist avant-garde free from traditional cultural hegemony. (2500w)

Something Said (1984)

F304 Anon. *Conjunctions* 7 (1985): 273.
SS presents the coherent and completely engaged polemic of one of the most unmuddled intellects working today. (25w)

F305 ———. *Kirkus Reviews* 52 (15 October 1984): 1001-2.
Partisan, headstrong, sophisticated yet antiacademic, GS's criticism appreciates form without losing its streetwise edge. GS is best when tackling thorny poets in the William Carlos Williams line and when dealing with talented but offbeat fiction. (400w)

F306 ———. *Journal of Modern Literature* 12.3-4 (November 1985): 421.
The critical perspective of *SS* is consistent with GS's highly literary, experimental novels, emphasizing writers from the sometimes rarefied atmosphere of little magazines and small presses. (150w)

F307 ———. *Progresso Italo Americano* [In Italian], 9 June 1985.
SS reveals GS's anger at ignorance, intellectual ignorance, and causes without sense; it also demonstrates his affection for works written with conscience and love for humanity. GS's principal commitment is aesthetic, and his major interest in the internal artistic process. (150w)

F308 ———. *Publishers Weekly* 226.15 (12 October 1984): 48.
Direct and open in declaring GS's biases, the pieces in *SS* describe his own creative practice, consciously—and sometimes tendentiously—

promoting kindred spirits to spite academics and their literary pantheon. (175w)

F309 Alix, Cleta M. *Library Journal* 109.20 (December 1984): 2280.
SS illuminates the varied influences on GS's own writing, among them Joyce, Flann O'Brien, and William Carlos Williams. (100w)

F310 Barone, Dennis. "You Get What You Pay For." *Contact II* 36-37 (Fall 1985): 41.
GS possesses both superior critical acumen and the praiseworthy willingness to take risks in his opinions. Though there are some disappointments in *SS*, usually GS's judgments are completely correct. (800w)

F311 Bianco, David. *Best Sellers* 44.12 (March 1985): 467-68.
Guided by his taste for neglected writers, GS offers in *SS* not only advanced, nonpedantic introductions to numerous underrated contemporary figures but also a critical apparatus for judging his own fiction and poetry. (250w)

F312 B[rosnahan], J[ohn]. *Booklist* 81.10 (15 January 1985): 680.
Never allowing personality or reputation to determine his judgment, GS develops in *SS* an aesthetic for modern literature. (75w)

F313 Carruth, Hayden. "Touring Parnassus." *New York Times Book Review*, 3 March 1985: 19.
Stepping beyond personal taste into the larger processes of the imagination, *SS* represents the most intelligent and readable criticism of neglected American avant-garde writers that we possess. Attempting to supplant the power of the academy's Great Tin Ear and Ouija Mentality, GS's essays spring from his belief that art is neither idea nor fantasy but reality. (750w)
Excerpted: *Contemporary Literary Criticism* 40 (1986) 390.

F314 Cornis-Pop, Marcel. "Some Other Sort of Sentence Making." *American Book Review* 8.2 (January-February 1986): 12-13.
Scorning the hysterical reliance of academic critics on humanism and interpretation, *SS* instead affirms the Williams-Zukofsky-Olson line as American literature's countercanon and celebrates their more authentic mode of postmodernism. Praising their opaque, antisymbolistic surfaces, GS forswears bourgeois hermeneutics and emphasizes the return of fiction to metonymy, the clash of codes, and the referential emptiness of linguistic signals. (850w)

F315 Dowell, Coleman. *Review of Contemporary Fiction* 6.1 (Spring 1986): 198.
SS, like GS's novels, reviews itself, thereby deliberately intimidating the would-be critic. Within GS's stringent aesthetic credo, art is inexplicable, artists somewhat divine, creation more important than artifact, and ideas the villain. (450w)

F316 Hyde, Lewis. "Style Is the Thing for Sorrentino." *Boston Globe,* 24 February 1985: A10, A12.
GS's aesthetic grounds itself in the assumption that reality is fixed, intractable, and utterly detached from personal desires and ideas. Consequently, only artists who refrain from imposing their sensibilities on the world can reveal it, and their basic tool of revelation is always form. Though GS's attack on romanticism and humanism is revealing, he never fully develops his arguments and *SS* remains essentially a book of opinions. (1100w)

F317 Kenner, Hugh. "Gilbert Sorrentino: A Critical Mass." *Washington Post Book World,* 10 February 1985: 3, 7.
Evidencing unity of mind, *SS* releases formidable energy and light, particularly in GS's discussions of less publicized writers. Throughout he argues for the inseparability of language and literature, heroically wrestling against the common misunderstanding that fiction and poetry are valuable because of their thematic content. (700w) Excerpted: "Current & Choice," *Washington Post Book World,* 17 February 1985; "Books of 1985," *Washington Post Book World,* 8 December 1985; and *Contemporary Literary Criticism* 40 (1986): 389.

F318 Myers, George, Jr. "Sorrentino's 'Something Said' Something Special." *Columbus* [OH] *Dispatch,* 3 February 1985.
Unlike the crystalline but dense nature of GS's novels, his critical essays are straightforward diamonds in the rough. (650w)

F319 Peters, Robert. "Sorrentino Speaks." *Los Angeles Times Book Review,* 3 March 1985: 7.
Fearlessly rejecting American snob culture, GS is a breed apart from the typical hack critic of contemporary literature. *SS*'s spirited defenses of Williams, Olson, Zukofsky, and Hubert Selby especially reveal GS's power. (1300w) Excerpted: *Contemporary Literary Criticism* 40 (1986): 389-90.
SS was also listed in the column, "And the Critics Commend," *Los Angeles Times Book Review,* 24 March 1985.

F320 Riggenbach, Jeff. "Inventive Novelist Proves a Splendid Critic As Well." *San Jose Mercury News,* 7 April 1985, "Arts & Books" sec.: 22.
One of the most prodigally talented and verbally inventive of contemporary novelists, GS is also a critic of astute judgment and coruscating wit. The distinctive voice that speaks throughout these essays resides not in their content but in their form. (750w)

F321 Rubin, Michael. "Strong Words." *Palo Alto* [CA] *Weekly,* 12 June 1985.
SS keeps strict critical time to the drumbeat of contemporary modernism, arguing that literature must be regarded as pure invention, the mirror of itself. Retaining their freshness and urgency, the essays in *SS* are especially strong in their treatment of William Carlos Williams's "signal-less" image

and his sensitivity to the desolation of American dreams. Opposing academic criticism and accepted authors, GS praises writers who use the American idiom uniquely, efface themselves within their poems, and achieve honest effects. (900w)

F322 Schaub, Thomas. "An Outsider's Look at Literary Culture." *San Francisco Chronicle Review*, 3 February 1985: 6.
Displaying a stern but entertaining impatience with artiness and the ingrown falsehoods of literary culture, GS grounds *SS* in a commitment to the work of art as a thing-in-itself. GS is particularly critical of sentimental writers and of those who regard art as a form of history or source of information. Insisting that the writer's job is not to interpret but to reveal reality, GS respects both language and the world as substantial but different things and urges the need to anchor human culture in the world, not ideas and verbal evasions. (1000w)

F323 Winders, James A. *Magill's Literary Annual* (1986): 847-51.
The range and diversity of GS's literary preoccupations allow him to comment forcefully on the arbitrariness of the academic literary canon. The index of greatness in writers GS champions is a stubbornly American quality that is capable of disclosing the nation's spiritual impoverishment. His analysis of the critical fates of William Carlos Williams, Jack Spicer, and Edward Dahlberg convincingly reveals the political grounds of their exclusion from the literary canon. But despite GS's commitment to resist the cultural prejudices that slight countercultural writers, he himself neglects women writers. (2300w)

Odd Number (1985)

F324 Anon. *Kirkus Reviews* 53 (15 July 1985): 671.
Existing ambiguously between murder mystery, pornography, and an examination of the fictive means for measuring reality, *ON* is a narrative Möbius strip that claims godlike authority for its own prose. Though mercilessly mocking contemporary forms of literary pretension, GS's novel is itself susceptible to the same charges it levels against others. (325w)

F325 ———. *Publishers Weekly* 228.4 (26 July 1985): 154.
So narcissistically self-referential as to alienate readers, *ON* is more jigsaw puzzle than novel. Though GS is a masterful stylist, the brilliance of his techniques is lost among *ON*'s boring characters and incoherent plot. (150w) Excerpted: *Contemporary Literary Criticism* 40 (1986): 390.

F326 Bill, Rise. *Best Sellers* 45.9 (December 1985): 331.
A conglomerate of fragments that challenges the reader's sense of reality, *ON* features a story that forms, disintegrates, and reforms in a web of unresolved contradictions. Though the novel's suggestion that truth lies

beyond human imagination has intellectual appeal, GS's language isn't cunning enough to deflect the reader's desire for a conventional plot. (325w)

F327 B[rosnahan], J[ohn]. *Booklist* 82 (15 October 1985): 314.
A mystery that expands and redoubles in yeasty obfuscation, *ON* is entertaining, whether it be read as literary gossip, intellectual puzzle, or a sublime example of high modernism. (50w)

F328 Green, Geoffrey. *Review of Contemporary Fiction* 6.1 (Spring 1986): 200-202.
A poignant and uncanny novel that effaces distinctions between imagination and reality, *ON* is structured in three parallel parts, each cast in the form of an interrogation. Though these sections rehearse the same events, their differing perspectives do nothing to clarify and their various interpretations serve only to obscure. (1000w)

F329 Hutchison, Paul. *Library Journal* 110.16 (1 October 1985): 115.
GS's masterful style transforms *ON*'s mundane, mass culture plot into a marvelous adventure, in which the characters' individual voices finally merge with the narrative itself. (100w)

F330 Kearns, George. "Revolutionary Women and Others." *Hudson Review* 39.1 (Spring 1986): 121-34, esp. 130-32.
The work of a sophisticated, meticulous artist with a gift for comedy and a deadly satiric eye for contemporary corruption, *ON* offers neither story nor characters but a scathing portrait of an inbred, commercialized New York culture scene. A jeremiad iced by every distancing device of post-modernism, GS's novel lavishes contempt on this sleazy world where art merges with crime. (800w)

F330a Mayhew, Jonathan. *VIA: Voices in Italian Americana* 1 (Spring 1990): 174-76.
A textbook of postmodern devices, *ON* flattens the modernist game of perspectivism: its multiple layers of narration deliberately do not illuminate each other but merely underscore the unreality of the characters' lives. *ON* continues *IQAT*'s parody of the fraudulence of American culture, but it is also a complex game of mirrors in which the reader can never be certain about language's representation of the world. (575w)

F331 Mobilio, Albert. *Village Voice Literary Supplement* 38 (September 1985): 3.
A self-assembling mystery with mismatched parts, *ON* employs techniques of French avant-garde fiction to upend the detective genre. Dumping plot and relying exclusively on narrative voice, GS's novel successfully blurs distinctions between fact and fiction but fails to create narrators capable of sustaining interest in such verbal spiraling and its aesthetic insights. (750w)

F332 O'Brien, John. "Third Degree." *American Book Review* 8.4 (May-June 1986): 11.
A triad of sessions, each involving unreliable narrators and all consisting of inexplicable questions followed by contradictory answers, *ON* is a formal aesthetic exercise intended not to make sense but to fulfill its own artificial design. A brilliantly comic novel, it is also terribly dark because of its monstrously corrupt characters. (1100w)

F333 Peabody, Richard. "The Funny, the Phony, and the Fabulous." *Washington Post Book World*, 20 October 1985: 10.
A master of artifice more concerned with methodology than message, GS attacks literature that strives for meaning and moral statement, emphasizing instead the integrity of language that precedes human interpretation. *ON* exposes one aspect of this general failure of truth by enacting the disintegration inherent in the investigative process. Designed as a recursive triptych in which each section repeats and subverts materials from the other sections, the novel uses gossip and hearsay to disrupt communication, ultimately rendering reality itself suspect. (850w) Excerpted: *Contemporary Literary Criticism* 40 (1986): 390-91.

F334 Taylor, Mark C. *Los Angeles Times Book Review*, 3 November 1985: 19.
Repeating characters and events in ways that dislocate identity and disrupt continuity, *ON* probes the mystery of writing and reading. Related to the literary preoccupations of Queneau and Blanchot, GS's art continues these French writers' exploration of the limits of experience and language. Focused on the impossible task of speaking the unspeakable, *ON* carries the reader into the strange territory that eludes language. Few contemporary writers are as demanding or as important as GS. (950w) Excerpted: "And Our Critics Commend," *Los Angeles Times Book Review*, 17 November 1985.

F335 Woodhams, Stephen. "Hey, What's This About?" *San Francisco Chronicle Review*, 15 September 1985: 3-4.
The verbal equivalent of a Möbius strip, *ON* is a postmodernist experimental job that tries good-naturedly to refer only to itself but ends by making a fool of itself. At once a high-minded novel about the structure of reality and a sleazy murder mystery, *ON* spoofs many conventions of fiction but provides less fun than literary sweat. (1600w)

Rose Theatre (1987)

F336 Anon. *Kirkus Reviews* 55 (1 September 1987): 1280.
This indecipherable exercise in automatic writing should be avoided. (75w)

F337 ———. *Publishers Weekly* 232.15 (9 October 1987): 77.
This self-indulgently discontinuous, fragmentary, playful fiction traces

the messy lives of some contemporary types squatting on the margins of the arts. Despite his difficulty, GS is amusing, even funny in his waggish way. (175w)

F338 ———. "Part Two of Sorrentino Trilogy Hits Stands." *Union Daily* [California State University, Long Beach], February 1988.
In *RT* GS writes using a montage of signifiers, which shows that he has said good-bye to his modernist masters Joyce and Flann O'Brien, and moved into a rich space of literature that is absolutely new. In *RT* language is put on stage to act out its possibilities, to question itself, and to question the possibility of ever telling the truth. (250w)

F339 B[rosnahan], J[ohn]. *Booklist* 84 (15 November 1987): 539.
A darkly comic metamorphosis of *ON*'s characters and scenario, *RT* continues GS's rigorous investigation of the fictional mode of narrative. *RT* is both demanding and rewarding. (75w)

F340 Cohen, Robert. *New York Times Book Review*, 20 December 1987: 16.
Alternately hilarious and infuriating, *RT* confirms GS's status as one of our funniest and most difficult writers. Representing the self-conscious reflexivity of postmodernism at its most French, *RT* focuses on unreliable perceptions and unknowable truths. (250w)

F341 Frank, Jeffrey A. "Sorrentino: Bitter and Beguiling." *Washington Post Book World*, 13 December 1987: 6.
Extending the utterly repulsive world of *IQAT*, *RT* continues GS's prolonged flirtation with the reader's expectations of realism. Hardly popular fiction but also neither self-indulgent nor nonsensical, *RT* engages its audience not with a narrative but with life itself. Though GS's daring leaps often end awkwardly, he is marvelous when aloft. (1000w)

F342 Hutchison, Paul E. *Library Journal* 112 (15 November 1987): 91.
Exploring the fertile region stretching between the writer's choice and the reader's awareness, *RT* is an evolving text that demands not just attention but also active participation. (100w)

F343 Messerli, Douglas. "Writers from the Diaspora of Truth." *Los Angeles Times Book Review*, 6 December 1987: 8.
A leading postmodern fiction writer who works against the grain of psychological realism, GS is also our most brilliant satirist. In *RT* he not only exposes the inanities and cruelties of American culture but mocks as well the pretensions of truth itself. *RT* enacts a diaspora of truth by systematically subverting the information presented in *ON*. The novel's characters are trapped in a language whose meaning constantly shifts, making stable representation impossible. *RT* successfully portrays our fall into both social and linguistic nonsense. (750w)

F344 Radner, Rebecca. "Thum May Not Wike Thith Witing at Aw." *San*

Francisco Chronicle Review, 8 November 1987: 7.
With both its characters and nonevents equally indistinguishable, *RT* does not strive for intelligibility. Though GS bullies the reader into taking his work seriously by attacking naturalistic fiction, *RT* is so completely written to formula that conventional narrative becomes attractive. (550w)

F345 Skiles, Don. "Major Author." *American Book Review* 9.6 (January-February 1988): 17-18.
RT sustains GS's amazing arc of creativity, which has included some of the finest innovative fiction written today. Elaborating the metatheme introduced by *ON*, the novel continues to explore information and the socio-cultural consequences of its processing. Using comic techniques that range from puns through burlesque to serious satire, *RT* humorously reveals how our personal lives increasingly mimic media events. More therapeutic and much higher voltage than most respected realistic fiction, GS's novel is uproariously funny without being strident or doctrinaire. GS's most immediate literary antecedent is Flann O'Brien. (1300w)

F346 Warren, Kenneth. "Novel Explorations of Ruinous Stereotypes." *Columbus* [OH] *Dispatch*, 6 December 1987: 9C.
Exploring the corrosive impact of the exhausted, artificial 1980s on the relations between men and women, *RT* centers on clothing and fashion's ability to transform identity, pervert character, and aggravate the word-play of eight married couples. (250w)

Misterioso (1989)

F347 Anon. *Kirkus Reviews* 57 (1 September 1989): 1278.
A book-length prose poem whose language play can be breathtaking in its virtuosity, *M* is as erudite, mannered, and frigid as its companion volumes, *ON* and *RT*. *M*'s ragtag collection of fabrication will dazzle GS's fans but baffle most others, who will conclude that a major talent has gone astray. (300w)

F348 ———. *Publishers Weekly* 236.23 (29 September 1989): 60.
M is a truncated series of frustrating anecdotes without a discernible plot. GS's evident wit might have been better diverted to character development. (150w)

F349 Brosnahan, John. *Booklist* 86.1 (1 September 1989): 37.
M mixes old ingredients from previous volumes with some piquant new additions to tantalize readers with fresh revelation and to disquiet them with further obfuscations. A delightfully witty summation of GS's trilogy. (120w)

F350 Coale, Howard. *New York Times Book Review*, 14 January 1990: 31.

At times hilarious and satirically on the mark, *M* displays GS's original and brilliant use of language. But in the absence of plot and character, the pleasures of pure artistic adventure wear thin, and the reader comes to suspect that GS has miraculously avoided taking risks, while cleverly pretending to risk everything. (225w)

F351 Frank, Jeffrey A. "The Best List-Maker Since Joyce." *Washington Post Book World*, 7 January 1990: 7.
M is a continuing collection of puns, one-liners, lists, and observations on the ways of mankind with no coherent plot. Taken together all this data becomes GS's most bracing look yet at the human condition. In *M* GS shows himself a perfect mimic of the information age, an era in which images appear and vanish, leaving only slight traces on the memory. (800w)

F352 Hutchison, Paul E. *Library Journal* 114.17 (15 October 1989): 104-5.
A novel of characters without plots, *M* is so dense in structure that only professional writers and readers will enjoy its achievement. (125w)

F353 Loose, Julian. "Alphabet Soup." *Times Literary Supplement*, 25-31 May 1990: 558.
M continues GS's dizzying pursuit of the postmodern logic of intertextuality and formal inventiveness, with a large cast of characters taking second place to formal pyrotechnics. Though *M*'s wild eclecticism affords amusing juxtapositions, GS's wit often palls and seems rather academic. But his long-term commitment to experimentation should still command our respect. (600w)

F354 McCaffery, Larry. "Foregone Inconclusions." *Los Angeles Times Book Review*, 10 December 1989: 3, 12.
M is a literary game in which ambiguity and enigma masquerade as fact and information. With its disparate materials united by GS's eye for detail and his savage wit, the novel not only imitates, parodies, and elaborates the fantasies and disappointments of American life, it also invents new and liberating possibilities for the culture. (1200w)

F355 Pekar, Harvey. *Northwest Extra!* [Olympia, WA] 1.11 (February 1990): 11.
One of the world's finest novelists, GS has a clear sense of himself in the context of Western literature. He responds to the challenges offered by Joyce and other modernists, extending their innovations to create a wonderful but difficult body of writing. A comic novel, *M* unites GS's encyclopedic knowledge of clichés with his prodigious command of technique to parody many things, including turn-of-the-century boys' stories and *Ethan Frome*. This review also offers a brief critical account of all of GS's prose works. (1400w)

F356 Schaub, Thomas. "A Supermarket That Caters to Imagination." *San*

Francisco Chronicle Review, 7 January 1990: 1, 10.
M resists the pull of narrative continuity that produces the effect of coherence but obscures the real itself. Using the imagination to liberate words and phrases from their transparent agency in everyday life, the novel is a hilarious and savage catalog of American language in which the words themselves are the chief characters. GS's real subject is the corruption of desire in American consumer culture, and *M* deliberately frustrates market-induced cravings, while also inviting its readers to recover true pleasure. (850w)

F357 Vitakis, Sophia. "Life, and Novels, Can Be Complicated." *Palo Alto* [CA] *Weekly,* 7 February 1990: 29-31.
M bravely attempts to delve into the misguided, disjointed, and strange lives of its many characters but finally leaves the reader with a feeling of vague incompleteness. Its unrelated paragraph style shows how hopeless is any attempt to organize facts. Though *M*'s characters come close to people in real life, they remain hopelessly inscrutable. (580w)

G. CRITICISM ON SORRENTINO

G1 Alcalay, Ammiel. "Gilbert Sorrentino's *The Orangery.*" *Review of Contemporary Fiction* 1.1 (1981): 85-87.
Argues that *O* employs formal means to escape the isolation and futility that typically beset the poet in American society. Proposes that this process culminates in *O*'s concluding poem, "The Crown," which demonstrates GS's knowledge that the poem's order is feigned. In *O* there is no interference from barriers erected between the world and the poet; rather there is persistent acknowledgment of the mysterious nature of the forces governing the world and the poet's obligation to accept his part in it.

G2 Aldridge, John W. *The American Novel and the Way We Live Now.* New York: Oxford Univ. Press, 1983, esp. 119-20.
Treats *MS* as an example of contemporary "fabulation," which blurs the distinction between fact and fiction. Argues that GS's belief in the interchangeability of fiction and reality leads to an arrogant disrespect for the integrity of both.

G3 Alpert, Barry. "Bricks and Swag." *Vort* 2.3 [also designated no. 6] (Fall 1974): 158.
Briefly compares the impact of the criticism of Donald Phelps and GS to that of Pound and Eliot.

G4 Armstrong, Peter. "Gilbert Sorrentino's *Imaginative Qualities of Actual Things.*" *Grosseteste Review* 6.1-4 (1973): 65-68.
Analyzes the psychological makeup of the characters in *IQAT*, observing how GS refuses to take his characters at their own valuation. Instead he situates their desires in the context of art and reveals how destructive to true poets are their needs. Argues that *IQAT* is a brilliant, often very funny book.

G5 Baraka, Amiri. *The Autobiography of LeRoi Jones.* New York: Freundlich Books, 1984, esp. "The Village," 124-201.
Briefly recounts Baraka's friendship with GS, who is referred to both under his proper name and the pseudonym, Paul Celento. Emphasizes GS's writings in *Yugen*, here called *Zazen*, and other works published by LeRoi Jones, including *BW*. Describes GS as "the classic debunker of the political in favor of the high aesthetic."

G6 Berman, Jaye Ellyn. "Parody as Cultural Criticism in the Postmodern American Novel: Donald Barthelme, Gilbert Sorrentino, and Thomas Pynchon." Diss. Univ. of Wisconsin, Milwaukee, 1988. Abstracted in *Dissertation Abstracts International* 49.8 (1989): 2217A.
A separate chapter analyzes GS's work chronologically. Focuses on parody as an instrument of oblique cultural criticism and argues that the energy of GS's work springs from the interanimations between the world

and the text. Explores the contradiction between the world as an enormous text from which GS draws his material and his desire to inhabit a pure, fictional space apart from social reality.

G7 Bronk, William. "The Person of Fiction, the Fiction of Person." *Sulfur* 4 (1983): 168-72.
Argues that the energizing tension of GS's work is the polarity between fiction and reality as set in motion by desire. Discusses the characters in *SC, SW, IQAT, MS*, and *CV*, examining the play between life, matter-of-fact fictions, and imaginative fictions.

G8 Brown, Harold. "Self-Reference in Logic and *Mulligan Stew*." *Diogenes* 118 (Summer 1982): 121-42.
Proposes that *MS* is an example of the "strange loop" phenomenon, which occurs in self-referencing works that deliberately tangle different levels of a text's hierarchy of discourses.

G9 Bruns, Gerald L. "A Short Defense of Plagiary." *Review of Contemporary Fiction* 1.1 (1981): 96-103.
Treats *MS* as a celebration of doubtful authorship that takes plagiary as its theme and plagiarisms of various sorts as among its most telling ingredients. Like the ancients, GS knows that writing is an art of memory, not of imagination. *MS*'s basic unit is the document, a writing-down of whatever is at hand. This intentionless practice of assembling pre-written discourses accounts for the randomness that is the novel's inescapable feature. Through *MS*'s central character, GS exposes the folly of the will to original creation. *MS*'s governing principle can be enunciated plainly: All writing is essentially anonymous and that which originates in an identifiable consciousness will either be worthless or mundane.

G10 Buzzard, Sharon Kay. "Reader Response Criticism and the Reflexive Narrative: The Reader/Viewer Role in Creating a Narrative." Diss. Univ. of Missouri, Columbia, 1985. Abstracted in *Dissertation Abstracts International* 46 (1986): 3348A.
Applies reader-response criticism to *MS*, demonstrating how the novel allows insight into the ways a reader helps create fictional characters and plot, while simultaneously being aware of the text and its artifice. Compares *MS* to the film *Singin' in the Rain*, showing how the two very different media reach the same phenomenological moment in the imagination, when narrative illusion becomes real and inner and outer merge.

G11 Byrne, Jack. "Sorrentino's *Steelwork:* Expanding Eddy Beshary's 'Annual Listing' (or) Beyond 'Besharyism.' " *Review of Contemporary Fiction* 1.1 (1981): 171-89.
Provides an alphabetical index of proper names, including chapter titles and subtitles, that appear in *SW*, with annotations derived from the novel.

G12 Cagidemetrio, Alide. "The Real Thing: Notes on an American Strategy." In *Critical Angles: European Views of Contemporary American Literature.* Ed. Marc Chénetier. Carbondale: Southern Illinois Univ. Press, 1986, 3-14.
Discusses *MS* as an example of the new poetics of fragmentation, reflexivity, and repetition. Argues that this aesthetic exposes the arbitrariness of all discourse by using fiction to explore the relation of sign to system and to examine the creation of meaning in the sign-object process. Focuses on GS's use of the detective story to exploit the distance between the genre's referential scheme and the consensual nature of truth. Also analyzes the way names in *MS* reflect the compromise between reality and fiction that characterizes any literary text.

G13 Caramello, Charles. *Silverless Mirrors: Book, Self, and Postmodern American Fiction.* Tallahassee: Univ. Presses of Florida, 1983, esp. 143.
Briefly comments on the alphabetical structure of *S-H.*

G14 Caserio, Robert L. "Gilbert Sorrentino's Prose Fiction." *Vort* 2.3 [also designated no. 6] (Fall 1974): 63-69.
Proposes that GS revives and revises the symbolist tradition by making the sensuous evocation of actuality compatible with a commitment to visionary experience. Examines *SC, SW, IQAT,* and *S-H* in light of this argument, showing how their density of concrete observation does not serve general socio-historical purposes but acts instead as the catalyst of desire's invention. Concludes that for GS imagination and reality are inherently discontinuous and that the terror of both art and life lies precisely in the absence of any saving communion between them. Excerpted: *Contemporary Literary Criticism* 7 (1977): 449-50.

G15 Charney, Mark Jay. "Reinventing Narrative: The Relationship of the Post-Contemporary Novel to the Cinema." Diss. Tulane Univ., 1987. Abstracted in *Dissertation Abstracts International* 49 (1988): 1136A.
Examines the filmic characteristics of surfictional narrative which disrupt conventional fictional form. Discusses GS along with twelve other contemporary American writers, specifically analyzing his use of different types of montage.

G16 Chénetier, Marc. *Au-dela du soupçon: La nouvelle fiction américaine de 1960 à nos jours.* [In French] Paris: Seuil, 1989, esp. 121-24, 133-35.
Analyzes *MS* as the ultimate metafictional text, whose parody destroys the conventions of both traditional and avant-garde narratives. Also discusses the alphabetic structure of *S-H* in relation to similarly organized works. Passing references touch briefly on other aspects of GS's work.

G17 Cioffi, Frank. "Gilbert Sorrentino's Science Fiction World in *Mulligan Stew.*" *Extrapolation* 21.2 (Summer 1981): 140-45.
Argues that *MS* at once draws on and parodies three basic variants of the serious science fiction/metafictional novel, as exemplified by Pynchon,

Robbe-Grillet, and Borges. This structure enables GS to contain the fragmented pieces of popular and sub-literary forms that usually comprise his work. By both rebarbarizing serious fiction with popular elements and satirizing metafiction, *MS* presents a metaphor of the fiction writer's inability to show all sides to his characters. GS thus achieves a convincing kind of mimesis, while simultaneously revealing that experience is ultimately not transcribable.

G18 Corn, Peggy Ward. "Functions of the Story within a Story in Twentieth-Century Literature." Diss. Ohio State Univ., 1983. Abstracted in *Dissertation Abstracts International* 44.11 (1984): 3380A.
Examines *MS* in the context of other twentieth-century novels and plays in which an inner story is contained by an outer one. Shows how *MS*'s story within a story is used to insist on the artifice of fiction by relentlessly exposing the conventions of realism.

G19 Cornis-Pop, Marcel. "Working Theories of New Fiction." *North American Review* 270 (1985): 66-70.
Briefly discusses *SS* in relation to the critical writings of Ronald Sukenick, John Barth, and William Gass, emphasizing GS's antimimetic stance and his rejection of the "interpretive fallacy."

G20 Creeley, Robert. "Xmas as in Merry." *Review of Contemporary Fiction* 1.1 (1981): 157-58.
With reference to *SC, SW,* and *AS,* emphasizes the moral disposition of GS's writing and his explicit concern with why the human world suffers so remarkably and so stupidly its persistent inabilities of judgment and perception. Argues that at the center of GS's work is the necessity to judge and define value, no matter the formal means employed or the technical pattern.

G21 D'Amico, Maria Vittoria. "Paradox Beyond Convention: A Note on Gilbert Sorrentino's Fiction." *Rivista di studi anglo-americani* 3.4-5 (1984-1985): 269-80.
Argues that paradoxes define GS's literary stance and production. Primary among these paradoxes is his linking artistic invention with plagiarism. Shows how this relates to GS's rejection of fiction's mimetic function and to his imitation of the styles of others. Suggests that despite GS's refusal to mirror life, his novels nonetheless render its actuality and process accurately. Furthermore his work is also highly moral, for it equates the search for a perfect language with the achievement of a better way to exist. Develops this argument through discussions of *S-H, MS, IQAT,* and *SC.*

G22 ———. "Sorrentino, Gilbert (1929-)." In *Postmodern Fiction: A Bio-Bibliographical Guide.* Ed. Larry McCaffery. Westport, CT: Greenwood, 1986, 505-8.
Proposes that GS gives preeminence to form over content and grounds

invention in absolute artifice, thereby basing his writing on unpopular aesthetic principles. Traces GS's faith in the power of the word to Sterne, Joyce, and especially William Carlos Williams. Argues that despite GS's reliance on such innovative techniques as color schemes and alphabetical sequence, his fiction successfully records the essence of American life. *SC, CS,* and *S-H* are particularly discussed.

G23 Domini, John. "Blue without Blues: Gilbert Sorrentino and the Subversion of the Novel." *Boston Phoenix,* 5 July 1983, sec. 3: 2, 14, 16.
Describes GS as an iconoclast of contemporary fiction and a leading exemplar of America's first homegrown modernist movement. Argues that GS's energy and imagination drive him to set up complex, unusual literary edifices, which join with his bitter sense of irony and his adamant denial of abstraction to distinguish his work in both poetry and fiction. Observes how GS's poetry unites formality and control with a powerful sense of loss, examining this pattern in *BW, O,* and *CS.* Divides the novels into realistic "familiar tunes" and experimental "unchained melodies." The former include *SW, IQAT, AS,* and *CV,* while the latter begin with *S-H* and *MS* and culminate in *BP,* where GS creates a surrogate world that displaces the debased, contemporary America it parodies.

G24 Dowell, Coleman. "Gilbert Sorrentino's *Aberration of Starlight.*" *Review of Contemporary Fiction* 1.1 (1981): 143-52.
Follows *AS*'s four-part structure, devoting separate sections to the psychology of the novel's principal characters. Emphasizes the change that occurs at the end of *AS,* when the reader puts aside amusement and recognizes the novel for what it has been all along: a form of anxiety, a submerged fear. Contrasts *MS*'s satiric humor with *AS*'s more insidious laughter, while also arguing that both offer generous room for rueful sympathy for all aspects of the human condition.

G25 Dunlap, Lowell. "Blue Indigo." *Review of Contemporary Fiction* 1.1 (1981): 130-31.
Offers an ironically inflated, philosophical analysis of the color blue in *MS,* with references to Sartre, Husserl, and Brooklyn Dodger "Duke" Snider. Argues that the novel's various shades of blue express the relations between the empirical and the transcendental ego.

G26 Durczak, Jerzy. "Gilbert Sorrentino." [In Polish] *Literatura na Świecie* 113 (1980): [262]-[267].
Provides a chronological overview of GS's career, beginning with a brief biographical sketch, followed by introductory comments on *SC, SW, IQAT,* and *S-H.*

G27 Eckstein, Barbara J. "On Being Male in America, or The Dancer in the Dance." *Southern Review* 19.1 (March 1986): [76]-88.
Analyzes Jim Harrison's *Farmer* and *CV* from a feminist perspective, arguing that both novels form pacts of despair with their male readers,

voicing the disillusionment of men whose longing for innocence and freedom is thwarted by the political contradictions of the American romance tradition. *CV*'s male narrators, victims of lost youth and disappointed desires, create a sanctuary from failed careers and marriages by projecting the image of a beautiful young woman whose ideal perfection imaginatively restores lost time. GS understands this dream to be a social construction and treats it analagously to the literary conventions that he both pursues and parodies. Faced with a relentless procession of social and artistic codes that are all unacceptable, the characters in *CV* finally escape their dilemma by absorbing themselves into the process of making their own text. This move overlooks, however, the inadequacy of their vision of lost American innocence and thus uncritically indulges male despair.

G28 Eilenberg, Max. "A Marvellous Gift: Gilbert Sorrentino's Fiction." *Review of Contemporary Fiction* 1.1 (1981): 88-94.
Argues that parody, conceived metalinguistically as writing about writing, focuses the project of GS's fiction, which extends the parodic function to comment not only on writing but also on the milieu which engenders it. Traces GS's attack on the clichés of conventional novels and the behavior of commercial publishers through *IQAT* and *S-H*, then closely analyzes *MS* as the culmination of this parodic process. Shows how *MS* operates through found texts and self-parody to set literature in the context of the powerful institutions of language and business that finally author and read it. Concludes by describing GS's success in reaching beyond the structuralist view of the text as a site traversed by codes and discourses in which the author is more a guest than an orginator. *MS* ultimately reinstates GS as author, his presence asserted implicitly in the monstrous overwriting and explicitly in the echoes of his earlier books. Also treats GS's uses of *Finnegans Wake*.

G29 Elman, Richard. "Reading Gil Sorrentino." *Review of Contemporary Fiction* 1.1 (1981): 155-56.
Explains a preference for GS's more modest works, particularly the early poetry and the novels, *SC, SW,* and *AS,* because they dramatize (though not in a slavishly realistic fashion) intense states of human interaction. Concludes that GS's most elementary concern is the fiction of language, pure and abstract, but also argues that this is a persona by which an artist of great seriousness, talent, and ability has shaped the pain of experience to animate language and show the limitations by which we live.

G30 Emerson, Stephen. "Imaginative Qualities of Actual Things." *Vort* 2.3 [also designated no. 6] (Fall 1974): 85-89.
Proposes that GS's fiction is an event in itself, whose import does not lie in its applicability to the phenomenal world. But also argues that GS's work respects the integrity of human experience, refusing to distort it through literary conventions. Insists that GS's work is committed to the actuality of human experience qua experience, a commitment which differentiates

his work from the grand artifice of such antirealist writers as Barth, Coover, Gass, and Nabokov. Illustrates this argument through analysis of *IQAT*, which devises fictive situations that reveal human lives within a context that recognizes that a work of literature is not a transcription of experience, but a linguistic construct. Excerpted: *Contemporary Literary Criticism* 7 (1977): 450-51.

G31 ———. "Three Thoughts About 'The Moon in Its Flight.'" *Review of Contemporary Fiction* 1.1 (1981): 81-82.
Argues that "The Moon in Its Flight" is attractive because the story legitimizes sentimentality and nostalgia through a combination of immaculately observed detail and aesthetic self-consciousness. "The Moon in Its Flight" joins *IQAT* and *S-H* as works that reflect upon the process of literary composition and its artifice at the same time that they cast light on the real world. This double purchase is absent from GS's other novels, including *SC*, *MS*, and *AS*.

G32 Emmet, Paul. "*The Sky Changes:* A Journey into the Unconscious and a Road into the Novels of Gilbert Sorrentino." *Review of Contemporary Fiction* 1.1 (1981): 113-29.
Argues that GS's fiction forms an intricate whole, bound together by his personal obsession with impotence. Treats *SC* as the seminal work, disclosing the relations between impotence and the creative process, the fear of castration, anality, the devouring female, and the dread of female sexuality. Detailed analysis of *SC* shows that the novel's adult characters form an Oedipal triangle, in which the husband is the son whose dominant mother and absent father result in homosexual tendencies. Traces this pattern not only in *SW* and *AS*, which share with *SC* a common surface language, but also in *IQAT* and *MS*. Concludes that GS's fiction is terrifying in its ability to expose the secret fears of mankind.

G33 Friedman, Lawrence. "Vision and Revision in Scorcese's *New York, New York* and Sorrentino's 'The Moon in Its Flight.'" *Literature/Film Quarterly* 9.2 (1981): 103-9.
Explains how Scorcese's film and CS's short story revivify the lifeless forms of the big band musical and the sentimental story, thereby overcoming the paralysis of self-consciousness suffered by many contemporary artists. Argues that "The Moon in Its Flight" transforms sentimental yearning for the vanished world of the 1940s into an ironic and critical perception of contemporary America, by filtering old-fashioned banality through the hip, self-reflexive style of the 1970s.

G33a Green, Rose Basile. *The Italian-American Novel: A Document of the Interaction of Two Cultures.* Rutherford, NJ: Fairleigh Dickinson Univ. Press, 1974, esp. 377-79.
Characterizes GS as an outstanding writer of the unstructured novel. Notes the formless form of *SW*, briefly describing its vision of senselessness through artlessness. Emphasizes the arbitrary arrangement of

incidents in *IQAT* and concludes that GS's good-natured indifference to his own worth conveys to the reader the need for values to sustain life.

G34 Greiner, Donald J. "Antony Lamont in Search of Gilbert Sorrentino: Character and *Mulligan Stew.*" *Review of Contemporary Fiction* 1.1 (1981): 104-12.
Argues that *MS* fosters active readers who understand that literature is a verbal construct, not a mirror of reality. Shows how Lamont is a parody of readers who cannot handle untraditional fiction, but also insists that GS's rejection of verisimilitude does not disregard content but rather reflects the collapse of the stable social norms that once sustained realistic fiction. Proposes that in *MS* order is created by the formal properties of the work itself, not by moral commentary. Illustrates these arguments through an extensive description of the interplay between GS, Lamont, and Lamont's characters.

G35 Hayman, David. "Surface Disturbances/Grave Disorders." *TriQuarterly* 52 (Fall 1981): 182-96, esp. 186-88.
Analyzes the macroparatactics of *MS*, comparing GS's continuously shifting styles to the narrative procedures of Joyce. Argues that *MS* is a complex, stylistic pun on all manner of printed texts, which not only disrupts the reader's expectations but also maintains coherence and interest.

G36 Herman, Luc. "Intertextualiteit in *Mulligan Stew* (1979) van Gilbert Sorrentino." [In Dutch] *Spigel der Letteren* 29 (1-2): 101-9.
Treats *MS* as an encyclopedia of literary genres and discourses, tracing GS's use of numerous writers, not only such major sources as Joyce, Flann O'Brien, Dashiell Hammett, and F. Scott Fitzgerald, but also his passing references to Nathanael West, Yeats, Malcolm Lowry, and others. Concludes that *MS* illustrates the condition of poststructuralist intertextuality outlined by Julia Kristeva.

G37 Hornick, Lita. "*Kulchur:* A Memoir." *TriQuarterly* 43 (1978): 280-97; also issued as *The Little Magazine in America.* Yonkers, NY: Pushcart Press, 1978. Rpt. in *Kulchur Queen.* New York: Giorno Poetry Systems, 1977, 119-33.
Briefly recounts GS's involvement with *Kulchur,* including his editorship of both issue no. 4 and the book review section for issues nos. 7-10.

G38 ———. *The Green Fuse: A Memoir.* New York: Giorno Poetry Systems, 1989, esp. "Kulchur Magazine," 23-39.
Provides a more personal account of GS's contributions to *Kulchur* than G37, while covering essentially the same events.

G39 Hume, Kathryn. *Fantasy and Mimesis: Responses to Reality in Western Literature.* New York: Methuen, 1984, esp. 45, 48.
Includes GS among the metafictionalists who understand literature as a form of criticism.

G40 Hutcheon, Linda. *Narcissistic Narrative: The Metafictional Paradox.* Waterloo, Ontario: Wilfrid Laurier Univ. Press, 1980, esp. 36, 87, 143, 152.
Draws on *IQAT* to develop an account of the assumptions and techniques of metafiction.

G41 Imhof, Rüdiger. "Self-Reflexiveness and Self-Reflection" and "Sternesque Jokes." In his *Contemporary Metafiction: A Poetological Study of Metafiction in English since 1939.* Heidelberg: Carl Winter Universitätsverlag, 1986, 80-97, esp. 84-86, and 197-224, esp. 199, 203-4, 211-12; also other brief references.
Analyzes the self-reflexivity of *MS*'s preliminary matter, GS's use of footnotes and inventories in *IQAT,* and his deliberate subversion of narrative authority in "The Moon in Its Flight." Also relates GS to other metafictional writers.

G42 Jacobs, Barbara. "The Art of Gilbert Sorrentino." Diss. New York Univ., 1984. Abstracted in *Dissertation Abstracts International* 45 (1984): 1752A.
Traces in detail the development of GS's art, showing how his concern to render authentically "the processes of the real" leads to experimentation. Discusses the interplay between emotion and space in *SC* and *SW.* Emphasizes the emergence in *IQAT* and "The Moon in Its Flight" of GS's preoccupation with the formal relationship between the narrator and his fictional material. Argues that *MS* represents GS's most fully realized expression of the novel as an imitation of the "processes of the real." Suggests that *AS* and *CV* do not advance narrative form as much as they testify to GS's recasting of materials, using original inventions to create new ones.

G42a Jacobs, Naomi. *The Character of Truth: Historical Figures in Contemporary Fiction.* Carbondale: Southern Illinois Univ. Press, 1990, esp. 132-34.
Argues that *FP* is a particularly hilarious demonstration of the random use of historical figures, whose lack of any discernible meaning in the narrative suppresses the reader's impulse to systematize the text.

G43 Jones, Hettie. *How I Became Hettie Jones.* New York: E. P. Dutton, 1990, esp. 75-76, 92-93, 151-54, 175-76.
Briefly recalls GS in the late 1950s and early 1960s as his life intersected with the group of writers associated with LeRoi Jones. Emphasis is on personal matters, especially GS's marriages.

G44 Karfiol, Judith Rachel. "New American Fiction and the Aesthetics of Camus and Robbe-Grillet." Diss. Univ. of Southern California, 1978. Abstracted in *Dissertation Abstracts International* 39 (1978): 2919A.
Analyzes GS's fiction in relation to the attack by Camus and Robbe-Grillet on rationalist fictional forms. Argues that GS's work continues the trend away from substantive meaning and order in human experience toward

an assertion of meaninglessness, based on an awareness of the absence of an ultimate order governing and unifying our world. Emphasizes GS's use of pastiche, which eliminates teleological significance by juxtaposing temporally or spatially oriented portions of his narratives in alogical sequences. Also compares GS to Steve Katz and Raymond Federman.

G45 Karl, Frederick R. *American Fictions 1940/1980: A Comprehensive History and Critical Evaluation.* New York: Harper & Row, 1983, esp. 554-55.
Discusses *MS*, emphasizing its parody and praising its use of lists, which serve GS as the means to transmute individual paranoia into cultural madness. Also argues that *MS*'s underlying thematic premises are fraternity house male-female antics, presented less as parody than titillation.

G46 Kern, Robert. "Composition as Recognition: Robert Creeley and Postmodern Poetics." *Boundary* 2 6.3-7.1 (1978): 211-30, esp. 219-20.
Considers GS to be a negative open formalist, who rejects the idea of the poet as witness standing in privileged relation to the immanent order of experience. Contrasts Creeley's modernist faith in art's self-sustaining reality with the skepticism of *PF.*

G46a Klähn, Bernd. " 'Brooklyners' oder Das Portrait Sorrentinos als junger Mann." [In German] *Schreibheft* 27 (April 1986): 106.
Situates *SW* in the context of GS's entire literary career, from *SC* through *CV.*

G46b ———. "Der literarische Exkurs der Moderne: Amerkungen zur Innovativen Nachkriegsliteratur der USA." [In German] *Schreibheft* 29 (May 1987): 41-47, esp. 47.
Briefly discusses *ON*, comparing its appropriation of detective fiction to Gaddis's use of it in *J R.*

G47 Klinkowitz, Jerome. "Avant-garde and After." In his *The Practice of Fiction in America: Writers from Hawthorne to the Present.* Ames: Iowa State Univ. Press, 1980, 114-28, esp. 118-19. Rpt. in *Sub-Stance* 27 (1980): 125-[138].
Briefly discusses *SC, SW, IQAT, S-H,* and *MS*, stressing their self-conscious attention to language's reality in itself and to the conventions of fiction.

G48 ———. "The Extra-Literary in Contemporary American Fiction." In *Contemporary American Fiction.* Ed. Malcolm Bradbury and Sigmund Ro. London: Edward Arnold, 1987, 19-37, esp. 20-26.
Discusses the impact of extraliterary forces, particularly those in the world of commercial publishing and commodity fiction, on the development of GS's art. Argues that *IQAT* transforms the inhibiting power of these forces into productive purpose by incorporating them within the writer's creative act, while *MS* systematically destroys them by its

exuberances of style. Regards *AS* and GS's later novels as exercises in the pure delight of language, which were made possible by *MS*'s success. Also treats *SS* and compares GS's critical work with Ronald Sukenick's.

G49 ——. "Gilbert Sorrentino's Super-Fiction." *Chicago Review* 25.4 (1974): 77-89. Rpt. with revisions in *Vort* 2.3 [also designated no. 6] (Fall 1974): 69-79.
Uses a collage of quotations from reviews, interviews, and GS's novels to discuss the aesthetic principles of GS's narrative art, emphasizing his efforts to subvert fiction's congenital illusionism. Treats *SC, SW, S-H,* and *IQAT,* arguing that the latter is GS's most fully realized expression of the novelist's proper role.

G50 ——. *The Life of Fiction.* Urbana: Univ. of Illinois Press, 1977, esp. 7-15.
Reprints G49, preceded by new biographical information about GS.

G51 ——. *Literary Disruptions: The Making of a Post-Contemporary American Fiction.* Urbana: Univ. of Illinois Press, 1975; 2nd ed. 1980, esp. 154-67, 188-94.
Rewrites the material in G49 and G50, supplementing it with discussions of *MS* and of GS's relation to other writers, including Creeley, Williams, as well as such metafictionalists as Barth, Federman, and Sukenick.

G52 ——. *Literary Subversions: New American Fiction and the Practice of Criticism.* Carbondale: Southern Illinois Univ. Press, 1985.
References to GS emphasize both his comic self-consciousness of the novel writing business as well as *MS*'s exhaustion of metafictional techniques.

G53 ——. "The New Fiction." In *American Literature since 1900.* Ed. Marcus Cunliffe. The New History of Literature 9. London: Sphere; New York: Peter Bedrick, 1987, 353-67, esp. 361-64.
Argues that GS shares with Gass, Sukenick a concern with fiction as language and language as fiction. Proposes that GS's work bridges the gap between Gass's abstractions and Sukenick's satire.

G54 ——. "Poetry in the Novel: American Fiction of the Last Eight Years." *Poetry Australia* 59 (1976): 61-69, esp. 66-69.
Briefly comments on the erasure of the mimetic by *S-H*'s alphabetical structure and discusses Williams's influence on GS's fiction, especially *IQAT.*

G55 ——. *The Self-Apparent Word: Fiction as Language / Language as Fiction.* Carbondale: Southern Illinois Univ. Press, 1984.
Cites GS as a leading theorist and practitioner of self-apparent fiction. Briefly discusses *MS*, arguing that the novel completely exhausts the self-reflexive techniques developed in American fiction of the 1960s. Also suggests that *MS*'s trivialization of content points to the need for avant-

garde writers to revive meaning and human sympathy in their works.

G56 Kuehl, John. *Alternate Worlds: A Study of Postmodern Antirealistic American Fiction.* New York: New York Univ. Press, 1989.
Reprints the analyses of *S-H* and *MS* from G57. Also examines reflexivity, defamiliarization, parody, and intertextuality in *MS* and *BP.* More generally, situates GS in the context of contemporary antirealistic fiction.

G57 ———. "The Ludic Impulse in Recent American Fiction." *Journal of Narrative Technique* 16 (1986): [167]-178.
Discusses the ludic elements in GS's work, particularly alphabetic play in *S-H* and *MS*'s use of lists and blending of genres.

G58 Krysl, Marilyn. "Lost Lecture in America." *Rolling Stock* 5 (1983): 19. Expanded version published as "Stein on Soul: Lost Lecture in America." *North American Review* 269 (1984): 58-62.
In a style imitative of Gertrude Stein, develops the thesis that narrative voice expresses the soul of an individual. Quotes Billy's letter to his father from *AS* to illustrate how even a few sentences can immediately tell everything about a person.

G59 LeClair, Thomas. "Avant-Garde Mastery." *TriQuarterly* 53 (Winter 1982): 259-67, esp. 260, 265.
Briefly describes *MS* as a continuation of Nabokov's illocutionary gamesmanship and argues that the true avant-garde has abandoned such play for perlocutionary acts.

G60 Longville, Tim. "Gilbert Sorrentino's *Corrosive Sublimate.*" *Grosseteste Review* 6.1-4 (1973): 91-95.
Suggests that the poems in *CS* are romantic, operating between assumption and fact, and making their living out of what results. The poems seek to create beauty and sense out of what possesses neither, or, if it does, does so only under the eye of death.

G61 Mackey, Louis. "Representation and Reflection: Philosophy and Literature in Gilbert Sorrentino's *Crystal Vision.*" *Noûs* 17 (1983): 23-33. Revised and expanded version in *Contemporary Literature* 28.2 (Summer 1987): [206]-222.
Shows how *CV* radically problematizes its own mimesis, both by foregrounding artifice and also by deconstructing within the fictional frame itself the difference between fact and fiction that renders fiction intelligible. This subversion of confidence in the representational power of fiction sets in motion an interminable circuit of reflections and representations that makes *CV* the ultimate postmodern novel. Thematically, *CV*'s seventy-eight chapters correspond to the seventy-eight cards of the tarot and explore the relations in American culture among the past, present, and future. From this perspective, *CV* is a budget of stories that adds up to absolute loss, revealing Americans to be a people locked in a

timeless limbo between false memories and vain aspirations, condemned to a pointless half-life. Also treats the epistemological consequences of literature's perpetual institution and deconstruction of the distinction between fact and fiction. Concludes by arguing that contemporary philosophy, by recognizing its own irreducible verbality, has become what literature is, an activity of language capable of neither totalization nor termination.

G62 Malmgren, Carl Darryl. *Fictional Space in the Modernist and Postmodernist American Novel.* Lewisburg, PA: Bucknell Univ. Press, 1985, esp. 169, 174.
Briefly discusses *MS* in terms of its foregrounding of narratival space and *S-H* as an example of alphabetic space.

G63 Marcotte, Edward. "Intersticed Prose." *Chicago Review* 26.4 (1975): 31-36.
Offers *S-H* as one of several examples of intersticed prose, where material is organized in short, paragraph-like segments, separated by space.

G64 Marowski, Daniel G., ed. "Gilbert Sorrentino: 1929- ." *Contemporary Literary Criticism* 40 (1986): 383.
Provides a brief, chronological overview of GS's literary career.

G65 McFarland, Ronald E. *The Villanelle: The Evolution of a Poetic Form.* Moscow: Univ. of Idaho Press, 1987, esp. 104-5.
Analyzes GS's experimentation with the villanelle form in *PF*'s "There is no instance that was not love."

G66 McHale, Brian. *Postmodernist Fiction.* New York: Methuen, 1987.
Briefly analyzes the metaleptical techniques of *IQAT*, particularly the interplay among reader, author, characters, and other literary texts that violates ontological boundaries. Also treats the stylistic devices of *S-H* and *MS* that obstruct the reader's path from text to reconstructed world.

G67 McMullen, Kim. "Necessary Fictions: Fictional Reflexivity in Works by Vladimir Nabokov, Flann O'Brien, Gilbert Sorrentino, and John Barth." Diss. Duke Univ., 1986. Abstracted in *Dissertation Abstracts International* 48.2 (1987): 388A.
Analyzes GS in relation to contemporary reflexive fiction, arguing that reflexive devices create an overtly dialogic structure that engages readers interactively in the self-critical production of meaning. A separate chapter on GS discusses *IQAT* and *MS* in detail; also treats less fully *AS* and *CV*, arguing that these later novels demonstrate how reflexive technique functions once the destruction of conventional reading habits and social codes has been accomplished.

G68 Messerli, Douglas. "Experiment and Traditional Forms in Contemporary Literature." *Sun & Moon* 9-10 (Summer 1980): 3-25, esp. 18-20.

Argues that *MS* reacts against the degenerate condition of avant-garde fiction. Not only does GS dissect the failure of twentieth-century literature, his linguistic energy opens new ground, by reaching beyond the objectification of experience to the expression of life in the action of writing.

G69 ———. "The Role of Voice in Nonmodernist Fiction." *Contemporary Literature* 25.3 (Fall 1984): [281]-304, esp. 294-99.
Presents *AS* as an indictment of the modernist novel and the voyeuristic vision inherent in its extreme objectivism. GS accomplishes this by juxtaposing two unreconcilable systems, modernist organicism with authorial intrusion, thus using the novel against itself.

G70 Monley, Keith. "The Good, the Bad, and the Ugly: Reflections on Recent Short Fiction." *New England Review* 2 (1980): 483-94, esp. 493-94.
Contrasts *MS* with "The Moon in Its Flight," "Land of Cotton," and "Decades." Argues that *MS*'s verbal acrobatics become boring, while the characters in GS's stories, though no less artificial, are nonetheless believable and engage the readers' sympathy.

G71 Mosley, Nicholas. "Gilbert Sorrentino and *Mulligan Stew.*" *Review of Contemporary Fiction* 1.1 (1981): 153-54.
Frames *IQAT* and *MS* within the challenge that Nietzsche posed for modern writers—namely, how to communicate in writing the realization that conventional writing has become a purveyor of lies. Though *IQAT* addresses this problem, only *MS* fully expresses GS's message that "either you, the readers, see that almost all your conventional ways of seeing things, reading about things, writing about things, are parodies; or you yourself will evaporate into a sort of parody yourself."

G72 Mottram, Eric. "The Black Polar Night: The Poetry of Gilbert Sorrentino." *Vort* 2.3 [also designated no. 6] (Fall 1974): 43-59.
Provides detailed analysis of GS's poetry, discussing his books in chronological order from *DSU* through *BW* and *PF* to *CS*, with comments on *S-H* as well. Explores the roots of GS's aesthetic in Pound, Williams, Creeley, and Olson. Argues that GS's poems exist on the edge between catastrophe and survival, working as acts of understanding and resistance to thrust off despair. Also emphasizes GS's conviction that the forms of art are absolute and real only to the extent that they are grounded in the actual. Concludes that GS's poetry affords the pleasure not only of astringent thought and feeling but also of shaped measures under the impulse towards proper artifact. Excerpted: *Contemporary Literary Criticism* 7 (1977): 499.

G73 ———. "Psychic Dismembering and Staying Sane: The Fiction of Gilbert Sorrentino." *Reality Studios* 3.3 (April-September 1981): 41-52.
Shows how *SC, SW, IQAT, MS,* and *AS* compose a collective text that voices GS's horror at love and sex wasted in lust, talent wasted in the

capitalist trap of life reduced to commodity, and energy leaked away in liquor and drugs. Argues that GS's social criticism is akin to William Burroughs's nonaligned satire and points out that GS's indictment of America is not founded in ideology and consequently refuses to offer any alternative vision of justice. Analyzes *SC, SW,* and *AS* as revelations of the criminal vulgarity of middle American life, with its lethal ignorance, clichéd fantasies, stock language as the mould of cheapened experience, and racism. Discusses how *IQAT* and *MS* elaborate the politics and erotics of wasted energy as they are exemplified in the art and literary world, where poetic production becomes personal seduction and consumption is paraded as a philosophy of life.

G74 Nijmeijer, Peter. "Sorrentino wil een dubbel fake-effect." [In Dutch] *De Volkskrant,* 2 October 1984.
Provides a general critical and biographical review of GS's career, with particular emphasis on *IQAT* and *SP.*

G75 O'Brien, John. "Every Man His Voice." *Review of Contemporary Fiction* 1.1 (1981): 62-80.
Analyzes *MS* in relation to the twin assumptions of twentieth-century American criticism: first that art, particularly fiction, is about the world outside itself, and second, that the artist himself is one who knows something. Argues that art is making rather than imitation, knowing, intuition, or expression. Shows how *MS* is a novel formed of the codes, conventions, and language of fiction, deliberately constructed to prevent explanation by way of reference to extrinsic fact. Examines GS's treatment of himself and his own writings as the material of fiction, and proposes that Lamont in *MS* is a burlesqued version of GS who should be understood as the author of everything in the novel. Also discusses the nature of the list and its evolving function in *SW, IQAT, S-H,* and *MS.*

G76 ——. "Gilbert Sorrentino (27 April 1929-   )." *Dictionary of Literary Biography Yearbook: 1980.* Ed. Karen L. Rood, Jean W. Ross, and Richard Ziegfeld. Detroit: Gale Research, 1981, 310-14.
Surveys GS's life and work into 1980, with brief, chronologically arranged critical accounts of *SC, SW, IQAT, S-H, MS,* and *AS.* Views GS as a synthetic writer whose drive to weld together disparate materials renders the list more important to his fiction than character or plot.

G77 ——. "Gilbert Sorrentino: Some Various Looks." *Vort* 2.3 [also designated no. 6] (Fall 1974): 79-85.
Features eighteen subtitled sections that address, sometimes playfully, other times anecdotally, a wide range of biographical and critical topics, including GS's artistic roots in past literature, his difference from fashionable metafictionalists, *IQAT*'s attack on artistic pretension, misreadings of *SC,* and the inappropriateness to GS of the critical concept of a writer's development. Excerpted: *Contemporary Literary Criticism* 7 (1977): 450.

G78 ———. "La otra narrativa norteamerican." [translation into Spanish by Miguel Martinón] *Syntaxis* 4 (January 1984): 28-30.
Presents GS as exemplary of a non/counterconventional tradition of fiction.

G78a Olsen, Lance. *Circus of the Mind in Motion: Postmodernism and the Comic Vision.* Detroit: Wayne State Univ. Press, 1990.
Briefly relates GS to the detotalizing effects of postmodernism's mixed style, particularly through the maximalism of plurisignification. Also cites *MS* as exemplary of the elitism of postmodern fiction.

G79 Olson, Toby. "Sorrentino's Past." *Review of Contemporary Fiction* 1.1 (1981): 52-55.
Argues that the past that is so prominent in GS's poetry and fiction is not autobiographical but invented, existing completely in GS's words. Suggests that GS is concerned less with any specific past than cultural matters. *IQAT* and *AS* as well as such poems as "Marjorie" in *CS* are properly social documents and aesthetic achievements that seek to redeem human loss through art, while also acknowledging that redemption is impossible in the real world.

G80 Owens, Rochelle. "To an Arrogant Fart." [poem dedicated "for Gil"] *Fuck You/A Magazine of the Arts* 3.5 (May 1963): [6-8].
Prompted by GS's negative review of Owens's poetry in *Four Young Lady Poets* (C64), attacks GS for his macho ways.

G81 Perloff, Marjorie. *The Poetics of Indeterminacy: Rimbaud to Cage.* Princeton: Princeton Univ. Press, 1981, esp. 6-7.
Briefly traces the origin of *S-H* to Rimbaud and relates GS's book to other contemporary homages to Rimbaud.

G82 Phelps, Donald. "Extra Space." *Vort* 2.3 [also designated no. 6] (Fall 1974): 89-96.
Evaluates GS's early work, arguing that romanticism, sentimentality, and willfulness define his literary voice. Praises GS's critical essays for their double ideal of form and authority, though faulting them for their morose veneration of fact. Regards *SC* as GS's bluntest act of self-projection, while attacking *SW* and *IQAT* as unsuccessful works that fail to reach beyond by GS's emotional insularity. Considers *PF* to be a successful declaration of identity and *CS* to be an act of genuine self-discovery. Excerpted: *Contemporary Literary Criticism* 7 (1977): 451-52.

G83 ———. "Loss of Space." *For Now* 6 (c. 1966): 39-42. Rpt. in Phelps's *Covering Ground: Essays for Now.* New York: Croton Press, 1969, 1-6.
Argues that GS's work is distinguished by his longing for the imaginative space displaced in contemporary culture by mathematical distance. Sees in *SC* a codification of this loss, describing the novel as an act of latitudinal journalism in which the imagination foregoes its independence, becoming

instead an elemental force commingling with the world. Notes the contradiction in GS's sensibility between his narrow-lensed intelligence and his moral dogmatism. Also remarks GS's passionately romantic conservatism and observes how it underlies *SC.*

G84 Robins, William Mattathias. "Gilbert Sorrentino (27 April 1929-)." In *American Poets Since World War II.* Ed. Donald J. Greiner. Vol. 5, Pt. 2 of *Dictionary of Literary Biography.* Detroit: Gale, 1980, 278-85.
After a brief biography of GS, discusses in chronological order each of his volumes of poetry, including *DSU, BW, PF, CS, WS,* and *O.* Argues that GS is a poet of survival, for whom art is a tool to ward off encroaching dangers, both physical and spiritual. An angry poetry that refuses to take insult to human dignity lightly, GS's verse is necessarily bleak in tone. It is also disciplined and tight in form, opaque in allusion, transcendent in intent.

G85 Roudiez, Leon S. "The Reality Changes." *Review of Contemporary Fiction* 1.1 (1981): 132-42.
Traces the Oedipal pattern in *SC, SW, IQAT, MS,* and *AS,* examining both explicit references to the Mother and the Father as well as transpositions of the conflict between maternal denial and desire onto other psychological planes. Connects the libidinal drive for the Mother with the process of writing and suggests how GS's decreasing concern for verisimilitude is rooted in the displacement of the Mother as a creative force. Also examines the chronological evolution of the relations among character, place, and reality in GS's novels through *AS.*

G86 Russell, Marie. " 'Yes, We Have No Bananas': Gilbert Sorrentino's *The Orangery.*" *Review of Contemporary Fiction* 1.1 (1981): 83-84.
Observes how the poems in *O* are verbal constructs written out of simulated memory, which explore the limits of language as well as the semantic range of individual words in different contexts. Argues that GS's poetry seeks to express neither feelings, ideas, or moral principles. Rather, his poems are objects of beauty made of words that respect the material world's independence of man's emotional needs.

G87 Russo, John Paul. "The Poetics of Gilbert Sorrentino." *Revista di studi anglo-americani* 3.4-5 (1984-1985): 281-303.
Argues that the absence of an Italo-American tradition forced GS to create his poetic identity out of international modernism. While recognizing that GS's temperament is suited to the impersonality of modernism, also suggests that GS remains obsessed with the memory of his ethnic past. Unable to resolve the conflict between his adopted and his ancestral cultures, GS typically represses it. Traces this pattern through close analysis of several poems, including "A Fixture" from *DSU,* "Ars Longa" and "The Fiction" from *BW,* and "Country and Western" and "Coast of Texas" from *CS.*

G88 Schäbler, Bernd. *Amerikanische Metafiction im Kontext der Europäischen*

Moderne. Beiträge zur Anglistik 7. [In German] Giesseen: Hoffmann, 1983, esp. 547-86.
Includes a long, detailed chapter analyzing *IQAT,* treating the novel as an exemplar of metafictional strategies and situating GS in the context of such other American writers as Federman, Sukenick, Brautigan, Barthelme, and Vonnegut.

G89 Schaub, Thomas. "Williams, Sorrentino, and the Art of the Actual." In *William Carlos Williams: Man and Poet.* Ed. Carroll F. Terrell. Orono: National Poetry Foundation, Univ. of Maine at Orono, 1983, [435]-449.
Examines the hostility of Williams and GS to mimetic realism and their common insistence on art's autonomy, arguing that for both writers, the products of the imagination are separate from life but also share with life an identity of composition and equality of being. Analyzes the resulting tension between familiar reference and internal autonomy in *IQAT* and *CV,* showing how GS's art deliberately enacts the process of the mind's engagement with reality and avoids moralizing commentary.

Carroll Terrell comments briefly on Schaub's argument in his introduction to the book, [15]-29, esp. 22.

G90 Selby, Hubert, Jr. "Gilbert Sorrentino." *Review of Contemporary Fiction* 1.1 (1981): 48-51.
Reminisces about GS in New York during the late 1940s, 1950s, and 1960s, including the years of *Neon.* Emphasizes GS's role as Selby's mentor, pointing out GS's ability to provide criticism without imposing his own point of view.

G91 Share, Bernard. "On Giving Up Fictioneering." *Review of Contemporary Fiction* 1.1 (1981): 168-70.
Argues that *IQAT* and *MS* replace the convention of the omniscient novelist with the convention of the novelist who knows nothing. Notes the problems associated with this strategy, including *MS*'s vanishing act in which everyone—characters, author, and audience—exit the book. Shows how *IQAT* and *MS* succeed in proving that humor and experiment are not incompatible and also suggests that both are more relevant to today's evaluation of experience than the self-sustaining fiction of *AS.*

G92 Skodnick, Roy. "Corrosive Sublimate/Beauty Is a Rare Thing." *Vort* 2.3 [also designated no. 6] (Fall 1974): 42-43.
Argues that the formality of GS's poetry is serious business, producing constructs of care that give readers their own privacies without destroying the experience. Characterizes GS's poetry as primers of feeling that also teach. Excerpted: *Contemporary Literary Criticism* 7 (1977): 448.

G93 Solotaroff, Ted. "Introduction." In *Many Windows: 22 Stories from American Review.* New York: Harper & Row, 1982. Rpt. as "*American Review* Fiction" in Solotaroff's *A Few Good Voices in My Head: Occasional Pieces on Writing, Editing, and Reading My Contemporaries.* New

York: Harper & Row, 1987, 194-203, esp. 197, 199.
Praises the emotional intensity of "The Moon in Its Flight," arguing that both the story's vividness of details and its ending reflect the strength of the narrator's experience.

G94 Stephens, Michael. "Gilbert Sorrentino." In his *The Dramaturgy of Style: Voice in Short Fiction.* Carbondale: Southern Illinois Univ. Press, 1986, esp. 85-101; also passages in other chapters.
Treats GS's literary career from *DSU* to *CV,* emphasizing his development of separate voices in poetry and fiction. Traces the evolving formality of GS's poetic stance from early Black Mountain roots to the later dominance of French models. Argues that the fiction embodies GS's vituperative temperament, with its combination of satire and improvisation. *CS, IQAT,* and *S-H* emerge as the high points of GS's achievement, until *AS* and *CV.* Also covers GS's connections with Hubert Selby as well as with the Cedar Bar artistic scene.

G95 Stevick, Philip. *Alternative Pleasures: Postrealist Fiction and the Tradition.* Urbana: Univ. of Illinois Press, 1981, esp. 75.
Proposes *SW* as an example of contemporary sentimentality because the novel is charged with nostalgia for the people and places of GS's youth.

G96 Sukenick, Ronald. "Nine Digressions on Narrative Authority." In his *In Form: Digressions on the Act of Fiction.* Carbondale: Southern Illinois Univ. Press, 1985, 66-82, esp. 74.
Locates *MS* within the Joycean use of epic, arguing that it is a novel whose only rationale is the tradition it mocks.

G97 ———. "Thirteen Digressions." *Partisan Review* 43.1 (1976): 90-101. Rpt. in his *In Form: Digressions on the Act of Fiction.* Carbondale: Southern Illinois Univ. Press, 1985, 16-33, esp. 23-24.
Briefly takes issue with GS's notion that art mirrors not the content but the processes of the real, arguing that this is simply another variant on the Aristotelian idea of imitation.

G98 Thesen, Sharon. " 'in the song / of the alphabet': Gilbert Sorrentino's *Splendide-Hôtel.*" *Review of Contemporary Fiction* 1.1 (1981): 56-61.
Shows how *S-H* is indebted not only to Rimbaud but also to William Carlos Williams and Jack Spicer. Proposes that all these writers share an operational language, a structure of belief in a world of particulars which "do not *connect,* neither in the poem nor in the life from which it springs, they correspond." This aesthetic contrasts with the Splendide-Hotel, which GS presents as a microcosm of contemporary American life where language and imagination are debased by their mistaken connection to politics and ideas. Concludes that *S-H* is both a defense of poetry and a statement of despair at the abundance of bad art and bad writers who think that their ideas, rather than language itself, will take them to the truth.

G99 Thielemans, Johan. "The Voice of the Irresponsible: Irresponsible Voices? On Gilbert Sorrentino's *Mulligan Stew.*" In *Representation and Performance in Postmodern Fiction: Proceedings of the Nice Conference on Postmodern Fiction (April 1982).* Ed. Maurice Couturier. Montpellier: Univ. Paul Valery, 1983, [113]-129.
Discusses *MS* in the relation to antimimetic narratives and their rejection of the Platonic notion that serious fiction accurately reflects external reality. Relates the techniques of *MS* to Flann O'Brien's *At Swim-Two-Birds* and shows how GS's numerous lists partake of the game-character of the novel as a whole. Argues that every element of *MS,* including its fragments, changes in direction, varieties of style, secondhand plot and borrowed universes of discourse, is drawn ineluctably, compellingly, and irrationally to the desire and creation of pleasure. Concludes that GS's refusal of the novelist's traditional responsibility to record the objective world is replaced by a new, revitalizing relation between writer and reader.

G100 ———. "The Energy of an Absence: Perfection as Useful Fiction in the Novels of Gaddis and Sorrentino." In *Critical Angles: European Views of Contemporary American Literature.* Ed. Marc Chénetier. Carbondale: Southern Illinois Univ. Press, 1986, 105-24.
Argues that both William Gaddis and GS see language as violently cut into two territories: an ideal pure language marked by referential precision and the debased language of the contemporary world, which emanates from a wounded society and stunted consciousness. Differentiates *IQAT,* which satirizes clichés and bad style while still sustaining the tie between language and reality, from *MS, CV,* and *BP,* where GS's fascination with corrupt language has become the dominant motivation of his text. Analyzes *MS* as a catalog of bad writing, *CV* as the negative face of idealistic writing, and *BP* as a system of text machines that operates to make language the center of attention. Concludes that in these novels GS becomes creative by escaping the linguistic superego of pure language and sinfully indulging his pleasure in debased discourse.

G101 Thiher, Allen. *Words in Reflections: Modern Language Theory and Postmodern Fiction.* Chicago: Univ. of Chicago Press, 1984, esp. 185.
Briefly characterizes *S-H* as a lexical primer and *AS* as a performance in ventriloquism.

G102 Tindall, Kenneth. "Adam and Eve on a Raft: Some Aspects of Love and Death in *Mulligan Stew.*" *Review of Contemporary Fiction* 1.1 (1981): 159-67.
Imaginatively responds to *MS* with a pastiche of memories, quotations, excerpts, and allusions, journalistic as well as literary. Elaborates *MS*'s attention to language and the fictionalization of ordinary life. Also discusses GS's use of demons.

G102a Unsworth, John. "Orchestrating Reception: The Hierarchy of Readers

in Post-Modern American Fiction." *Centennial Review* 34.3 (Summer 1990): 413-32.
Associates GS with a generation of American postmodernists who publically double as privileged First Readers of their own work and thereby attempt to set the terms of their own critical reception. Argues that the reputations of this group of writers are promoted by academicians who uncritically adopt the writers' own language of self-description. Compares John O'Brien's interview with GS (E6) with his essay on *MS* (G75) to illustrate the contention that such academic criticism is thinly disguised intellectual advertisement which lacks independent judgment.

G103 Varsava, Jerry Andrew. "The Mimetic Function in Postmodernist Literature." Diss. Vanderbilt Univ., 1984. Abstracted in *Dissertation Abstracts International* 45 (1984): 1392A-94A.
Emphasizes the phenomenology of reading in order to construct a non-normative, reader-response model of mimesis. Applies it to postmodernist fiction to demonstrate the latter's mimetic function. Analyzes the intertextuality of *MS* to show how narrative innovation encodes ontological, moral, and epistemological issues.

G104 Viscusi, Robert. "Debate in the Dark: Love in Italian-American Fiction." In *American Declarations of Love.* Ed. Ann Massa. London: Macmillan, 1990, 155-73, esp. 165-66.
Suggests that *AS* adopts the obsessive repetitiveness of the *nouveau roman* to evoke the dilemma of Italian-American children haunted by the cultural conflicts caused by the heterogeneity of American society.

G105 Waugh, Patricia. *Metafiction: The Theory and Practice of Self-Conscious Fiction.* London: Methuen, 1984.
Numerous passages use GS's work to illustrate various techniques of metafiction. Discusses *S-H*'s view of literature as pure formalism, concerned solely with its own linguistic process. Cites *IQAT* to exemplify metafiction's problematizing of names and characters. Briefly describes *MS*'s parodic intertextuality.

G106 Weichselbaum, Lehman. "Shapes of Feeling: The Poetry of Gilbert Sorrentino." *Home Planet News*, November 1979: 9-10.
Observes that Sorrentino is a poet working very specifically out of the modernist tradition formed by Pound, Williams, and Creeley. Illustrates GS's mastery of the projective short lyric with examples from *BW* and *O*, noting how GS tracks his minutest neural impulses through purely verbal means, with a microscopic precision that is uncanny and unmatched. Argues that what differentiates GS from other interesting but neglected poets is "Coast of Texas" in *CS:* this suite is a true masterpiece, the most brilliant realization of the projective aesthetic in print.

G107 Weinfield, Henry. "The Image in Time: An Essay on *Corrosive Sublimate* by Gilbert Sorrentino, Black Sparrow Press, 1971." *Mysterious Barricades* 3 (Spring 1973). Rpt.: *Vort* 2.3 [also designated no. 6] (Fall 1974): 41-42. Argues that *CS* explores the bitter paradox that "there is no truth / but in dead event." Shows how GS conceives the image as discontinuous with the world, since its integrity depends on isolation from the flow of experience. Concludes that GS's poems do not intimate immortality but record the loss which attends the achievement of wholeness. Excerpted: *Contemporary Literary Criticism* 7 (1977): 448.

G108 ———. "'After the Deluge': An Essay on *Splendide-Hotel* by Gilbert Sorrentino, New Directions, 1973." *Vort* 2.3 [also designated no. 6] (Fall 1974): 61-63.
Contrasts Rimbaud's idealism with GS's cynicism and argues that *S-H* succumbs to the self-hatred and impotence that are typical of the modern world. Describes *S-H* as a reification of the most deplorable elements of contemporary culture. Excerpted: *Contemporary Literary Criticism* 7 (1977): 449.

G109 Werner, Craig Hansen. *Paradoxical Resolutions: American Fiction since James Joyce.* Urbana: Univ. of Illinois Press, 1982, esp. 197-200.
Argues that *MS* is at once a part of the mainstream of post-Joycean writing and an important new current. Emphasizes the allusive nature of GS's humor as well as its ability to critique the mythologies, both popular and elitist, of American culture. Concludes that *MS*, like *Finnegans Wake*, demonstrates how art inevitably reflects its culture.

G110 Williams, Jonathan. *Uncle Gus Flaubert Rates The Jargon Society in One Hundred One Laconic Présalé Sage Sentences.* 8th Hanes Lecture. Chapel Hill: Hanes Foundation, Rare Book Collection, University Library, Univ. of North Carolina at Chapel Hill, 1989, esp. 16.
Two-sentence comment on *DSU*.

G111 Winkelman, Aaron. "Authorial Presence in American Metafiction: The Novels of Coover, Federman, Sorrentino, and Sukenick." Diss. Univ. of California, Los Angeles, 1986. Abstracted in *Dissertation Abstracts International* 47.7 (1987): 2588A.
Treats literary foregrounding as the hallmark of metafiction and argues that this technique makes authorial presence conspicuous. A separate chapter about GS features individual discussions of *S-H*, *MS*, *AS*, and *CV*, focusing on three areas of authorial presence in his work—the writing of fiction as subject matter, form, and voice/persona.

G112 Wright, Martin. "Gilbert Sorrentino's *Imaginative Qualities of Actual Things.*" *Grosseteste Review* 6.1-4 (1973): 61-64.
Notes that GS's wit in *IQAT* is less comic diversion than a tragic response to a meretricious artistic world. Also shows how GS's distinction between prose and reportage informs the style of *IQAT*.

G113 Young, Thomas Earl. "Mirror, Mirror: Dimensions of Reflexivity in Postmodern British and American Fiction." Diss. Michigan State Univ., 1980. Abstracted in *Dissertation Abstracts International* 41.9 (1981): 4031A. Offers a theoretical and historical overview of self-reflexive fiction in the post-World War II period, briefly treating GS as one of the younger disruptivists within the vigorous American tradition of self-conscious narrative.

INDEX

COLOPHON

This book was designed by Steven Moore
and typeset by Shirley Geever in July-September 1990
in Caledonia on an Itek Quadritek Phototypesetting System.
600 copies were printed and bound by BookCrafters
of Chelsea, Michigan, in October-November 1990.
Of this edition, 550 copies were intended for sale and
50 copies reserved for complimentary and promotional use.
Published January 1991 for the Dalkey Archive Press.